AF709471

SHADES OF ṢULḤ

Pittsburgh Series in Composition, Literacy, and Culture

David Bartholomae and Jean Ferguson Carr, Editors

صلح

SHADES OF ṢULḤ

The Rhetorics of Arab-Islamic Reconciliation

RASHA DIAB

UNIVERSITY OF PITTSBURGH PRESS

Published by the University of Pittsburgh Press, Pittsburgh, Pa., 15260
Copyright © 2016, University of Pittsburgh Press
All rights reserved
Manufactured in the United States of America
Printed on acid-free paper
10 9 8 7 6 5 4 3 2 1

Library of Congress Cataloging-in-Publication Data

Names: Diab, Rasha, author.
Title: *Shades of Ṣulḥ: The Rhetorics of Arab-Islamic Reconciliation* / Rasha Diab.
Description: Pittsburgh: University of Pittsburgh Press, 2016. | Series: Pittsburgh Series in Composition, Literacy, and Culture | Includes bibliographical references and index.
Identifiers: LCCN 2016007244 | ISBN 9780822964018 (paperback)
Subjects: LCSH: Rhetoric—Political aspects—Arab countries. | Arabic language—Rhetoric. | Dispute resolution—Arab countries. | Persuasion (Rhetoric)—Political aspects—Arab countries. | Reconciliation—Political aspects—Arab countries. | Conflict management. | BISAC: LANGUAGE ARTS & DISCIPLINES / Rhetoric. | SOCIAL SCIENCE / Islamic Studies.
Classification: LCC P301.5.P67 D53 2016 | DDC 303.6/909175927—dc23
LC record available at http://lccn.loc.gov/2016007244

for Awatef and Khairy,
for Aya and Ahmad,
with love and appreciation

CONTENTS

ACKNOWLEDGMENTS

I am grateful to many colleagues, teachers, mentors, and friends, whose help and advice contributed to the successful completion of my book. Thanks go first to Awatef, Aya, and Ahmad whose unconditional love and support made this work possible. Thank you for your unwavering belief in me, your endless support, and for patiently listening to my incessant talk about this book project. Thanks also go to Khairy, my father, who taught me lessons about justice, some of which I continually feel too young to understand.

I owe much of my intellectual growth before and during the numerous writing phases of this book to intellectual communities that welcomed my work and asked me questions or pointed out connections that helped me think longer and deeper about *ṣulḥ*. My three main communities include members of the Composition and Rhetoric Programs and Communication Arts at the University of Wisconsin-Madison as well as my colleagues and students at the Department of Rhetoric and Writing at The University of Texas at Austin.

Colleagues, mentors, and teachers at the University of Wisconsin-Madison helped me during the initial phase of this project. I am grateful to Melvin Hall, Rhea Lathan, and Kate Vieira for our long conversations about rhetorical traditions. I want to especially thank my colleagues Shifra Sharlin and Mary Fiorenza for generously extending their hearts and ears to listen to early iterations of my research questions and dilemmas. Thanks also for making me feel the warmth of family far away from home. I also owe many thanks to Michael Bernard-Donals, David Fleming, Ceci Ford, Brad Hughes, Marty Nystrand, Morris Young, and Sue Zaeske for helping me understand the arts and responsibilities of communication. My work at Madison would have never been possible without Rob Asen and Deborah Brandt's continuous support and belief in my work.

As my thinking on ṣulḥ continued to deepen, many more colleagues added to my work through illuminating discussion and challenging questions: Samir Ali, Davida Charney, Diane Davis, Barbara Harlow, Jacqueline Henkel, Meta Jones, Mark Longaker, John Ruszkiewicz, Clay Spinuzzi, Snehal Shingavi, and Margaret Syverson. I especially appreciate the support of Linda Ferreira-Buckley, Patricia Roberts-Miller, and Jeff Walker who have patiently listened to and read varied iterations of different sections of the continuously evolving and changing manuscript.

Across different institutions, my work was enabled by the insightful support of librarians, archivists, conference organizers, and institutions. Thanks go to the conference organizers for arranging panels in ways that alerted me to different intersections and possibilities of studying the questions of violence and peace as well as the study of rhetorical traditions across cultures and time. Most important, the Rhetoric Society of America's Summer Institutes and Workshops offered a unique environment to work through and reframe my project in its different phases. I owe a great debt to the "Comparative Rhetoric" seminar led by Lu Ming Mao and Arabella Lyon, the "Possibility and Limits of Human Rights Discourse" seminar led by Erik Doxtader and Gerard Hauser, and the "Rhetoric and the World" seminar led by Susan Jarratt, Gwendolyn Pough, Susan Romano, and Sharon Crowley. Seminar leaders and participants provided me with rigorous intellectual engagement that had positive impact on my work.

Institutional support for my book came in different forms. Early on in my explorations of ṣulḥ, I was fortunate to have a fellowship from the American Association of University Women. Later on, I was granted a College Research Fellowship and a Summer Research Assignment Grant by The University of Texas at Austin. This time was priceless in helping me undertake the research necessary for chapters 3 and 5. I also recieved a University of Texas at Austin Subvention Grant awarded by the Office of the President.

Throughout the years and across different institutional affiliations, I have also come to appreciate hours of debate, study, insightful advice, and long chats with Beth Godbee, Tanya Cochran, Thomas Ferrel, and Eric Pritchard. My heartfelt thanks especially go to Beth Godbee—a friend and sister of many years. Thank you for insightful and encouraging feedback, carefully reading numerous drafts and different iterations of ideas, being generous, and holding my hand throughout the ups and downs of the process of writing this book.

I want to offer two final thanks. The enduring presence and sage advice of Deborah Brandt continue to enrich my life. And to my mom, Awatef, I am indebted for grounding me every time I come home with a tornado, especially those in my teacup, and for reminding me to settle in my very best.

SHADES OF ṢULḤ

INTRODUCTION

Discursive Spaces for Peace

This project began as an interest in al-Sādāt's 1977 peace initiative and sought to capture an elusive rhetorical dimension of al-Sādāt's Knesset address, which I first recognized as exemplary and savvy presidential rhetoric and then as a strategic fusion of epideictic and deliberative rhetoric. Little did I realize that I was intrigued by the invisible presence of a culturally inflected peacemaking practice called *ṣulḥ*, especially as it intersects with and is potentially eclipsed by diplomatic discourse. *Shades of Ṣulḥ* moves beyond this early interest in al-Sādāt's Knesset address and explicates the variegated nature and flexibility of ṣulḥ practices using a variety of illustrative cases. Because our world continues to be beleaguered by violence, this book addresses a great need. The study of ṣulḥ practices contributes to a better understanding of our collective history of peacemaking practices, shedding light on untapped resources of peacemaking.

Shades of Ṣulḥ responds to two interrelated sets of questions. First, the book engages the questions of violence and peace. Second, the book is equally energized by and engages other enduring dilemmas in rhetoric and composition studies. For example, it addresses questions raised by calls to revisit the rhetorical tradition, which invite us to "study the rhetoric of traditions—the ways that political parties, ethnic groups, social movements, and other discourse communities constitute and maintain the shared values and assumptions that authorize discourse" (Miller 26). These two seemingly dissimilar lines of inquiry interrelate in this book, which responds to a long-standing, cross-cultural, disciplinary investment in rhetoric's potential for countering violence—an investment revived in rhetorical scholarship, especially since World War II. The book also responds to increased attention to the rhetorics of reconciliation around the world. This increased attention is indicated, for example, by rhetorical studies of South Africa's Truth and Reconciliation Commission and transitional justice (Doxtader, *With Faith*; Mack, *From Apartheid*). Scholarship on the rhetorics of reconciliation and peacemaking, however, remains informed mainly by Judeo-Christian models of peacemaking. This gap dovetails with yet another. To date, there is no book-length rhetorical exploration of Arab-Islamic rhetorics, let alone of Arab-Islamic rhetorics of reconciliation.

Seizing the opportunity to address both gaps, this book explicates the ways in which ṣulḥ is a cultural, rhetorically mediated resource for peace that complements and extends our scholarship on Arabic rhetoric and the rhetorics of peacemaking and reconciliation. To address these two interrelated areas of research, the book argues that ṣulḥ taps into the potential of rhetoric in numerous ways to counter violence. Like restorative justice models (i.e., nonpunitive justice measures), ṣulḥ provides us with a critique *against* violence/conflict and articulates a critique *for* justice and peace. Uniquely, however, it organizes the work of peace pursuers and (a) initiates peacemaking using forgiveness, apology, or simply a commitment to make amends; (b) interpellates a community that pursues peace; and (c) names witnesses to the peace process as a way to foreground the discourse of accountability. As such, ṣulḥ engages the dialectic of conflict and conflict resolution.

To engage research on peacemaking rhetorics and on rhetorical traditions, the book is informed by and draws on a variety of bodies of literature. In addition to rhetoric and communication studies, two growing areas of inquiry inform this project, namely comparative and cultural rhetorics and peace studies. Together, these bodies of literature inform the book's exploration of the shades of ṣulḥ and inform the analysis of the cases studied.

THE RHETORIC OF VIOLENCE AND THE VIOLENCE OF RHETORIC: FINDING AN ANTIDOTE?

The phenomenon of violence has attracted the attention of researchers from different disciplinary walks (Lawrence and Karim). Similarly, the relation among violence, justice, and rhetoric continues to raise enduring questions. A vibrant stream of scholarship testifies to a persistent need and ongoing exploration, especially since World War II. This scholarship includes most recently the 2013 forum on violence (Engels) and numerous articles on specific forms of violence, such as gendered or racialized violence (e.g., McCann, "Entering the Darkness"; "On Whose Ground?"). This growing scholarship demonstrates yet again that rhetoric and violence can be neither reduced to the assumption that rhetoric is/enables violence nor that rhetoric is readily antithetical to violence. We see daily this inextricable, intricate connection in violent and often militarized, yet normalized, metaphors we live by (Tiles) when we "take a stab" at a project or, in our own disciplinary discourses, in "violent metaphors we use to conceptualize argumentation and debate: as battle, strife, and war" (Engels, "Introduction" 180).

The complex, subtle, and incessant relation among violence, justice, and rhetoric energizes scholarship, which explores the violence of rhetoric and the rhetoric of violence and invites further consideration of the responsibilities of rhetoric and rhetoric studies. For example, Erin J. Rand urges, "Our work should be driven by this tenuous balance between, on one hand, the responsibility to criticize violence and alleviate real suffering and, on the other hand, the necessity of considering the productive potential of violence" (475–76), which can catalyze solidarity, strategic thinking, and deep reflection on cultural norms that anticipate/support the *emergence*, *normalization*, and *sustenance* of violence. Accordingly, scholars have paid attention to power (ab)use (e.g., Burbules; Foucault); (coercive) silencing, exclusionary practices, the politics of persuasion, and power relations embedded in genres; and discursive practices and expectations (e.g., Foss and Griffin; Gearhart; Perelman and Olbrechts-Tyteca). In addition, scholars have sought ways to better understand linguistic violence (e.g., Gorsevski "The Physical"; Hallet; Tiles), counter rhetorical hegemony, and enable the move toward understanding and more equitable rhetorical interaction that would realize, for example, the duty to dialogue (Perelman and Olbrechts-Tyteca) or an ideal speech situation (Habermas).

In addition to scholarship motivated by the critique against violence, there is a growing body of literature on the rhetoric of peacemaking, reconciliation, and human rights. This scholarship intersects with peace studies and calls for a systematic study of "discursive opportunities" or "discursive spaces for peace" (Bruck; Rivenburgh). This work seeks to underline facilitative conditions as well as reflective, communicative practices that seek and promote identification, cooperation, and duties to dialogue, listen, assume prudence, and reflect on and embrace silence (e.g., Booth; Burke; Crosswhite; Glenn; Kelley; Ratcliffe). All seek to develop nonadversarial rhetorical skills and stances. They also suggest ways interlocutors can develop/embrace more peaceful communicative practices while affirming their right to dignity, as in Gerard Hauser's *Prisoners of Conscience*, claiming their grievances and resisting being co-opted (Gorsevski, "Nonviolent"; *Peaceable Persuasion*).

With increasing scholarly attention to (racial) reconciliation, transitional justice, and truth and reconciliation commissions (e.g., Beitler, *Remaking Transitional Justice*; Doxtader, *With Faith*; Hatch, *Race and Reconciliation*; Mack, *From Apartheid*), rhetoric scholars and others have seized this opportunity to shed light on the exigence, limitations, and potentials of rhetoric and reconciliatory interventions. Their work critiques the limited relational payoff of apologia and the need for national apologies (Hatch, "Beyond Apologia"), dutiful listening to grievance claims (Tully), or confessional accounts—as a measure of (transitional) justice—that promise but often fail to recognize, let alone heal, the harm done to victims (Doxtader, "A Question of Confession's Discovery"). This attention to the rhetorics of reconciliation, rights, and witnessing is manifest in books and edited collections on memory and forgetting (Phillips, *Framing Public Memory*; Vivian, *Public Forgetting*), the *Rhetoric Society Quarterly* special issue on traditions of testimony and witnessing (Lyon and Olson), and Arabella Lyon's *Deliberative Acts*. This work invites an exploration of modes of deliberation and reconciliation in different cultural traditions, an area of scholarship that must claim much more of our disciplinary attention.

INVISIBLE RHETORICAL TRADITIONS AND REVISIONARY HISTORIOGRAPHY: REVISITING ARABIC RHETORIC

This book is equally informed by calls to revisit our conception of the "rhetorical tradition" (e.g., Miller) and calls to explore rhetorical practices and theories around the globe (e.g., Lipson and Binkley, *Rhetoric Before and Beyond*; *Ancient Non-Greek Rhetorics*). These calls seek to further disciplinary reflection by "interrogat[ing] how our own dispositions and epistemologies shape our perceptions of the past and press us toward new methodologies and sites of inquiry" (Agnew, Gries, and Stuckey 110). These calls have energized two hard-to-separate bodies of scholarship. The first focuses on historiography and its impact on how we account for, represent, envision, and pass down rhetoric. The second attends to the intersection of culture and rhetoric.[1] I address each of these bodies of literature briefly to underline how both invite and inform my exploration of Arab-Islamic rhetorics and the rhetorics of ṣulḥ.

Increasingly, scholars have been calling for rigorous reflection on the ways we tell and are informed by the history of rhetoric and its development.

Recognizing the process/product of writing history as a political enterprise, James Berlin underscored the importance of critical reflection, explaining that "historians must become aware of the rhetoricity of their own enterprise, rhetoric here being designated as the uses of language in play of power" (cited in Murphy et al. 6).[2] The rhetoricity of the history of rhetoric impacts—if not determines—our selection of texts, rhetors, and communicative spaces/activities we consider worthy of rhetorical exploration. Our attention to this rhetoricity foregrounds a question. As Victor Vitanza puts it, "The central question is one of whose interests, in a given history, are being served and whose are being deflected or forgotten" (324). Scholarship explicating the rhetoricity of the history of rhetoric and its far-reaching, formative impact, therefore, invites increased attention to un(der)recognized assumptions that influence how we perceive of, define, represent, and study rhetoric. In turn, this question has energized scholarship that sheds light on, recovers, and questions the invisibility of texts, rhetors, and whole regions of enduring rhetorical knowledge and practice.

Not only does this scholarship pay attention to historiographic methods and typology (Vitanza), but it also attends to our rhetorical landscapes (e.g., Glenn, "Remapping"; Royster, "Disciplinary Landscapes"), which illuminate what is deflected and forgotten. Reflective attention to such landscapes helps reveal how space, location, and position inform how we *other* rhetorically. With the goal of recovering what is forgotten or ignored and increasing disciplinary reflection, Jacqueline Jones Royster ("Disciplinary Landscapes"), for example, provides a multidimensional framework that models and guides the process of rereading, revisiting our uptake of rhetoric's history, and rewriting our rhetorical histories. Royster's model entails shifting where we stand, shifting rhetorical subjects, shifting the circle of practice, and shifting the theoretical framework. The growing recognition of such possibilities has resulted in vibrant feminist and revisionist historical research, which calls for and models increased self-reflexive attention to *what* and *who* is excluded (archives, rhetors, texts, peoples, traditions, and practices) and *how*. This investment in the histories and historiographies of rhetoric continues to grow and to chart paths seldom frequented.

Alongside these developments, scholarly attention has been focused on the intersection of culture and rhetoric. This line of research attempts to counter the invisibility of culture and increase commitment to (a) shed light on invisible rhetorical traditions; (b) recover what's on offer in terms of differing understandings of rhetoric, rhetorical practices, activities, texts, the rhetor, and the responsibilities of rhetoric; (c) reflect on disciplinary perspectives and methods that have eclipsed such traditions; and (d) invite disciplinary discussion on how to improve and sustain this recovery/reflection project (e.g., Mao, " Reflective," Royster, "Disciplinary Landscaping"). There has been to date a steady stream—even if slow—of scholarship on different rhetorical traditions and practices.

Starting with the late 1960s, we see work addressing rhetorical traditions of the Far East while recognizing the challenges of comparative/cultural analysis of patterns of communication, rhetorical traditions, and values as well as social and political forces at play (e.g., Oliver, *Culture and Communication* and *Communication and Culture*). Along the road there have been other publications, like George A. Kennedy's *Comparative Rhetoric*, that have attempted to acknowledge ignored rhetorical traditions. More important, this work's attention to rhetorical practices and traditions has energized critical reflection on "Doing Comparative Rhetoric Responsibly" (e.g., Mao, "Reflective Encounters", "Doing Comparative Rhetoric"; Hum and Lyon), underlining the responsibilities to deeply interrogate ideological stances and interpretive and analytical choices. Only then do we move toward understanding cultures on their own terms and have a reflective encounter with othered rhetorical traditions and practices.

This reflective, interpretive, and analytical stance is consistent with the aforementioned transformational shifts that Royster called for: it interrogates "the assumption that the dominant Western rhetorical paradigms must be somehow universally valid and applicable in all contexts, known, unknown, and yet-to-be known" (Mao, "Doing," 64). In addition, this stance models an art of deep contextualization. As LuMing Mao explains and charges, "We have to learn to develop an etic/emic approach ("Reflective") or to practice the art of recontextualization ("Searching") by troubling our own modes of thinking and being and by deftly moving between self and other, the local and the global, and the contingencies of the present and the historical imperatives of the past" ("Doing," 66). Increased awareness of the need to work differently in order to shed light on forgotten traditions has invited and authorized work on different rhetorical traditions. Such emerging scholarship is not additive, for it has a deep impact on our understanding of moments of origin, rhetoric's timeline, the image of the rhetor, and the importance and multidirectionality of cultural encounters (oppressive and otherwise). All affect differently the recession or development of rhetorical practices and increase our understanding of rhetoric.

The growth of scholarship on cultural rhetorics and the charge to shed light on different rhetorical traditions inform this book on ṣulḥ, even if indirectly. In a sense, this growing literature invites attention to Arab-Islamic rhetoric, an underexplored tradition. To illustrate, I touch briefly on some of the important work done and the gap in our knowledge of Arabic/Arab-Islamic rhetorics. We are collectively building bodies of knowledge on African-American rhetorics (e.g., Atwater; Jackson and Richardson, *Understanding*; Pough; Richardson and Jackson, *African American*; Royster, *Traces*); Asian-American rhetorics (e.g., Mao and Young); Chinese rhetorics (e.g., Mao, "Studying"); American-Indian rhetorics (e.g., Lyons; Powell; Stromberg); rhetorics of the Americas (e.g., Baca and Villanueva); and Near East rhetorics (e.g., Lipson and Binkley). Among the work on the rhetorics of the Near East, there has been limited work on Arabic/Arab-Islamic rhetorics.

Although there has been some interest in Arab-Islamic—mainly medieval—rhetoric, it is fair to say that to date, rhetoric scholarship does not represent the complexity, richness, and longevity of Arabic/Arab-Islamic rhetorics. Interest in Arabic rhetoric situated in translation and language studies, contrastive rhetoric, Middle Eastern studies, and medieval and Renaissance studies has shed light on poetics and philosophic rhetorics, mostly by exploring commentaries on translations of Aristotle (i.e., the reception of Aristotle). The interest in the reception of Aristotle is manifest in, for example, Deborah Black's *Logic and Aristotle's Rhetoric and Poetics in Medieval Arabic Philosophy* and Salim Kemal's *The Philosophical Poetics of Alfarabi, Avicenna and Averroës*. The translation movement in both the East (i.e., Baghdad) and the West (i.e., al-'Andalūs) of the Arab-Islamic world has indeed attracted scholarly attention (e.g., Baddar; Borrowman; Butterworth; Ezzaher, "Alfarabi's *Book of Rhetoric*"; Lameer). For example, there are studies of Arab commentators/translators who engaged the work of Plato and Aristotle, such as al-Kindi (Baddar, "From Athens (Via Alexandria) to Baghdad"), Ibn Rushd or Averroes (Shaub; Ezzaher, *Three Commentaries*), and al-Farabi or Alpharabius (Ezzaher, "Alfarabi's *Book of Rhetoric*"). This scholarship remains invisible despite its role in charting numerous paths for the study of Arabic/Arab-Islamic rhetoric. On the one hand, this scholarship opens the door for rhetoricians to study the long history of Arab/Arab-Islamic poetics and philosophic rhetoric and to complicate our understanding of translations and commentaries as derivative (Baddar, "The Arabs Did Not *Just* Translate Aristotle"). On the other hand, because it sheds light on just a sliver of Arabic rhetoric, it invites us to think about the invisibility of other strands of rhetorical knowledge and practice, like religious oratory, organizational rhetoric, the teaching of rhetorical arts as part of an educational mission, and peacemaking practices as rhetorical knowledge and practice.

For this reason, Philip Halldén's article, "What Is Arab Islamic Rhetoric?"

which foregrounds and critiques such a narrow scope, is a welcome intervention. Halldén powerfully sheds light on other bodies of work relevant to rhetoricians, including religious oratory and homilies. Halldén's critical, revisionary assessment of the state of scholarship on Arabic rhetoric is a much-needed reminder of the treasures to be mined in relation to religious dialectic, religiopolitical text and talk, *khuṭbah* (i.e., religious oratory) manuals, instructions, exemplars, organizational writing, among others.[3] Considering the long history of the Arabs and the expansive territory of Arab/Arab-Islamic communicative activity, the continued invisibility of Arabic/Arab-Islamic rhetorics and the tendency to focus on medieval translations is surprising. Yet it is not: to some extent rhetoric is perceived as philosophic rhetoric. Though philosophic rhetoric is just one line of rhetorical development in the European tradition (Kennedy),[4] this perception informs expectations and, therefore, the study of Arab-Islamic rhetoric as manifest in studies of the commentaries/translations. Around the globe, however, rhetorical traditions manifest numerous lines of rhetorical development. This is made clear in Lipson and Binkley's two edited collections. Similarly, the Arab world demonstrates numerous strands of rhetorical practice and knowledge. The gap in rhetorical scholarship, concerning the different strands of Arab/Arab-Islamic rhetoric, warrants disciplinary attention.

Seizing this opportunity, my work on ṣulḥ goes beyond poetics, translations, commentaries, and philosophic traditions and focuses alternatively on a variety of rhetorical practices. In exploring Arab-Islamic peacemaking rhetoric, my book is unique in three ways. First, this is a book-length study of Arab-Islamic rhetoric grounded in rhetorical *scholarship* and *methodology*. Book-length works on Arab/Arab-Islamic communicative practices exist but they do not draw on rhetorical scholarship, methodology, and history/historiography (e.g., Abdul-Raof, *Arabic Rhetoric*; Bassiouney, *Arabic Sociolinguistics*; and Hoigilt, *Islamist Rhetoric*). These works are informed by and situated in sociolinguistics, systemic functional grammar, and pragmastylistics, which are areas of linguistic analyses. Second, current scholarship tends to focus on the Arab-Islamic rhetorical tradition in terms of style (*balāghah*) and translations of or commentaries on the classical cannon, as noted earlier. Scholarship on style/poetics and (translations of/commentaries on) philosophic rhetoric are important strands in the history and development of Arabic rhetoric. My book extends this scholarship on Arabic rhetoric and engages other strands of rhetorical knowledge and practice by looking at rhetoric as a way of *knowing*, *doing*, and *being*. Third, though scholarship on the rhetorics of reconciliation and peacemaking abounds, it remains mainly informed by Judeo-Christian models of peacemaking. To date, there is no rhetorical study of peacemaking practices informed by the Arab culture and Islam. These three gaps created a space for my book, which attends to and critiques long-standing Arab-Islamic rhetorical practices of conciliation and explicates the ways in which ṣulḥ is a culturally inflected, rhetorically mediated resource for peace.

As a rhetorical study, this book explicates Arab-Islamic peacemaking practices as occasions for rhetorical work that manifests in different types of text/talk and contributes to conversations concerning the question of violence and the imperative to find peace. Generally, much work is needed to study rhetorics of peacemaking and their cultural roots.[5] Though we recognize the transcultural, transpatial, and transtemporal exigence for conflict resolution, we still need to shed light on "discursive spaces for peace" and develop a body of literature on the cultural rhetorics of peacemaking around the globe. Traditional peacemaking practices, like ṣulḥ, are grounded in a worldview that elevates relational responsibility and understands justice and peace after violation as exceeding the punishment of a wrongdoer (i.e., punitive justice). Rather, they seek to "restor[e] victims, [repair] harm, and re-weav[e] the fabric of human relationships in a community," and hence are referred to as models of restorative justice (Coben and Harley 245).

Despite the importance of this three-dimensional healing work, ṣulḥ and other restorative traditions continue to be invisible in rhetoric scholarship. This invisibility of ṣulḥ is matched with its limited visibility in peace-studies scholarship, despite its enduring presence. The role culture plays in reconciliation in peace studies and international relations has generated increased interest (Funk and Said; Hudson; Irani and Funk; Kriesberg) and subsequent interest in and recognition of traditional and restorative peace practices. Despite this recognition, there is a dearth of scholarship on what ṣulḥ as a reconciliation model and method has to offer. This invisibility calls for scholarly investment.

As a case in point, I have noted earlier how this project started with an attempt to analyze al-Sādāt's Knesset address. To date, there is only one *rhetorical* exploration of al-Sādāt's 1977 peace initiative (Littlefield). Though the study sheds light on balance as a key feature of the speech, it doesn't relate this feature to restorative justice, which seeks to address and balance the differing restorative needs of stakeholders. Similarly, without naming or recognizing the cultural framework that informs his peace initiative, scholarship in political science and international studies analyzing the speech notes crucial features of al-Sādāt's peacemaking initiative, which I contend are features of ṣulḥ. For example, Zeev Maoz and Dan S. Felsenthal focus on al-Sādāt's use of voluntary, self-binding commitment to peacemaking to resuscitate stalled peace talks. Their study neither recognizes nor links self-binding commitment to ṣulḥ's enduring practices. Likewise, Arnold Lewis's anthropological study analyzes the peace ritual invoked by al-Sādāt's trip to Jerusalem without identifying the process as ṣulḥ, a traditional practice that has a history and characteristic features.

Uniquely, ṣulḥ offers a resilient, generative, and flexible model of peacemaking (e.g., Drieskins; Lang; Funk and Said; Smith); it is multifaceted, rhetorically and typologically rich, and characterized by a remarkable rhetorical longevity. Not only does ṣulḥ discourse converge with (extra)juridical and human rights discourses, but it also draws on an expansive array of rhetorical practices, including constitutive rhetoric, suasion, and visionary articulations of moral orders. It is worth noting that this flexibility is also a source of challenge: ṣulḥ can be eclipsed by our attention to other juridical/extrajuridical or political practices that similarly seek justice and peace, a challenge I underline in chapter 4. In addition, ṣulḥ cases transcend time and space limitations; practices have been documented in medieval Medina (in modern-day Saudi Arabia) and contemporary Cairo, Egypt, as the chapters illustrate, guiding stakeholders as they negotiate publicly communal conflict in the former and interpersonal conflict in the latter.

As ṣulḥ travels across time, space, and spheres of interaction, it shares features with other restorative justice models and retains some conspicuous features. Ṣulḥ shares two dominant features with other restorative models, all critique injustice and violence and advocate for conflict resolution and peace. For short, I refer to the former as critique *against* and the latter as critique *for*. Both modes of critique are interdependent; investing in the critique against violence/injustice is not enough, for we equally need to invest in the critique for peace, an investment that articulates and makes actionable a vision for peace and justice. The need for both modes of critique emanates from their different affordances: the critique against is mainly deconstructive, whereas the critique for is revisionary and reconstructive. The second aspect of restorative justice conspicuous in ṣulḥ is the move toward balancing, at best, the seemingly irreconcilable demands of peacemaking stakeholders, including wrongdoers. Restorative justice models seek to reverse conflict (i.e., a moral need) and to heal all stakeholders and relations violated by an act of aggression (i.e., a relational need). Similarly, ṣulḥ manifests the critique for and critique against and attempts to balance the moral and relational needs of stakeholders and the community.

Three unique features characterize ṣulḥ. First, it can be initiated using apology-forgiveness discourse, but it can also be initiated by declaring commitment to the pursuit of peace. This alternative initiation model, despite seeming atypical, is useful in protracted, multiparty conflicts where parties share responsibility and the brunt of conflict/violence. Second, ṣulḥ discourses interpellate and reconstitute stakeholders into a deliberative community, which comprises peace pursuers and beneficiaries who grapple with the possibilities and risks of negotiating their peacemaking needs and responsibilities. Third, ṣulḥ enlists the community who witnesses the resultant agreement to support the move toward peace; members of the community, if you will, become commissive witnesses.

To explicate ṣulḥ's rhetorical richness, I have carefully chosen illustrative cases. Each sheds light on ṣulḥ's aforementioned unique features, namely (1) initiation using commitment in addition to apology-forgiveness discourses, (2) reconstitution of a deliberative community comprised of different stakeholders, and (3) mobilization of commissive witnesses. Additionally, the cases analyze ṣulḥ's varied rhetorical activities and settings, demonstrating how it is malleable enough to address interpersonal, (inter) national, and intrapersonal needs. To illustrate, for interpersonal ṣulḥ, I draw on published ethnographic studies of ṣulḥ practices in rural and urban settings. For national ṣulḥ, I shed light on and analyze the Constitution of Medina. This is a seventh-century document, comprising several merged ṣulḥ pacts; together, they are recognized as a charter and constitution. As to international peacemaking, I show how ṣulḥ blends easily with diplomatic discourses. To this end, I analyze political speeches and reference a number of international instruments like Security Council Resolutions. Finally, to illustrate ṣulḥ's potential for resolving intrapersonal conflict, I analyze a literary dramatization and epistemic dialogue on peacemaking. As such, the cases demonstrate the malleability, success record, and the variegated range of reach of ṣulḥ as a ritual and practice. Put differently, ṣulḥ travels well across spheres of activity (juridical/extrajuridical and political/diplomatic); time (medieval, modern, and contemporary); and geopolitical borders (Cairo, Galilee, and Medina).

Because I wanted to highlight how ṣulḥ easily flows across the various spheres of interaction, the cases are not organized chronologically. Rather, the book is organized conceptually. This organization recognizes how we tend to experience reconciliation and ṣulḥ's typological richness, warding off a potential misreading: in our everyday lives, conflict with others is the most conspicuous form of conflict, and the exigence for interpersonal conflict resolution is more immediate. In contrast, conflict and the move toward communal, national, and international conflict resolution is typically experienced as more impersonal, elusive, and distant, as well as mediated. Moreover, intrapersonal ṣulḥ is the most taxing and least visible. The chapters address the more obvious forms of conflict/conflict resolution first and then address the least obvious and more taxing form of peacemaking last. Because ṣulḥ practices are so varied they invite a typological rather than chronological reading; they engage interpersonal, communal, and political imperatives to counter violence; resolve conflict; and heal individuals and communities. Such a conciliatory engagement can manifest in unilateral, bilateral, or third-party-initiated conciliatory processes. Intriguingly, these processes can be either victim or wrongdoer initiated. This richness implies an expanded repertoire of peacemaking endeavors and calls into question the assumptions that peace is necessarily or typically initiated by apology and by the wrongdoer. Ṣulḥ, as a culturally inflected and relationally driven peacemaking discourse, problematizes such assumptions; the peacemaking repertoire can be limited neither to apology-forgiveness discourses nor to addressing only bilateral or third-party modes of intervention, for peace discourse can also manifest as unilateral, self-binding commitments).

More important, because the book is about ṣulḥ as a cultural resource for peace that is informed by Islam, it neither attempts to historically or typologically survey all ṣulḥ practices nor to provide a historical account, even if short, of Islam or Arab-Islamic rhetoric; these goals are not feasible while maintaining the focus and unique character of this project. Considering the current state of scholarship on the rhetoric of ṣulḥ, it will take a huge disciplinary—not individual—endeavor to attain a critical mass of scholarship, currently unavailable, that would help a rhetoric scholar provide a historical survey like Conley, Kennedy, or Murphy (Classical). Much more orchestrated disciplinary work will be necessary to realize the goal of providing a history of Arab-Islamic rhetoric. As to shedding light on the history of Islam or the history of Muslims, scholars of Middle Eastern studies, history, and theology have been for years doing this important work. However, history is a key player in many of the ṣulḥ cases addressed in this book. Accordingly, it is crucial to highlight aspects of the historical moment that fostered the exigence to mobilize the discourse of ṣulḥ. For example, in chapter 3, I zoom in on the life of a relatively small, emergent city-state known as Yathrib and then Medina. Because Medina's tribes shared the brunt of a long history of conflict, the city's history, its tribes, and their conflict is presented. As the backdrop, the history helps us read the rising exigence for peacemaking and the coauthoring of the Constitution of Medina, a document that brings together the discourses of ṣulḥ, rights, and interpellation of a unified citizenry.

Another reason for the typological/conceptual rather than chronological order is to prevent a crescendo, or march of development, which would be a misrepresentation of ṣulḥ, an unwarranted celebration of one instantiation of ṣulḥ (al-Sādāt's address), and a closing off of the need to continue critical thinking about ṣulḥ in the (inter)national arena. This is especially important considering debates about the current state of affairs in several countries in the Middle East. By contrast, the conceptual arrangement aims to foreground ṣulḥ's rhetorical richness, malleability, and unique features.

As the book sheds light on ṣulḥ's different discursive practices, it provides a multidimensional story of how ṣulḥ is fluid, for it relates to and supports other discourses. This fluidity and multifariousness invite an eclectic method that combines analytical terms and disciplinary perspectives. I combine, therefore, the global discursive insight of rhetorical analysis with the microanalytical precision of critical discourse analysis, which draws on other linguistic disciplines, including pragmatics and sociolinguistics. When combined, rhetorical and critical discourse analyses provide a particularly detail-oriented method. Such an analytical approach is consistent with the complex nature of reconciliation discourse, which mandates astute synthesis of different analytical tools and bodies of scholarship. This combination is conspicuous in chapters 3 and 4 where I combine (1) interpellation, constitutive rhetoric, and categorization of membership to illustrate how people are interpellated as peace pursuers and (2) rhetorical listening with the representation of locution to demonstrate how claims of grievance are listened and responded to. In order to provide a nuanced study of "discursive opportunities" or "spaces" (e.g., Bruck) that promote the possibilities for peace as well as constitute and galvanize peace pursuers, I draw on research in communication (e.g., Bruck; Rivenburgh) and rhetorical studies (e.g., Booth; Doxtader; Hatch; McPhail). I complement this scholarship with studies of the role of culture in peace studies (e.g., Abu-Nimer; Lederach; Kriesberg; Shaw) and foreign policy (e.g., Hudson). Using these cross-disciplinary perspectives, I explicate the rhetorical nature of efficacious ṣulḥ processes across interpersonal, communal, national, and international spheres; ṣulḥ's contribution to the study of culturally inflected peacemaking rhetorics; and the richness of ṣulḥ deliberations that can blend political, religious, and social registers. This exploration unfolds in the chapters that follow.

Chapter 1, "Peacemaking Topoi: Cultural Iterations of Relational and Moral Needs," underlines cross-cultural commonplaces of peacemaking rhetorics and demonstrates that culture plays a central role in shaping peacemaking expectations, processes, articulations, and outcomes. Across varied models of conflict resolution, reconciliation pursuers debate (a) punitive/restorative/transitional conceptions and modes of justice; (b) perceived/real tensions among justice, (political) prudence, (moral/social) recognition, and calls for remembering/forgetting; and (c) measures that translate peacemaking endeavors into a stable/formalized relation (e.g., binding peace pacts/treaties). These cross-cultural commonplaces *emanate from* and *address* culturally inflected relational, ethical, and political imperatives, seeking ways to resolve conflict and move forward. Additionally, this chapter argues that these topics are also analytical tools that can capture the generative potential of debates about peacemaking as a goal and process. Using exemplary moments from cases that range from contemporary Egypt (after the January 25, 2011, revolution) to Sierra Leone in the wake of its civil war, this chapter explicates the rhetoric of peacemaking as a sphere of discursive activity. This discursive sphere hinges on a repertoire of culturally inflected, rhetorical uptakes of the aforementioned commonplaces. In shedding light on these recurring and culturally inflected topoi, the chapter sets the stage for the study of central terms of the manuscript and grounds ṣulḥ in its cultural imperatives and doctrinal roots.

Chapter 2, "The Power of Sweet Persuasion: Cultural Inflections of Interpersonal Ṣulḥ Rhetorics," draws on and revisits ethnographic accounts of ṣulḥ from Cairo, Lebanon, and Galilee and explicates how ṣulḥ exceeds typical apology-forgiveness conciliation. Specifically, cases range from transgressor (Lang) and third-party-initiated (Abu-Nimer *Nonviolence*) to wronged-initiated ṣulḥ (Ayoub). Therefore, the chapter argues that articulations of apology, forgiveness, and/or commitment-driven ṣulḥ are motivated by relational goals (relations with self, others, and community). In addition to arguments from (religious) authority and precedent, the chapter captures how reconciliation pursuers debate, among themselves and with others, the possibilities and stakes of pursuing peace or taking revenge. To further draw out the relational dimension, as I analyze different interpersonal ṣulḥ cases, I shed light on dimensions of what I refer to as performative open-hand rhetoric. For example, *muṣāfaḥah* (shaking hands), *muṣālaḥah* (reconciliation), and *mumālaḥah* (eating together) are crucial social acts with conspicuous relational goals that counter the logic of violence/violation/alienation and begin the work of peaceful coexistence.

Chapter 3, "*We* the Reconciled: The Convergence of Ṣulḥ and Human Rights," focuses on the Constitution of Medina (622 CE), the first Arab-Islamic constitution. This chapter demonstrates that the constitution, a composite text of ṣulḥ pacts, weaves together rhetorics of reconciliation and human rights by ratifying a prolonged reconciliation between tribal communities of different faith traditions (polytheists, Christians, Jews, and Muslims) and of relative political power. More important, the chapter explicates how the constitution established Medina as a city-state, an act that constituted a unified citizenry based on equal rights and obligations. Medina's constitution affirmed the rights of new immigrants and their equal standing and peaceful relations with the native inhabitants; outlined everyone's right and obligation to the pursuit of justice; recognized the religious freedoms of all citizens of Medina; and obligated all to the protection of the city-state. My analysis demonstrates that the forty-seven articles of the constitution capture a relationally driven, albeit political, conciliatory investment in the welfare of individuals (citizens) and communities (bound either by tribal affiliation or religious traditions)—an investment that draws on and realizes a discourse of human rights. "*We* the Reconciled," therefore, explicates a historical precedent of the successful convergence of discourses of ṣulḥ and rights, which could efficaciously counter the tribal logic that often denied rights by foregrounding tribal interests, privileges, and status. This chapter —in the context of recent debates in Cairo about writing a new constitution; the rise of political Islamist movements calling for a religious state; and ongoing religious conflicts—sheds light on the political imperative that informs ṣulḥ and engages enduring rhetorical questions: How can the discourses of conciliation and (transitional) justice best realize the discourses of citizenry and equal rights? What are the discursive conditions manifest in historical precedents that can enable their realization?

Chapter 4, "From the Egyptian People's Assembly to the Israeli Knesset: al-Sādāt's Knesset Address, Ṣulḥ, and Diplomacy," analyzes al-Sādāt's Knesset address and a series of speeches and statements given by Muḥammad Anwar al-Sādāt before and after the Knesset address to shed light on the symbolic and procedural dimensions of his peace initiative and how ṣulḥ practices are invoked, initiating what led to the Camp David Accords in 1979. Consequently, the chapter identifies culturally influenced rhetorical moves that proved to be efficacious in the international arena. Calls for accountability and openness to the other are traceable rhetorical moves. al-Sādāt used rhetorical tools, like constitutive and epideictic rhetorics and speech acts of promise while signaling rhetorical listening to the needs and fears of the other. Together, these tools were potent enough to initiate peace and to reconstitute a community of peace pursuers who share the *responsibility for* and *rewards of* peacemaking. As such, the chapter provides a detailed, case-driven exploration of (1) policy measures that peace pursuers embraced as a crucial part of their conflict resolution and (2) the mobilization of international imperatives for peace (using public diplomacy). A case in point is the way in which policy discourse interpellates subjects as participants in deliberation who are shaped by and influence foreign policy.

And within today's Egyptian context, there are calls for revisiting the Camp David Accords and equally forceful calls for honoring international treaties, a rhetorically rich political situation that invites further exploration of the discourse of the 1977 peace initiative and its interpellated subjects. If peacemaking rhetoric hinges on a discursive sphere of activities that actualize formalized and binding conciliatory work and relations, what conditions recycle the phase of articulating grievance claims, and what short-circuits or affirms peace?

Chapter 5, "To Gather at Court: Ṣulḥ as Rhetorical Method," analyzes an overlooked dialogue titled *The Great Court of Ṣulḥ*. The chapter argues that the dialogue (1) brings together the different dimensions of ṣulḥ, highlighting its spiritual roots and (2) dramatizes a humanistic, dialogue-driven, interventionist approach to reconciliation. The approach is applicable to personal, interpersonal, communal, and international conflict. The lucidity and broad applicability of this rhetorical approach to reconciliation come from the fact that *The Great Court of Ṣulḥ* is responsive to its times—written after World War I, the Versailles Treaty, and the establishment of the League of Nations—while being attentive to the recurring problem of *power over* that results in marginalization, domination, and denial of rights. By analyzing the dialogue, this chapter shows how ṣulḥ is a rhetorical resource for conciliatory intervention. *The Great Court of Ṣulḥ* makes a simple argument: internal reconciliation between warring factions of the self is a *precursor to*, *condition of*, and *model for* the resolution of world conflicts and the establishment of a cooperative international community of peace pursuers. Intriguingly, from the dialogue, we can extrapolate a culturally inflected, rhetorical method for reconciliation, comprising a functional interaction of three discourses: (1) a bidirectional, reciprocal discourse of expressing and listening to grievances; (2) introspective, reflective discourse; and (3) a visionary/devotional discourse. In unique ways, each discourse articulates a vision for peace. As such, the dialogue presents a functional, collaborative move from grievance claims to the establishment of a restorative peace. At the same time, this chapter illustrates how dimensions of ṣulḥ rhetoric are grounded in traditional, Islamic philosophy, which entails a reconceptualization of virtues, the nature of the self, the value of moderation (*wasaṭīyah*), and the pursuit of justice and excellence.

Each of the book's chapters explicates ways in which ṣulḥ is a rhetorically mediated model for reconciliation, and each seeks to underline a dimension of ṣulḥ. Together, these dimensions provide an account of ṣulḥ, a culturally inflected, rhetorically mediated process and practice of reconciliation. This account complements and extends current scholarship on Arabic rhetoric, which is invisible and does not represent well the richness of its rhetorical traditions. But more important, by shedding light on the iterative, responsive, rhetorical labor of conciliation, my account of ṣulḥ addresses concerns we all share. On a daily basis, the news strikes us yet again with horrifying images and details of escalations of violence and impending war in the world. This project on ṣulḥ invites us to acknowledge the history and richness of reconciliation practices like ṣulḥ. These practices chart a different, a more peaceful path.

1

PEACEMAKING TOPOI

Cultural Iterations of Relational and Moral Needs

> However painful the experience, the wounds of the past must not be allowed to fester. They must be opened. They must be cleansed. And balm must be poured on them so they can heal. This is not to be obsessed with the past. It is to take care that the past is properly dealt with for the sake of the future.
>
> —*Desmond Tutu*, TRC's Final Report

Tutu's words underline the desire to heal, loosen the grip of grim realities, and chart a new future. As he seeks to transform the realities of South Africa's apartheid, Tutu encapsulates an enduring exigence for peacemaking. Across different cases of conflict/conflict resolution, across cultures, and across multidisciplinary scholarship, people attempt to counter conflict/violence and embrace the journey toward healing. In their work, pouring balm over wounds, we can discern recurring reconciliation topoi. Each focuses on a central question: How do we confront/deal with the past? How do we attain justice and balance the needs of stakeholders? and How do we prudently manage and transform the political moment? These questions underline three topoi as they address the roles memory, justice and balancing stakeholders' restorative needs, and political prudence play in the pursuit of justice and peacemaking.[1]

These topoi are interdependent, and they share the goal of healing individuals, communities, and nations. This is why Tutu draws on metaphors of healing and medicinal intervention (*wounds*, *balm*, and *healing*). Metaphors of medicinal intervention condense, "highlight and make coherent our own pasts, our present activities, and our dreams, hopes, and goals as well" (Lakoff and Johnson 232–33). Healing metaphors, therefore, condense the bidimensional critique *against* injustice and the critique *for* peace. This bidimensional critique is motivated by a moral imperative to bring about justice to *all* community members and a relational imperative to recover from/heal broken relations. In few words, Tutu captures this bidimensional critique and yearning of peace pursuers when reconciliation is "called forth to heal, transcend, and (re)constitute" (Doxtader, "Reconciliation," 267). In the wake of violence, conflict, and injustice, their voices deliberate conciliation goals and measures that best address the wounds of the past, vindicate victims, punish and/or integrate perpetrators, heal the community, and restore justice.

To understand the rhetorical dimension of these deliberations, this chapter studies the aforementioned three reconciliation topics and introduces the imperatives (or logic) that underwrite them from the perspective of peace pursuers and discourse analysts. As the chapter focuses on these topics and their instantiations across varied conflicts and peacemaking practices, it builds up a vocabulary for studying the discourses of reconciliation. In the process, the topoi's cross-cultural inflections and analytical potential are underlined. This same vocabulary is used to introduce *ṣulḥ*, explicating its meaning and cultural and doctrinal roots, and demonstrating how ṣulḥ manifests the topoi of justice and recognition as well as memory, moral modeling, and prudence. These topoi help underline how ṣulḥ converges with and diverges from other reconciliation models.

RECONCILIATION TOPOI AND RECONCILIATION IMPERATIVES

As a sphere of rhetorical activities, reconciliation draws on a variety of discourses and topoi. All contend with the multidimensional consequences of aggression and orchestrate rhetorical work toward the pursuit of reconciliation. To initiate reconciliation, people negotiate their reconciliation needs and expectations, recruit community members (e.g., elders) who can mediate/intervene to resolve conflict, and set the terms of and expectations for the processes, events, and outcomes of their desired reconciliation. To do this work, they engage questions about the past and whether it is best forgotten or remembered; justice and which form of justice vindicates victims, recognizes their violation and restorative needs, heals the community, and balances the needs of pursuers of justice; and political prudence or how to avert the danger of the community tearing itself apart in its professed pursuit of justice and peacemaking. Scholars draw on these topoi to study how people resolve conflict and initiate peacemaking. The different topoi, therefore, offer a useful vocabulary to study peacemaking and explicate how peacemaking processes are rhetorically mediated and culturally informed.

This is a key contribution of rhetoric to peace studies, albeit an underrecognized one.

The specific nature of each conflict (resolution) calls for a creative process that efficaciously ends conflict but, more important, restores and heals. Everett L. Worthington explains, "Couples, families, or public officials can learn to resolve conflicts, but that does not eliminate problems. Nor does it heal wounds incurred during conflict. People must still deal with the aftermath of conflict—the hurts and offenses that have produced unforgiveness and ruptured trust" (166). As Worthington speaks to the differing and far-reaching consequences of aggression, he underlines how ruptured trust shakes the relational and moral foundation of people's lives. Because this ruptured trust results in great social, psychological, and political damage, it calls for complex, creative, and iterative reconciliatory and reparative work.

For peace seekers, restoring the violated relational and moral universe is crucial to any conciliation endeavor. The former seeks to recover from the sense of betrayed trust with those whom we deem the same (e.g., relatives, compatriots). The latter captures more than a comforting imaginary. It is rather a matter of faith, an unwavering commitment and belief in what's good, just, and beautiful. In "Souls of Black Folk," W.E.B. Du Bois captures the force of the moral universe when he writes, "Through all the sorrow of the Sorrow Songs there breathes a hope—a faith in the ultimate justice of things. . . . Sometimes it is faith in life, sometimes a faith in death, sometimes assurance of boundless justice in some fair world beyond" (261). It is this "faith in the ultimate justice of things" that inspires our attempts to enact justice via social contracts or agreements and to reimagine relations shattered by acts of violence. The aforementioned topoi address the need to restore the "moral tone" and reinvigorate the "moral fabric" of the community (Stovel).

However, the process is arduous because relations, too, play a crucial role in conflict and conflict resolution. Realizing conflict resolution entails multifaceted processes that address experiential and material consequences of violence on individual, communal, or (inter)national levels. Social or political relations (between victims and wrongdoers) complicate reconciliation, often intensify hurt, and harden unforgiveness. Conciliation pursuers reckon with recurring tensions among justice, memory, and political prudence. These recurring tensions can be considered relational in nature in the sense that they foreground and attempt to recognize/refashion the relation between transgressor/victim, restore/repair the victim's sense of self and standing in their community, and restore the community's sense of a moral universe. Such fraught situations mandate creative peacemaking processes that enable and sustain peaceful coexistence.

Recognizing the consequences of aggression and holding on to "faith in the ultimate justice of things" can make involved parties more accepting of tasking peacemaking deliberations, a process that mandates an understanding of the "inclusive, comprehensive nature of reconciliation" (Hurley 2) and tolerance of the iterative nature of reconciliatory discourse. At best, this discourse sustains "the will to change things for good" and brings about change that is fair, just, and acceptable to all involved parties.

Concomitantly, literature on reconciliation consistently demonstrates that it is not possible to attain any of the reconciliation goals without attending to the recurring topoi of dealing with the past by remembering/forgetting, realizing justice and vindicating victims (often through apology-forgiveness, reparation, and/or punitive measures), and prudently maintaining a healthy political community where the needs of stakeholders are realized. Sandra Rafman explains that peace pursuers must contend with the "moral dilemmas where relational, moral and survival imperatives conflict and permit no resolution" (217). Because these topoi help individuals and communities address their relational and moral needs, they are deemed central.

For scholars, the relational and moral imperatives serve as an analytical lens that helps us study the relational, ethical, and political forces that call forth reconciliation. These topoi, then, provide an analytical vocabulary that facilitates recognition of the restorative needs of conciliation pursuers and foregrounds lines of argument that can lead to division or rhetorical coordination of action. This vocabulary makes us more attuned to conditions apt to promote or tensions that can impede reconciliation processes. In rhetorical scholarship, restoring the moral universe manifests in questions about remembering, forgetting, moving forward, and justice. The relational imperative surfaces when interlocutors address standing and recognition as well as the conundrum of reaching an efficacious political rhetoric that avoids cooptation and instead balances the demands of different stakeholders. The questions of memory, justice, political prudence, and balanced response to reconciliatory needs recur and often conflict with one another. Their articulation across the globe underlines varied value systems that inform different approaches to peacemaking. Despite the differences, it remains instructive to look at these topoi to which conciliators, peace pursuers, and scholars continue to gravitate, and to initiate a reflection on how culture influences how they are taken up. I now turn to memory, justice, and political prudence.

PEACEMAKING AND THE POLITICS OF MEMORY

> When, or under what circumstances, a public decides to forget elements of its shared past is a fundamental determining factor in allowing members of a community to begin again, to release one another from burdensome or corrosive dimensions of their common history and mutually enter into new and improved relations.
>
> —*Bradford Vivian*, Public Forgetting

In this quote, Vivian underlines the relational and political dimension of the rhetorical work of remembering/forgetting. Memories, histories, and cultural artifacts may encode oppression and violence that individuals, communities, and nations face.[2] In the wake of traumatic events, memories of acts of violence hardly recede. Rather, as Judith Herman explains, "It is as if time stops at the moment of trauma" (*Trauma and Recovery* 37). Attempts to deal with such troubled and troubling ever-present memories are riddled with questions concerning the limits and potentials of remembering/forgetting: Who is served by the choice to remember/forget? How does the choice effect reconciliation? The dilemma—whether to remember or forget—is best expressed by two seemingly contradictory conciliation slogans: "Forgive and Forget" and "Remember and Forgive" encode two different models for engaging memory. What binds the two slogans, however, is what scholars refer to as the presentist orientation of deliberations concerning memory (e.g., Mack, *From Apartheid to Democracy*, 138; Phillips; Vivian, *Public Forgetting*). We can neither obliterate memory nor sever its (partially constitutive) bonds with the present and the future. Each one of the slogans encodes a stance in deliberation concerning moving forward and the possibility of "mutually enter[ing] into a new and improved relations" (Vivian, 117).

Communities and individuals reckon with their past in diverse ways. Scholarship reflects the complex, varied relations among public forgetting, remembering, and reconciliation (Phillips; Shriver; Vivian, *Public Forgetting*). Scholarship also provides case studies of the tension between remembering and forgetting in dealing with past violence and conflict in South Africa (Shriver), Taiwan (Shriver), and Sierra Leone (Shaw), for example. Some case studies demonstrate the positive impact of verbal truth telling (e.g., South Africa's Truth and Reconciliation Commission [TRC]), while others reject that possibility in favor of rituals of social forgetting, aiming at reintegration (e.g., Sierra Leone). These studies alert us to the fact that the tension between remembering/forgetting and reconciliation operate at individual, communal, and national levels; demonstrate how culture can define what role memory (forgetting/remembering) plays in the pursuit of truth, justice, and healing (Shaw); and explicate how the choice to remember or to forget grapples with survival imperatives, albeit differently defined. The choices to forget or remember in this regard are similar in the sense that both are motivated by an investment in restoring relations or faith in the moral universe. Those who choose to forget argue that "acts of forgetting make possible new memories" (Vivian, *Public Forgetting,* 117). New memories can realize their survival and relational imperatives. Alternatively, others argue that "a past that has not been properly reckoned with cannot be properly buried, and . . . sooner or later, it will rise up and demand *just* attention" (Biggar, "Concluding Remarks," 271; emphasis added). Put together, the path from memory to truth telling and the path from social forgetting to community rebuilding demonstrate how reconciliation processes are complex, case sensitive, and culturally mediated. In what follows, I address the politics of memory by explicating arguments for remembering—as manifest in truth telling—and healing and forgetting as an alternative route to remembering or reintegration of wrongdoers.

Remembering: "Revealing Is Healing"

> Forgetfulness is the enemy of justice, unless one takes refuge in that untrue truism: There is nothing we can do to change the past.
>
> —*Donald W. Shriver*

Arguing for remembering, Donald Shriver underlines the relation between remembering and justice. Like Tutu ("Foreward"), who warns that "the wounds of the past must not be allowed to fester," Shriver refutes the "untrue truism" and affirms that we can intervene: "We can change our relation to the past, and the first step for doing so is *uncovering* its dreaded secrets" (emphasis added). Revealing the horrors of the past, survivors testify, uncover their oppression, detail their grievances, and (in)formally assert their claims of rights. In the case of South Africa, "as they told their own and others' stories before the TRC, victims have frequently said that the very telling has been a step toward their own personal healing and a certain reentry into civic society" (27). The rhetorical work of retelling fulfills—for them—immediate and pressing ethical and relational imperatives, hence catalyzing a survivor's personal healing, which is crucial to their reintegration into society and pursuit of ways to counter violence. But more importantly, their testimony—an act of bringing memory to the public—is more than shared subjective truth; it becomes part of the public record shaping public knowledge. In addition, testimonies (as a manifestation of the "publicness of memory")[3] function rhetorically as a new account(ing) or an "interpretive lens" (Lucaites and Condit) that foregrounds *what was* and brings into sharp relief *what should never happen* and *what can* and *should be done.*

Remembering can be healing; remembering is rhetorically functional and powerful when it helps communities reckon with past horrors. It becomes rhetorically powerful when the community addresses the causes of and ways to counter violence. Remembering and revealing the truth disrupts a period of dysfunctional silence and oblivion to violence and violation.[4] Members of a community, then, initiate recovery when they recognize victims and attend to their restorative needs; they initiate accountability when recognition is complemented with institutional interventions that counter future acts of violence and seek redress. Remembering can also catalyze a vision for a better future. Put differently, rhetorical testimony enables collective, critical reflection, and reimagining. Shriver touches on this briefly when he notes that survivors of Nazi Germany and South Africa's apartheid "remember[ed] a past that serves as a warning for their own future and the world's" (27). Such a mode of remembering can be named *revisionary memory*, which facilitates the work of collective reimagining. In contrast to the cases of Nazi Germany and South Africa's apartheid, Sierra Leone's conciliation experience, which I detail below, reminds us that forgetting can also be functional and thus challenges the popular South African slogan "Revealing Is Healing."

Forgetting: "Cooling the Heart"

If forgetting is considered "a symptom of absence, lack, or loss; of apathy, neglect, or inaction; of ruin, destruction and death" (Vivian, *Public Forgetting*, 168), Sierra Leone's case challenges "the categorically positive status of memory" (169). Sierra Leone suffered from 1991 to 2002 from civil war that involved gross violations of the population's moral universe. In Sierra Leone, acts of aggression included mutilation, amputation, and civilian execution. What made the situation even more complex and gruesome was that gross violations were perpetrated by male and female children-soldiers and youth who "were abducted, conscripted, and often compelled to commit acts of killing, mutilation, rape, and abduction" (Shaw 3). After eleven years of atrocities, Sierra Leoneans wanted to forget. Their desire was motivated by a relational dilemma and a relational imperative: the child excombatants returned, and the community needed to focus on recovery and reintegration. Shaw's ethnographic research documents their relationally driven, deliberate, and constitutive recuperation practice, which she condenses in the phrase "cooling the heart."

> In Temne-speaking areas, when child ex-combatants were returned to their home communities after demobilization, their family members adapted or created rituals to "cool the heart" of the child [ex-combatant]. "Cooling the heart" reversed the work of the combatant groups that had made the child into a fighter, restoring the child's relationship with God and the ancestors—and thereby also with the family and community—through prayer, the application of consecrated water, and small offerings. In some rural communities, religious leaders introduced group rituals or church ceremonies for returning combatants (both child and adult) involving confession, prayers, and offerings, in which the whole community participated. (9)

Religious practice mediated their deliberate(d) choice to forget, which also entailed a choice to remember differently: as they chose to remember that the child ex-combatant was a victim, too, they engaged memory's revisionary potential and re-membered ex-combatants. Sierra Leone's ritual and practice of "cooling the heart" challenges the assumption that remembering or revealing—memory that helps build the forensic archive—is the only path to healing. At times, remembering will be the way for communities to uncover both subjective and forensic truths and enable healing. However, other routes can do the work of memory and reconciliation. The Sierra Leonean practice of "cooling the heart"—as an act of social forgetting—is neither a dysfunctional absence nor a complicitous amnesia. Rather, the practice mandates transformation of both the child ex-combatant and the whole community. To actualize this transformation, the community's communicative practices changed to affirm the rituals of social forgetting.

> Because having and maintaining a "cool heart" requires a transformation of social identity, ex-combatants were discouraged from publicly talking about the war after these rituals, and reciprocally community members were enjoined not to call child or adult ex-combatants "rebels" or other combatant labels, not to ask ex-combatants about their past actions, and not to discuss the war in public after rituals of reintegration. This was not merely a top-down directive from leaders: most people I asked in these and other communities—including child ex-combatants—said that they wished "to forget" the war and to get on with their lives. (Shaw 9)

To reintegrate ex-combatants, Sierra Leoneans' communicative choices had to, on the one hand, resist fixating on ex-combatants' older subject positions and past actions. On the other hand, their new communicative choices had to allow and support the process of refashioning. Shaw clearly identifies and speaks to the rhetoric of naming and refashioning as a crucial part of the rhetorical consequences of memory. She explains that "such a process of social forgetting 'unmakes' past violence and 'remakes' ex-combatants as new social persons. It is not a panacea, but rather a practice that enables and sustains ongoing processes of healing and social recovery" (9). "Cooling the heart," therefore, condenses the rhetorically mediated social processes of refashioning identities and relations. As transformative interventionist acts, these processes enable ex-combatants and community members to transcend their former adversarial relation and move toward their reconstitution.

"Cooling the heart" is just a different mode of handling the past and seeking reconciliation. Sierra Leoneans still have their memories of past atrocities (i.e., individual remembering). They were, however, encouraged to socially forget. Shaw explains that individual remembering and social forgetting worked in tandem because they had different goals (9). Their dynamic interdependence and rhetorical nature are worth dwelling on. First, Sierra Leoneans' choices to privately remember and publicly forget were deliberate(d): "People in the northern Sierra Leonean communities . . . discussed the war within their families and inside their houses, but often reminded each other not to 'pull it outside' and thereby risk endowing it with reality" (9). Second, their silence was equally deliberate and purposeful. As people retained their personal memories of the events and losses, they resorted to forgetting (a form of silence), which became, as Kierkegaard explains, "the sheers with which you cut away what you cannot use, doing it under the supreme direction of memory" (qtd. in Shriver 28). Sierra Leoneans' choice to socially forget was not a dysfunctional silence, for they believed that speaking about the war was like "pulling it outside," resuscitating discourses of violence and violation.[5] Rather, Sierra Leoneans' choice of a mode of public social forgetting *spoke to* and *of* a responsibility and faith in beginning anew. Via social forgetting and individual remembering, they employed a memory technique that provided a functional response to the horrors and ramifications of the past, "cooled their hearts," and reintegrated child ex-combatants. In South Africa, Archbishop Tutu answered the question differently by calling for a functional remembering that would uncover the past so the wounds could be healed. In this way, he argued, "the past is properly dealt with for the sake of the future."

Scholars warn us against the seduction of dysfunctional memory or "willed forgetting" (Shaw; Vivian, *Public Forgetting*, 178). As such, the Sierra Leonean and South African cases reiterate a recurring wisdom. Equally, they warn against dysfunctional memory that traps us in old subject positions, reducing us to amnesiac subjects who refuse to acknowledge and learn from their history. The stances of denial and resistance to learning are toxic and impede a future-oriented pursuit of healing and reconciliation. Concomitantly, peace pursuers need to undertake a toxicity purge, which hinges on "draining the memory of its power to continue to poison the present and future" (Shriver 28). In addition, they need to embrace a stance of recognition and openness to foster conditions consistent with a moral judgment that reconciles and heals. Whether conciliators and peace pursuers choose rhetorical remembering or rhetorical forgetting, their decisions seek and enable an interventionist rhetoric that counters violence, refashions their subject positions, and remembers that the ultimate goal is reconciliation and justice, another central topos of reconciliation. In general, attaining justice is crucial for a stable, peaceful society. Because justice is a decisive factor in the pursuit of an enduring and mutually acceptable reconciliation, it is the focal point of the following section, which underlines (1) the differences and similarities between restorative and punitive justice and (2) how justice entails the vindication and recognition of victims and perpetrators, which in turn hinge on (3) the functional use of listening and speech acts.

JUSTICE: A FUNDAMENTAL PIECE OF THE PUZZLE

> From the villages of Cambodia to the newly formed states of the former Yugoslavia to the hills of Rwanda, there are strong calls for justice emanating from survivors and an obvious need for trauma healing and reconciliation among survivors, perpetrators and bystanders in the conflict.
>
> —*Wendy Lambourne*

Because justice is the cornerstone of a stable, peaceful society, calls for justice proliferate around the globe, as Lambourne notes. The consistent and systematic actualization of justice strengthens the moral tone of a community, as Laura Stovel puts it. Because of its centrality, conciliators can neither ignore justice nor forgo prudential exercise of justice mandated by complex conflicts. Nevertheless, responding to calls for justice, which is vital for the life of a community (i.e., survivors, perpetrators, community members, and bystanders), is thorny and complicated by varying conceptions of justice and conflicting needs of community members. Though resolving conflicts to make things right is a central premise in justice systems, justice discourses differ greatly in how they respond to the questions:

Whose justice? Justice for whom? Justice to what end? To address these questions, conciliators deliberate the type of justice and measures that realize the form of justice they seek. Their questions demonstrate how discourses of justice, which seek to end violence, diverge in their conceptions of justice and the relation between the perpetrator and victim; the responsibility and imperative to pursue and enforce justice; and the measures used to attain justice. These variations may be informed by dissimilar and culturally specific understandings of justice, its practices, and individual needs (Lambourne 312–14). These variations, therefore, warrant scholarly attention. In what follows, I focus on the goals and actors of punitive or retributive and restorative justice. I also shed light on the influential roles played by recognition of victim and perpetrator, listening, and speech acts (e.g., apology) in realizing reconciliation.

Retributive Justice: Perpetrator vs. State

In the Western legal tradition, retribution, restitution, and procedural justice are central concepts.[6] Retribution focuses on punishing perpetrators. More important, crimes are defined as "any act or omission to act that the authoritative governing body has declared punishable and hence lawbreaking" (Estrada-Hollenbeck 66). Accordingly, crimes are perceived as being committed against the state. Within this system, justice is pursued when violations of laws are precisely determined, violators identified, punishment specified, and court decisions enforced (68). Restitution and procedural justice are key terms within this model.[7] "Restitution, meaning the recovery of losses or compensation to rectify harms, generally takes the form of a financial payment made to the victim either by the offender or by the state" (Lambourne 312–13). Procedural justice "is concerned with fair treatment in making and implementing decisions that determine the outcome of a court case" (313).[8] In litigation, these central terms inform retributive justice, a model in which victims are invisible and their needs are irrelevant or secondary at best.

A war tribunal, for example, is a legal instrument used to bring about justice and enforce accountability. Yet, in war tribunals—which adopt a legalistic model and therefore a punitive legal discourse—the restorative needs of the victims are discounted. This limitation is addressed in Martha Minow's critique of international trials: "Reconciliation is not the goal of criminal trials except in the most abstract sense. We reconcile with the murderer by imagining he or she is responsible to the same rules and commands that govern all of us; we agree to sit in the same room and accord the defendant a chance to speak, and a chance to fight for his or her life. But reconstruction of a relationship, seeking to heal the accused, or indeed, healing the rest of the community, are not goals in any direct sense" (Minow 26).

Minow underlines a key difference between punitive and restorative justice as manifest in war tribunals. Because legalistic justice aims to "maintain rules, laws, and civil order" (Estrada-Hollenbeck 68), its main goal is punishing violators of the law rather than vindicating victims (Biggar, "Making Peace," 10). Their vindication hinges on meeting the restorative needs of those violated, wrongdoers, and the community at large. Thus, as Minow rightly states, (punitive) justice is divorced from reconciliation, which renders victims visible and centers their restorative needs.

Restorative Justice: "Making Right the Wrong"

In contrast to the punitive/legalistic model, restorative justice values and centers the needs of those violated, wrongdoers, and the community. For this reason, it behooves us to heed the call for a reorientation by scholars like Zehr who explain that "to understand restorative justice, the praxis of legalistic justice must be set side, and a reorientation of how we think about crime and justice must be embraced" (qtd. in Estrada-Hollenbeck 74). The difference between retributive and restorative conceptions of justice centers on the perception of right, violation, and measures used to counter violation.

Restorative justice encodes an investment in a relational potential, which influences how justice is conceived and pursued. Defining crime as resulting from "a conflict relationship" (Hudson and Galaway 286) underscores how a crime "is primarily [a] conflict between individuals that results in injuries" (Estrada-Hollenbeck 74); restorative justice seeks to heal the consequences of this violation. Also, because restorative justice models attend to and "involve, to the extent possible, *those who have a stake* in a specific offense" it recognizes and involves those who are indirectly impacted by violence to "*collectively* identify and address harms, needs, and obligations, in order to heal and put things as right as possible" (Zehr 37; emphasis added). Not only do the impacts of the injury extend beyond the victims to include communities and offenders, but the state also may be decentered (Estrada-Hollenbeck; Stovel); the crime mainly involves the individuals violated and community members whose moral universe is violated, and the crime is considered "only secondarily as a violation against the state" (Estrada-Hollenbeck 74). Rather than punishing perpetrators (i.e, the aim of punitive justice), the main goal of restorative justice is to "restor[e] relationships between parties" as Tutu, who was referencing South Africa's *ubuntu* tradition, explained (Tutu qtd. in Lambourne, 313).[9] Restoring relations begins by recognizing the humanity and restorative needs of victims, perpetrators, and the whole community (Stovel). Since restorative justice aims to "making right the wrong" done (Wemmers 400), peace pursuers have to address multiple justice needs. Restoration and healing are "the most important justice needs" (Lambourne 314) and they exceed punishment. This is why scholars like James Tully underscore the centrality of acknowledging the hurt, restorative rights, and needs of victims. Whether the pursuit of justice entails "acknowledgment," "recognition," or attending to the "needs" of victims (Doxtader, "On the Turn"; Lambourne; Tully), it is both a central topic and an arduous task that mandates reflexivity and prudence (Tully). Yet, the questions remains: How do we recognize victims? Can/should perpetrators be recognized?

Recognizing Injury, Recognizing Victims

Numerous scholars have explained the polarizing (us vs. them), exclusionary, dehumanizing, and adversarial interactional dynamics that precede violence (Daye; Galtung). Reconciliation resorts to recognition of the humanity, worth, and dignity of individuals and peoples to reverse this discourse. Current reconciliation literature deals with attaining recognition in two different ways. Firstly, it underscores the need to restore the dignity of victims through justice, truth finding, acknowledging acts of violence/violation (Biggar, "Making Peace," 10) and their claim(s) of right(s). Secondly, the literature points to vindication processes that can go a step further. In such cases, the root causes of conflict are addressed, which entails an investigation of cultural and structural modes of violence that may support and engender situations resulting in questioning, overlooking, or stripping away someone's dignity, thus objectifying them. There are numerous ways to address both goals. In what follows, I address how symbolic and procedural measures rhetorically address injury.

Recognition of victims and survivors can manifest in the form of substantive and/or symbolic forms of vindication.[10] Substantive forms of vindication typically entail the use of procedural/institutional forms of justice like reparative measures (Biggar, "Making Peace," 10; Doxtader, "Faith and Struggle," 128–40). It is possible to offer compensation—as a form of restitutive justice (Lambourne 313).[11] However, often no compensation (or punishment) can provide a worthwhile gesture toward responsibility/response-ability. Especially in these situations, symbolic justice needs to be pursued, and it "can be achieved when victims perceive that authorities or perpetrators acknowledge the injustice that they have experienced" (314).

One way to acknowledge injury symbolically is through affording surviving victims and/or perpetrators a space to tell their stories and testify to the atrocious violence. Disclosing the past can offer what Doxtader ("Faith and Struggle" 134) refers to as a "(metatransitive) turn," a beginning. In disclosing the past, interlocutors seek to promote a better understanding of atrocious deeds and ensuing hurt and harm: ideally, "this (meta-transitive) turn is one that calls those subjected to historical violence to the work of subjectivation, a 'coming to terms' through the (re)presentation of those words that are claimed to hold the potential for understanding" (134). As a case in point, the South African TRC "routed its definition and defense of recognition through the potential of public speech, an interchange and exchange dedicated to disclosing and narrating one's *'own account'* of history, accepting responsibility for past transgression, (re)presenting self interest, and fostering the mutual understanding needed for the 'restoration of our humanity'" (I, 112 qtd. in Doxtader, "Faith and Struggle," 133). Public speech helped bring truth to light in order to account and be accountable. Defined as such, symbolic justice is a complex product of the pursuit of justice and vindication that enlists forms of memory/forgetting. This memory is critical for victims' (and the community's) healing and reckoning with an atrocious past. Both symbolic and substantive vindication measures acknowledge victims' suffering and affirm their dignity, rights, and equal worth (Tully).

Testimonial disclosures, however, do not imply that reconciliation is realized, for as Biggar aptly put it, "Bringing the truth to light is but the first step in a long process of reconciliation that will take generations to complete" ("Making Peace" 6). In addition, these testimonial disclosures are fraught with difficulties when testimony leads to neither recognition nor healing. Numerous case studies document the limits of disclosure testimonials that resulted in neither a wrongdoer's contrition nor their ability to listen rhetorically to victims' accounts. To illustrate, when an account of past atrocities is part of a discourse of amnesty in which perpetrators are required to share their "own accounts," the rhetoric of disclosure is reduced to merely an instrumental requirement for amnesty (as in South Africa's TRC). Thus, it is stripped of its potential gesture toward the other, recognizing their humanity and restorative needs. This impedes accountability.

Paulina's mis-/underrecognition is yet another case in point. Paulina, a Chilean woman who discovered that Doctor Roberto (her neighbor) was her torturer and rapist under a former military rule, felt misrecognized when he failed to communicate contrition. In response, she kidnapped him, put him on trial in her living room; her cross-examination reached a climactic point at which she underlined the unassailable tension among misrecognition, healing, and restoring humanity.

Paulina: . . . I'm not going to kill you because you're guilty, Doctor, but because you haven't repented at all. I can only forgive someone who really repents, who stands up amongst those he wronged and says, I did this, I did it, and I'll never do it again.

Roberto: What more do you want? You've got more than all the victims in this country will ever get. What more do you want?

Paulina: The truth, Doctor. The truth and I will let you go.
(Biggar, "Making Peace," 11)

Contrition—implicitly or explicitly articulated—seizes the possibility of recognizing victims and hurt incurred. Paulina yearned for recognition of her humanity. Failing to recognize his violence, embrace accountability to his victims, and commit to "never do it again," Roberto failed Paulina again. Like Paulina, many South Africans felt unrecognized, underrecognized, or misrecognized because they were not heard.

The "Duty to Listen"

Wrongdoers fail victims a second time by refusing to recognize them as grievable subjects (Butler) whose grievances should be listened to. Doxtader cogently explicates this limit of testimonials when victims' rhetorical truth telling, uncovering violation, falls on deaf ears: "At the TRC, in hearing after hearing in which the testimony of victims failed to produce any reaction from or interaction with perpetrators, the problem of the word's capacity to sever and isolate in the name of setting like only and always with like is the question of how reconciliation might indemnify the unraveling of recognition's narrative promise into a string of claims that is neither coherent nor heard" (Doxtader, "Faith and Struggle," 135). Telling one's story, then, fails to lend itself to recognition when its recipients—especially those who are made accountable by the narrative account—refuse to listen rhetorically.

The absence of listening exacerbates conflict, silences grievance claims, makes victims nongrievable subjects (Butler), and short-circuits conflict resolution endeavors. When wrongdoers refuse to listen to victims, they void victims' accounts of their rhetorical power; a narrative's potential is then nullified when it neither generates recognition, is not listened and responded to rhetorically, nor results in an interruption, a new interpretive lens. Conversely, active listening, a rhetorical practice (Ratcliffe), allows for truth(s) and contested memories to surface and belligerent parties/peace pursuers to voice their grievances and to listen to the grievances of others, which are essential actions in cases of double victimization. Thus, it enables functional contact that promotes peaceful conflict resolution. Then, listening and responding transform testimony from a monologic to a dialogic encounter; the wrongdoer listens and assumes accountability, hence engaging in reconciliation.

Because of its decisive role, the power of listening is ascertained across varied disciplines that consider it central to processes of reconciliation (Booth, "Rhetoric of War and Reconciliation"; Ratcliffe; Stovel; Tully; Villa-Vicencio). For example, Nicolas Cull and James Tully (public diplomacy and political philosophy, respectively) underline the importance of listening. Tully advocates for "dutiful listening," emphasizing "the maxim *audi alteram partem* (always listen to the other side)" (Tully 94–95), which translates to "the duty to listen and respond" (99). Cull ("Seven Lessons") asserts its crucial role in promoting understanding and establishing trust and meaningful diplomatic interaction. Similarly, Charles Villa-Vicencio ("Reconciliation") and Laura Stovel (sociology and religious studies, respectively) affirm active listening's decisive role in political reconciliation since it creates opportunities for understanding, which in turn promote conflict resolution. Likewise, Wayne Booth and Krista Ratcliffe affirm its role in reducing tension, leading to peaceful negotiation of contentious issues. This scholarship calls attention to the duty to listen, explaining that we are bound to listen, especially when it is difficult to listen to rights claims, which are generative. These affect not just those violated but the whole community: whether right claims are (perceived as) invisible or dismissed, they become part of the conversation on (in)justice. As such, recognition claims must be complemented with the "duty to listen" (Tully 99) for the way they inform our collective take on the moral universe, which allows for/impedes recognition of victims and their rights. Ultimately, recognition of victims by disclosing their own accounts affords victims/survivors respect, acknowledges their injuries, and counters the logic that enabled/justified an act of violence. But what of the perpetrator? Do perpetrators have rights or restorative needs to be recognized?

Recognizing the Humanity of Perpetrators

> It takes training to peer through a dark lens long enough to begin to see one's neighbors as essentially inferior to oneself. Harder for most of us, perhaps, is training in the habit of seeing the worst of neighbors as still

> humans like ourselves. To adopt that latter habit is to acquire empathy for the "repulsive" . . . , a habit quite different from either sympathy or excuse. To explain and understand is not to justify; but to empathize is to discover the common humanity that links victims to their perpetrators.
>
> —*Donald W. Shriver*

Recognizing a transgressor's humanity (especially a perpetrator of [mass] violence and violation) is difficult, as Shriver soundly explains in the epigraph. To understand transgressors' humanity is to recognize the fragility of our own, which indeed entails self-consciousness and rhetorical work. To reckon with the repulsive in our neighbor empathetically, we need to recognize our shadow—a Jungian concept that basically underlines the hidden or repressed dimensions of the self. As Carl G. Jung explains, "No one can become conscious of the shadow without considerable moral effort. To become conscious of it involves recognizing the dark aspect of the personality as present and real. This act is the essential condition for any kind of self-knowledge, and it therefore, as a rule, meets with considerable resistance" (8).

The imminent presence of and the need to recognize our shadow—and accordingly the humanity of a wrongdoer—was expressed by many, but not as simply as the psychiatrist supervising Nazi defendants: "We must conclude not only that such personalities are not unique or insane, but also that they could be duplicated in any country of the world today" (qtd. in Shriver 36). In recognizing transgressors' humanity, we can and should remember their horrendous acts. Yet in order to recognize their humanity, we must continue to learn about our own fragilities so we do not fall into the trap of dehumanizing perpetrators, thus reviving the rhetoric of violence.[12] This complex task is central to restorative justice, which emphasizes the restorative rights of wrongdoers, too. Many will refuse to consider the restorative needs of perpetrators. Yet calling for "the *just* affirmation of the humanity of victim and perpetrator" (35; emphasis added) while vindicating victims is the only way to heal and restore the moral tone of a community. However, attaining the goals of affirming victims' humanity and vindicating them hinges on understanding the complexity and limits of the speech acts that result in recognition. Only then can an enduring reconciliation be attained.

Speech Acts and the Rhetoric of Recognition

The rhetorical work of recognition can be actualized differently, depending on whether we choose speech acts of apology, forgiveness, or commitment. Each is rich with possibilities and fraught with complications. To illustrate, Marc Gopin underlines the complexity and contradictory characterizations of forgiveness:

> There are many contradictory characterizations of "forgiveness" that include, for various peoples: verbal acts and formal gestures; confession; apology, repentance, and acknowledgment of past; a willingness to suffer punishment as part of forgiveness; ritualized bilateral exchanges that give efficacy to forgiveness only in a prescribed set of interactions; unilateral expressions; bilateral expression of the gesture; forgiveness that is offered and received that concedes all other obligations; forgiveness only in the context of legal compensation, justice, restoration, or the righting of past wrongs; and finally, interpersonal versus collective executions of remorse, apology, and forgiveness. (88)

The complexity and centrality of apology-forgiveness to reconciliation discourse has led to philosophic, linguistic, sociopolitical, and theological questions—some captured by Gopin—that explore key features of apology-forgiveness, their relation, and their role in efficacious conciliation. These recurring questions demonstrate our differing perceptions of the role apology and forgiveness play in interpersonal and political conflict resolution.

Across different orientations, scholarship converges and affirms the undeniable utility of apology and forgiveness as interventive measures that can heal severed relations, solve conflicts, and restore communities. Though scholars agree on this interventive, problem-solving potential, they disagree on their assessment of (1) the kind of rhetorical work done, (2) the nature of the relation between apology and forgiveness, and (3) the ensuing obligations. If apology and forgiveness are "measures" that ultimately pursue justice, they are different acts and entail different rhetorical work. The rhetorical work done can entail unilateral and/or bilateral interactive—often ritualized—communicative gestures that include verbal utterances (e.g., "sorry"), stances (i.e., accountability or forgiveness), and commensurate actions (e.g., reparations as a gesture toward making amends). Underlining their interdependence, some scholars define apology and forgiveness as a form of exchange or deal in which the latter is conditioned on the former. However, other perspectives transcend this exchange/pact model. As a pact or exchange, apology-forgiveness relations center (the identification of) culpability. Alternatively, Derrida presents forgiveness as neither conditional nor dependent on apology, and Tutu (*No Future*) considers forgiveness as necessary for reconciliation, which he refers to in relation to the open stance of magnanimity and ubuntu that many South Africans exuded. When forgiveness is seen as independent of apology, the discourse decenters identification of culpability and punishment and seeks to invest in recognizing the restorative needs of all involved.

The rhetoric of forgiveness is generative. Biggar ("Concluding Remarks" 277) explains that paradigmatically, reconciliation "is an intimate business," underlining the dyadic nature of "granting and accepting of forgiveness." However, beyond the intimate sphere of dyadic interaction, scholars underline the limitation of political forgiveness (Biggar; La Caze), explaining that the rhetorical work done by peace pursuers is typically responsive to and affected by their spheres of interaction (e.g., [extra]juridical or political). For example, "in the paradigmatic sense, a state cannot forgive. . . . only victims have the authority to forgive" (Biggar 277–78). In addition, this paradigmatic, dyadic configuration ignores crucial dimensions of conflict, violence and hence reconciliation. First, the dyadic paradigm fails to recognize cases of double or multiple victimizations (Elshtain; Estrada-Hollenbeck; Montville) in which the patterns of exchange of apology and forgiveness are neither neat nor unidirectional. Second, it deflects attention from the fact that apology does not necessarily lead to healing or forgiveness and underrecognizes the dire impact of an act of violence on a whole community (Biggar, "Making Peace"; Stovel): apology and forgiveness reconciliation can leave victims feeling sorely betrayed. For example, in Sierra Leone's and South Africa's reconciliation experiences, critiques of the limitations of apology-forgiveness shed light on how, despite giving voice to some victims and enabling their healing, recipients of violence and communities were left vulnerable when an apology was directed to the state; they neither knew the perpetrators of violence nor were recipients of perpetrators' expressions of repentance (Biggar, "Concluding Remarks," 277–78). Further, if we consider an (official) apology as a deliberate act of recognition of those injured (i.e., a speech act based on and exuding a disposition of respect), which is the perfect duty of the wrongdoer (La Caze), we cannot assume or require that an apology necessarily result in forgiveness. La Caze argues that forgiveness, unlike apology, is an imperfect duty premised on love.

As such, the power of apology for past injustices can neither be overemphasized nor dismissed. Reducing apology, forgiveness, and reconciliation to "sentimentalism" or discrete utterances of confession/acknowledgment of responsibility (Elshtain 41) means their potential and relevance as political instruments is dismissed. Alternatively, while recognizing how and to what extent both concepts serve communities and nations in their pursuit of justice and peace—despite being fraught with limitations—we can build a richer understanding and repertoire of interventive modes of engaging, if not countering, violence and moving toward peace interpersonally and (inter)nationally. Public (representative) apology has brought some accounting, if not healing, to nations (e.g., the British and Irish according to Elshtain); minority groups around the world (e.g., Clinton's apology for the Japanese internment camps); and colonized subjects of war crimes (e.g., Japanese Prime Minister Tomiichi Murayama), to mention but a few.[13] Yet, while studying apology-forgiveness on a political level, we must be cognizant of the consequences of reducing all reconciliation to a dyadic paradigmatic model. Such consciousness certainly calls for further exploration of how the rhetoric of reconciliation meets the restorative needs of victims and informs citizens of the nature and meaning of reconciliation on a political level. However, political life is often driven by the logic of expedience, a logic that might be in tension with the pursuit of punitive justice. This is why speech acts of commitment (i.e., commissives) to making amends become crucial.

Commitment surfaces in study after study, underlining the value of stakeholders' commitment to peace. For example, Catherine Barnes underscores the value of commitment in a report titled *Owning the Process: Mechanisms for Political Participation of the Public in Peacemaking.* Based on her experience in a workshop held with peacemaking consultants, Barnes asserts that "conflict dynamics are not transformed by agreements alone—they also need a *commitment to address ongoing problems* through political means. It is possible that this challenge will be addressed more easily if most elements of the society have had an opportunity to *engage* in and *take responsibility* for the peace process" (15). Barnes thus affirms the role of assuming responsibility and committing to sustain the move toward peace. In specific terms, she underlines how commissives make peace pursuers own the process, persist in the processes of identifying the real causes of conflict by listening to their and the others' grievances, and stand up to the challenge of confronting the realities of violence, their rippling effects, and enduring consequences. In cases of multiple victimization, as well as cases of unaccountable perpetrators, commitment to peace can help communities move forward. Commitment can open a door for accountability that can be closed by stark power asymmetries, dysfunctional justice systems, or lack of laws to vindicate victims. This limitation recurs and invites us to think about how the pursuit of justice might be limited by political realities, a situation that requires an attempt to address together justice and prudent response.

POLITICAL PRUDENCE

The need for prudence persists; political prudence has been a concern in political thought (Dobel; Ruderman) since antiquity.[14] Contemporary scholars—invoking the Aristotelian tradition—explain prudence as a flexible, practical knowledge that aims at "having us live 'well,' bringing us closer to our ends as humans" (Ruderman 409–10). At moments of conflict resolution, leaders work toward peace, and justice is one of its cornerstones. However, realizing justice and peace is often elusive and poses difficult moral dilemmas, for in pursuing justice, community members might disagree about how they define justice (ends) and the way to attain it (means), as noted earlier; unfortunately, in their pursuit of justice and peace, community members can tear the community apart.

At best, a community aspires to collective support of a peace agreement after it is reached. However, sometimes peace agreements are perceived as unjust. Because justice is fundamental to the attainment of peace, perceptions of reluctance to pursue justice or resorting to insufficient or inefficacious measures jeopardize reconciliation. In other words, "insofar as people regard a political settlement as unjust, they will not support it; and if enough people regard it as unjust, it will cease to be viable" (Biggar, "Making Peace," 7). Alternatively, besides questions concerning the efficacy of different modes of justice, peace pursuers contend with the consequences of (in)justice and the (in)compatibility of justice and political prudence; both can manifest in impunity—defined as both a lack of punishment and insufficient punishment—justified as politically expedient. The absence of justice has devastating impacts that transcend victims to affect the whole community. Because justice protects a community from repeated aggression, "[Amnesty International] condemned impunity as negating the value of truth and justice and leading to further violation" (Daye 107). Impunity distorts political life when it undermines equal rights, including the right to fair punishment, standing, and obligations, which includes being accountable to others. Thus it "confuses and creates ambiguous social, moral and psychological limits" (107). Because justice and (collective) memory intersect, impunity authorizes dysfunctional forgetting for "the lies and denials are institutionalized and are defended by the laws of the country" (107). As such, impunity distorts public memory and foils the possibility of citizenship in the full sense because "impunity affects belief in the future and may leave a historical 'no man's land' in which there is both an official and an unofficial version of events—something that may give rise to historical stagnation, limiting the possibility of moving ahead and creating a common just society" (107). Thus, on the one hand, impunity violates collective memory and becomes a festering presence, distorting perceptions of justice, order, equity, and reciprocity of rights and obligations—crucial variables for the (re)formation of community. On the other hand, impunity has an impact on interpersonal and intrapersonal social dynamics, for it impedes full engagement: "Impunity strengthens powerlessness, guilt and shame" and "invalidates and denies what has happened and thereby limits the possibility of effective communication between fellow citizens. This hampers collective mourning and the collective working through of what has happened" (107).[15]

Perceived tension between peace and justice results in a difficult situation for community leaders[16] or political rhetorical agents who need to continually strike a balance between justice and political prudence. And at times of escalating violence when peace becomes an end to be promoted and pursued, leaders need prudence to frame suasive discourses that can problematize retaliation while offering alternative justice measures that can "cool the hearts." This will entail processes of deliberation. To illustrate, because, "there are two divergent motives behind calls for public remembering, . . . politicians are morally bound to make some choices between them: Is the purpose of recall to be the nourishing of revenge? Or is it the nourishing of public purpose not to repeat the evil? The justice of truth telling needs the justice of forbearance from revenge" (Shriver 29). Conciliators, then, need both restraint and creativity, two features of wisdom (Crosswhite) to coinvent alternatives to violence that generate collective support and celebrate the cultural values that would make this alternative meaningfully coherent and consistent with the community's moral fabric.

In our attempt to attain reconciliation, we must ensure that means lead to ends pursued, so prudence (in the sense of pursuing means consistent with desired goals) is a decisive factor for attaining reconciliation. Prudence aspires to efficacy, and reconciliatory efficacy entails self-reflexivity, a move toward the other, and actualizing stances that embrace the risk of recognizing violence and violation for what they are. Subsequently, we can dutifully listen to and engage claims of rights, knowing that reconciliation is more than addressing claims of rights. Efficacious and prudent conciliatory discourse will come to fruition when it creatively offers an alternative to retaliation and its logic; a culturally sensitive mode of dealing with the past; and a meaningful recognition that is—in Doxtader's and Tully's terms—coherent and *dutifully* listened to. But because of the intricate nature of healing on individual, communal, and (inter)national levels, it is prudent to consider reconciliation not as a one-time event. Rather, reconciliation must be a dynamic and organic formation capable of iterative, self-reflexive, reciprocal, and dialogic processes of vindication and restoration. This reconciliatory response hinges on knowledge of and a willingness to engage memory, justice, and prudence. Ṣulḥ pursuers, too, attend to the same topics.

ṢULḤ

Ṣulḥ pursuers, too, grapple with these reconciliatory topoi; they grapple with justice, memory, and the mandate for prudence as they seek to vindicate victims, to hold accountable and reintegrate wrongdoers, and to restore a community's faith in the ultimate justice of things. As an Arabic word, ṣulḥ / صلح/ literally means "reconciliation." The word captures the practices, rituals, processes, and goals of ṣulḥ, a very old sociopolitical traditional reconciliation practice in the Arab world that relies heavily on mediation. The reconciliation tradition attempts to realize the rights and needs of people in the wake of acts of aggression. Like other reconciliation modalities, ṣulḥ recognizes that: "humans are deeply motivated to satisfy their basic needs for recognition, security, and identity. If any of those needs remains unfulfilled, individual or group conflict will result. A genuine resolution of conflict occurs only when those basic human needs are fully satisfied" (Abu-Nimer, *Nonviolence*, 9). Abu-Nimer's quotation underlines the need for "recognition, security, and identity." For this reason, ṣulḥ is sometimes translated as "reconciliation," "forgiveness," or "cooperation" (Lang 53). Though all three translations communicate ṣulḥ's general impetus to resolve conflict and regain social harmony, they are all partial synonyms that fall short of effectively and unambiguously translating ṣulḥ: the words ṣulḥ and reconciliation are not full equivalents. In English, reconciliation has a connotation that is not part of the Arabic word. Michael Hardimon elucidates how the word reconciliation has two meanings: "In its ordinary use, *reconciliation* can mean 'submission' or 'resignation'" (173). The use of either the preposition *to* or *with* after the verb *reconcile* (reconcile *to* and reconcile *with*) implies power (a)symmetry between involved participants and therefore implies a different type of act: "The negative tone of *reconciliation* is especially clear when the verb is used with the preposition *to*, a usage that suggests that the process of reconciliation is asymmetrical and that the object of reconciliation is a state of affairs that is viewed negatively. One becomes reconciled *to* the loss of a child. The use of the preposition *with*, on the other hand, suggests that the process is symmetrical and the object of reconciliation is a person who is viewed positively. I become reconciled *with* my friend" (Hardimon 173).

In Arabic, there are two different words for each sense of reconciliation:

the first is communicated in Arabic using the word *riḍā* (i.e., contentment), which is equivalent to *acceptance*, *toleration*, or *resignation*. The second is ṣulḥ or *muṣālaḥah*, which is equivalent to reconcile *with*. It is very important to distinguish ṣulḥ from reconciling *to*. In Arabic, there are words that refer to submission, surrender, and coercion, and, unfortunately, numerous cases of ṣulḥ practices reduce ṣulḥ's potential when people settle for submission, surrender, and coercion. The difference is consequential because, as Hardimon explains, "if reconciliation is a matter of submitting to the powers-that-be or resigning oneself to the status quo, who wants it?" (173). Reconciliation certainly entails transformation, which includes change in subject position and, potentially, relations, but such change needs to affirm one's power—not relegate reconciliation pursuers into positions of subjugation, for then reconciliation recirculates power *over* and ceases to be; subjugation reproduces violence.

Cultural and Doctrinal Roots

Numerous scholars, theologians, and promoters of peace have studied ṣulḥ and peace in Islam. Their scholarship sheds light on religious (Abu-Nimer, *Nonviolence*; Fitzmaurice), social, and political viewpoints (Irani; Lang; Smith), and this literature continues to grow, especially with increasing investment in traditional knowledges of conflict resolution (Kreisberg, "Reconciliation"). This scholarship traces the call for ṣulḥ as a recognized relational and moral good (i.e., *al- ṣulḥ khayr*) to al-Qur'ān (e.g., al-Nisā' 128). Additionally, this scholarship goes as far back as *Ṣaḥīḥ al-Bukhārīy,* which can be considered a ninth-century, secondary source of insight into ṣulḥ.[17] The book on ṣulḥ (Book 49) provides a collection of prophetic sayings and accounts of events that survey ṣulḥ practices and addresses questions pertinent to ṣulḥ. These include the significance of and rewards of ṣulḥ as a conflict resolution method (Book 49, No. 870); the obligation to pursue ṣulḥ (Book 49, Nos. 855, 858); examples of Prophet Muḥammad's comments on, mediation, and arbitration to resolve disputes over marital affairs, loans, and retaliation versus restitution (Book 49, Nos. 859, 866, 868–69, 872–73); conditions or situations that could jeopardize or render ṣulḥ unjust and, hence, nullified (Book 49, Nos. 861–63); acts that neither nullify ṣulḥ nor make a conciliator a liar (Book 49, No. 857); and what can be written in a treaty (Book 49, Nos. 863–65, 867), referencing the ṣulḥ al-Ḥudaibiyah, the ṣulḥ with Khaybar, and Prophet Muḥammad's prophecy of ṣulḥ al-Ḥasan. As such, *Ṣaḥīḥ al-Bukhārīy* provides a historical record of compiled evidence that documents the practice of and belief in the good (relational, business/monetary, societal, political, etc.) attained by ṣulḥ. More recent scholarship has studied the conception of reconciliation in Islam as presented in the *Qur'ān* (Fitzmaurice), explicating its doctrinal dimensions, conditions for success, value as a good to be pursued in the relationship between human beings and God, and value as an effective dispute-resolution measure among Muslims and between Muslims and non-Muslims (Fitzmaurice 164–65). Though some studies focus on the interventive dimension of ṣulḥ, numerous studies explicate ṣulḥ's proactive potential by situating it in relation to a multidimensional investment in relational good, harmony, and balance—essential characteristics of a reconciled self/community (for more on this, see chapter 5).

To illustrate, providing a nuanced framework for nonviolence and peacebuilding in Islam, Abu-Nimer ("A Framework") explains how ṣulḥ is embedded in a culture of peace that is invested in resolving social, economic, and political conflicts: "Islam yields a set of peacebuilding values that . . . can transcend and govern all types and levels of conflict, values such as justice (*'adl*), beneficence (*iḥsān*), and wisdom (*ḥikmah*), which constitute core principles in peacemaking strategies and frameworks" (220). Ṣulḥ—as a relational and moral good—is rendered meaningful by its relation to the values of *'adl, iḥsān,* and *ḥikmah.* A central piece of 'adl is truth telling. The obligation to truth telling and its relation to justice is very clear in the following verse: "O you who have believed, be persistently standing firm in justice, witnesses for Allah, even if it be against yourselves or parents and relatives. Whether one is rich or poor, Allah is more worthy of both. So follow not [personal] inclination, lest you not be just. And if you distort [your testimony] or refuse [to give it], then indeed Allah is ever, with what you do, Acquainted" (al-Nisā' 136). In addition to the obligation to rightfully testify and pursue justice, ṣulḥ is grounded in doctrinal principles that mandate nonviolent conflict resolution. These are "the unity of humankind, the supreme love of the Creator, the obligation of mercy, and Muslims' duty of subjection of their passions and accountability for all actions" (Abu-Nimer, "A Framework," 227).

More important, peace is not just an intrinsically valued good for the individual and community; it must be actionable. Because "the essential thing in life is peace, it is toward the achievement of peace that all human effort must be sincerely diverted" (Abu-Nimer, "A Framework" 228).[18] This obligation is the reason Islam unequivocally discourages people from using violence and firmly regulates its use when *absolutely* necessary "to avert worse disasters" (228) and to enable reconciliation afterwards. Since "the essential thing in life is peace" (228), which is defined as "a state of physical, mental, spiritual and social harmony" (243), peace is the default—not aggression. Consequently, the doctrinal aspect of reconciliation and peacebuilding is not just responsive to situations of conflict. Rather, at best, it is a proactive, forward-looking system that tries to subvert violation, violence, and oppression at institutional and individual levels. Accordingly, Abu-Nimer asserts that "Islamic teachings go beyond intervention to reach a settlement in a specific dispute; they aspire to achieve the value of one human family" ("A Framework" 241); peacebuilding at times of conflict and at times of stability hinges on the pursuit of justice (233–37), social empowerment through doing good (237–39), the universality of human dignity (239–41), equality (241–42), the sacredness of human life (242), and the active and passive pursuit of peace (243–45). In this pursuit, justice is central.

Justice and Recognition

Unlike typical juridical systems, ṣulḥ acknowledges and tries to balance the needs of all involved parties. When people resort to ṣulḥ, whether in tandem with their juridical system or as an extrajuridical "ritualization of peace-making" (Smith 394), the process typically involves mediation: family or community elders form a committee, intervene, and work toward reconciling belligerent parties. As an expression of restorative justice, ṣulḥ is often manifest as a practice and ritual across the Arab world that sets off the crucial process of healing the victim, enabling the atonement and at-onement (i.e., making two conflicting parties one and returning to God) of the offender, and restoring the community's "moral tone" (Stovel). All these goals are indeed extrajuridical (Smith 394).

Ṣulḥ is a restorative iteration of justice. It differs from punitive models in which "punishment serves as an enlargement of the relative value of the victim by diminishing the value of the offender, the defeat of the wrongdoer can be directly at the hands of the victim or through an agent, such as the state" (Daye 106). Ṣulḥ neither considers punishment as its main focus nor considers retributive and restorative justice as mutually exclusive. The relationship among ṣulḥ, restorative justice, and retributive justice is well documented by ethnographic studies of ṣulḥ in Galilee and Cairo, for example, (Ayoub; Drieskens; Lang; Smith) that demonstrate how ṣulḥ is often used "in tandem with the state justice system" (Lang 52). Ṣulḥ neither dismisses nor settles for the goals of retributive justice because it recognizes the complexity of justice needs (see chapter 2). Accordingly, scholars and practitioners underscore the importance of ṣulḥ's attention to the restorative (read social, psychological, and ethical) needs of the victim, perpetrator, and community. This attention recognizes the need for and implications of (not) having a just and fair resolution to conflict: only when "sulha alleviates emotional and social pressures [does it serve as] a legitimate alternative to retaliation" (Lang 54). As such, ṣulḥ manifests the principles and goals of restorative justice: it does not settle *just* for punitive demands but rather attempts to meet the restorative needs of all involved as a ṣulḥ mediator interviewed by Smith succinctly underscored:

> I want to say something about court ruling, however, including Rabbinic courts or civil courts. Somebody always loses in the court. The person who loses in the court always leaves unhappy, because he lost the case. The person who wins the case leaves the court happy, because he has gained. A court cannot satisfy two sides, it can only satisfy one side. Making the Arab Sulha satisfies all parties—there is no loser, and no gainer. No happy and unhappy—all are happy in the end. Even the whole village is happy. (391)

As the informant asserts, ṣulḥ is attentive to all stakeholders because of its investment in reintegration: "Restorative measures are designed to reintegrate both victims and offenders into society" (Daye 110). This investment is informed by an ethic of care for others and a relational worldview. Within a relational perspective, "humans are relational beings" and "crime is a violation of a relationship, an injury inflicted on another person that harms the people involved and the community" (Stovel 3). People are related, and "an ethic of care which argues that people are ethically responsible for those around them with whom they have a relationship" (Kiss qtd. in Daye 2) motivates them to be response-able.

These restorative goals and resultant response-ability are orchestrated through a strategic, rhetorical engagement that ameliorates conflict and guides people's co-construction of conflict resolution; the former critiques and counters injustice, whereas the latter seeks to envision an alternative (i.e., the critique for peace). Ṣulḥ as a process or as an event manifests a cultural and doctrinal framework of peacebuilding that seeks not only to solve a problem but also to address the grounds that enabled an act of violence or oppression. To mobilize both moves, reconciliation pursuers enlist the help of community elders who guide/support their collective pursuit. The wrongdoer or someone on their behalf initiates a ṣulḥ process, which typically entails mediation. Depending on its (urban/rural) setting, ṣulḥ might result in a public event—called *ṣulḥa*—"strictly dictated by traditional steps" (Smith 387). As an event, ṣulḥ becomes an intricate ritualization of peacemaking (for more on this, see chapter 2). Mediation, traditional steps, and ritualized peacemaking are key features of ṣulḥ that manifest ṣulḥ's restorative and reintegrative rhetoric.

Many consider mediation a condition of possibility for ṣulḥ. Because mediation is capable of realizing the relational imperative, which becomes one of the mediator's key responsibilities, "a 'solution' to a dispute [is not recognized] until the mediation process is realized" (Smith 394). The unique interventive potential of mediation stems from the fact that it is a humanistic, dialogic, and context-sensitive communicative model that transcends punitive justice and aspires for reintegration; the mediator—a rhetor par excellence—"must construct an outcome in the light of the social and cultural context of the dispute, the full scope of the relations between the disputants and the perspectives from which they view the dispute" (Felstiner 74). As mediators attend to these sociopolitical dimensions of ṣulḥ, they distinguish ṣulḥ from other conflict resolution practices like peacekeeping, which tends to be perceived as a short-term measure for social control that mainly focuses on containing conflict (Fetherston). Alternatively, ṣulḥ is long-term oriented, promotes change, and entails social reconstitution; all imply a rhetorical dexterity to dissuade people from retaliation and to foreground the potential of ṣulḥ. Mediators' tasks, therefore, are indeed complex: in addition to creating a space for the meeting of parties involved, they need to (1) recognize and balance the needs of all involved parties, which transcends punishment, (2) heal victims by affirming their rights, (3) enable the atonement/at-one-ment of the offender, (4) find out what will hold the wrongdoer accountable for their aggression and reconciliation, all while (5) maintaining communal solidarity (Ayoub), restoring the "moral tone" (Stovel), and enabling conflict resolution and transformation.

Often the process of ṣulḥ is inextricably linked to a *ṣulḥah* (i.e., ṣulḥ event). In a full-fledged ṣulḥ, a public meeting can be used to actualize, affirm, and hold peace pursuers accountable to their stances of recognition and responsiveness. A public meeting/ṣulḥ event typically relies on ritualized acts, which in turn facilitate the reconciliation process, increase openness to the co-construction of a mutually accepted resolution, and may help sustain ṣulḥ. Though the rituals are typically seen in rural settings where the relational ties are stronger, they manifest crucial aspects of ṣulḥ that might be expressed differently in other settings. Across different settings, ṣulḥ seeks to reconstitute relations and heal communities. Smith captures the reconstitutive dimension of ṣulḥ and elucidates how the tradition and practice of the Arab ṣulḥ—like the Hawaiian Ho'oponono and Kpelle Moot (Smith 393–94)—move beyond acts of retribution to acts of interpersonal recognition and intrapersonal healing: ṣulḥ like these restorative models guides people as they address the emotions of hurt and shame and seek to coordinate a public ritual that reclaims the victims' honor—as a sense of and affective stance toward the self as well as a representation of good standing in relation to the community (394). Ritual and observing traditional steps seek to recognize victims, reverse power abuse, and regain a community's moral tone. This is why cases of ṣulḥ events proliferate.

As evidence, *Al-Masry Alyoum*, an Egyptian daily paper, reported a ṣulḥ case on February 13, 2014. The news story, "Five Shrouds End Blood Vengeance between the Families of Ḍāḥī and al-Masāwīy," reported the effective ṣulḥ that ended an eight-month conflict, which started when five men of the Ḍāḥī family fought with and were later indicted for the death of a man from al-Masāwīy family. Because ṣulḥ seeks the reintegration of all involved members in a healthy community, it endeavors to reclaim the dignity of the victims and orchestrates a process and public event that recognizes their unrightful violation and gives them their due apology and restitution. The Ḍāḥī and al-Masāwīy ṣulḥ entailed a public event. The title of the story and an accompanying photograph underline several key features of ṣulḥ. The title clearly taps into the use of visual and symbolic reservoirs of peacemaking rituals. In the worst-case scenario, a killer, who is the most likely candidate for revenge (or a member of their family), goes to the victim's family carrying the killer's *kafan* (shroud). The Ḍāḥī family's performative gesture (i.e., carrying shrouds) signaled their contrition and earnest pursuit of forgiveness. Carrying one's kafan and humbly facing the bereaved is part of the visual and symbolic reservoir of ṣulḥ rituals.[19] Also, the event is witnessed by hundreds of community members (2,000 is the number reported in the piece). The story includes a photograph, which demonstrates a huge crowd; at the center, men from both families embrace one another. Likely, one of them is the bereaved father. These public rites do not just recognize the rights of those violated, but they also discourage further victimization mainly by reversing power performatively; the wrongdoers are bound by the forgiveness/magnanimity of those bereaved. While reversing the trivialization of the rights and needs of those dehumanized and violated and acknowledging the ensuing hurt and anger, rites guide and help involved parties (those violated, perpetrators, and witnesses) to reinitiate a peaceful coexistence. The reconstitutive goal of ṣulḥ's public rites is demonstrated by the three "main pillars" of this "pre-Islamic custom" (Lang 53). Ṣulḥ pursuers shake hands *(muṣāfaḥah)*, forgive one another (*muṣālaḥah* or *muṣāmaḥah*), and eat together (*mumālaḥah*). These pillars (Smith 391) exceed the parameters of a legal, formal agreement and fulfill ṣulḥ's social-reconstitution goals. Ṣulḥ is irreducible to a "public performance of ritual action" (Smith 394), for it comprises a very long and intricate process, which is informed by a doctrinal and restorative value system. This process might end with a "public performance or ritual action." Ritual—whether fully expressed or reduced—is not just an efficacious reconciliation method, for it provides access to and a remembering of a rich repository of collective knowledge. Ṣulḥ pursuers often tap into this collectively remembered knowledge as a common ground and model of prudential intervention.

Memory, Moral Modeling, and Prudence

When a community chooses to continuously remember and draw on a particular tradition or peacemaking practice like ṣulḥ, the community taps into a cultural reservoir, which functions as its interpretive horizon. Within this cultural reservoir community members find models and precedents that guide future decision-making processes. Unlike forensic memory (i.e., remembering aggression acts) geared toward the pursuit of justice, this form of collective memory readjusts the interpretive compass in order to refashion one's response. Numerous suasory techniques manifest this form of memory. Mohammed Abu-Nimer's ethnographic account (*Nonviolence and Peacebuilding in Islam*) refers to frequent use of (1) Qur'ānic verses, (2) Ḥadīth (i.e., recorded statements made by Prophet Muḥammad), and (3) a "repertoire of saying, statements and stories" (101); each provides a condensed argument that promotes the value of forgiveness and peacemaking. In cases of ṣulḥ, involved participants bracket off the retributive tradition and choose to evoke the restorative one. This is evident in Abu-Nimer's ethnographic account; "the [sulha] process begins with the reading of three Qur'anic verses that support the mediation efforts" (99), but throughout the process not only Qur'ānic verses are resorted to, for ṣulḥ participants draw on a rich cultural reservoir that results in both persuasion and dissuasion. Recourse to this cultural reservoir is more complex than arguments from authority (Perelman and Olbrechts-Tyteca 306–10); rhetors strategically remember, evoke Qur'ānic verses, Ḥadīth, or conciliatory narratives to deliberately recall and foreground a peacemaking tradition that offers an alternative to hostility and retaliation. This rhetorical work can be better explained using addressivity and resourcement.

The act of recalling an alternative frame manifests addressivity—a Bakhtinian term pointing to "the quality of turning to someone else" (Murray 137). Addressivity allows encoders to relate to other utterances in a bigger discourse that is limited in neither place nor time. This rhetorical recall can be also considered a form of resourcement, which facilitates the process of disengaging from the logic of the initial violence and the reactive logic of punitive revenge. Therefore, the rhetor "deliberately draws energy from a new resource—a source other than the individual or system that provided the initial frame for the issue" (Foss and Griffin 9). Accordingly, as elders, mediators, and pursuers of ṣulḥ disengage from the logic of violence and revenge, as rhetors, they creatively reframe the situation from intractability to possibility. In the process, they, too, are subject to change from belligerent parties to peace pursuers. As such, peacemaking knowledge is not just an interpretive horizon, for it has a constitutive potential.

To illustrate, a Gazan intervener—interviewed by Abu-Nimer—had clear suasory goals: not only did he seek to channel ṣulḥ participants' thoughts and actions toward a peaceful and satisfactory conflict resolution, but he also sought to bring them to a state of remembrance:[20]

> We remind the parties about God and faith in God as the basis for all behavior. We remind them of death and of the futility of earthly life. Therefore, how can they quarrel about worldly things? We remind them of the following: destiny and fate; that Islam is the religion of justice, it treats justly both victims and offender; the neutrality of *shar'a* [Islamic regulations] and its encompassing blessing; that a person who refuses *shari'ah* [Islamic law] is placing himself in the circle of *kufur* [denial of Islam or God]; that sulh is *khayr* (reconciliation is good); that you should "be to people like trees, when a stone is thrown at them, fruit is thrown back" [Ḥadīth]; that returning aggression with *ihsan* (doing good) will bring good and reconciliation; and that by doing good to people, you will own their hearts, as often a human has been owned by his own good doing (*ihsan*). (Abu-Nimer, *Nonviolence*, 100)

The Gazan intervener resorts to the "the prophet's tradition and an accompanying set of traditional and cultural sayings that call for good actions" (101). In reminding involved parties of doctrinal premises that affirm peace, he highlights cornerstones of community building in the form of religious institutions (like Islamic law) that guide (proactive function) and regulate (responsive function) human action. His rhetoric underlines valued behavior: unlike the impulse of immediate, retaliatory acts, the intervener foregrounds action based on iḥsān, which implies responding peacefully and in kindness (not responding in kind). The Gazan intervener's account illustrates how memory in the sense of remembrance of what is *khayr* (good) has a sobering effect, for it provides a transformative re-modeling.

In an attempt to coordinate peaceful action, the intervener's rhetoric combines the spiritual with the pragmatic; he persuades and dissuades. The intervener seeks to influence the stakeholders' affect, thought, and action when he draws on a religiously charged vocabulary that can resist the language of retaliation and allay fears of repeated victimization. Dissuasion often leads to the use of warnings: an intervener/mediator can "warn people against lies, aggression, false oaths, and doing harm to others" (Abu-Nimer, *Nonviolence*, 101) in addition to promoting sayings that promote "social harmony" and restore order (96). Examples of sayings often cited include "Forgive when you are able" (*al-'afu 'inda al-makderah*); "every aggressor will pay the price for the[ir] aggression" [*'ala al-bāghī tadūr al-dua'ir*]; "God gives time but does not neglect" [*yumhil wa lā yuhmil*]; "a mistake is not a reason for another mistake;" and "all people will lose by fighting" (99–101). All these statements foreground a peaceful resolution that realizes the values of forgiveness, justice (even if delayed), and faith in the immanent goodness of people. In remembrance of this faith, peace pursuers spell out the good pursued (i.e., *al-ṣulḥ khayr*), invoke the commonplace of justice, and "[appeal] to the good that resides in all parties" (101). Because "the disputants have to be convinced that harmony is better than victory" (101), one of the goals of suasion (in the ritual phase of ṣulḥ) is to accentuate priorities and spell out the good pursued. Put differently, the cultural reservoir of sayings acts as an alternative interpretive lens that negatively evaluates retaliation and positively evaluates peacemaking, thus providing ṣulḥ participants with grounds and precedent for seeking peace.

More important, recalling well-recognized, wise reconciliatory intervention models what can/should be done. Ṣulḥ participants may call on narratives, which are appealing probably because of the subtle unfolding of "depropositionalized argument" (Hart, "Narrative Reasoning") for a particular mode of action. Abu-Nimer reports a religious narrative, which was used by an intervener: "A believer bought a piece of land and, after paying the price, found a pot of gold. He took it back to the man who sold him the land and told him: I bought the land and not the gold. But the man said: I sold you the land and everything in it. They went to Solomon, who said: Marry the boy and girl from each family and give them the gold" (*Nonviolence* 100). This narrative demonstrates how Prophet Solomon models prudence; he found a mutually acceptable solution for disputants. In addition to this narrativized model for prudential intervention to solve interpersonal problem, there are other narrativized precedents of political leaders who prudently choose communal peace over the pursuit of justice only.

A historically momentous case of ṣulḥ known as Ṣulḥ al-Ḥasan exemplifies this form. After a military confrontation, al-Ḥasan—one of the early

Muslim caliphs who had a legitimate right to rule—gave up leadership to Mu'awīyah, who also, albeit unfairly, claimed right to leadership. al-Ḥasan voluntarily accepted peace and proposed a framework for formal agreement.[21] al-Ḥasan's decision to give up leadership saved community members on both sides from fragmentation and prevented grave losses to civil war (al-Bukhārīy). Ṣulḥ initiators or pursuers mobilize the process as responsible members of a community who consider impending loss graver than potential gains or victory resulting from sustained conflict. The process does not have to begin with forgiveness; it can begin with a commitment to peacemaking. Ṣulḥ al-Ḥasan is often recalled as a formative historical moment and as a model for the willingness to prioritize the community's good, especially at times when right and might collide. A recalled historical account becomes a "depropositionalized argument"; the act of remembering is strategically used in ṣulḥ processes and events to ground, frame, and validate deliberation and model action consistent with ṣulḥ.

MOVING FORWARD: ṢULḤ ENACTMENT

As described, ṣulḥ manifests and draws on the topoi of justice, memory, and prudence, albeit differently. Like other peacemaking practices, ṣulḥ seeks to counter violence and resolve conflict. In the following chapters, I zoom in on cases that shed light on the rhetorical work entailed by ṣulḥ at interpersonal, communal/national, international, and intrapersonal levels. Together, these chapters depict a story in which ṣulḥ and ṣulḥ pursuers are key players. What makes the story unique is that the arduous process of peace is often initiated by committing to peace without fully knowing how the process unfolds, its entrapments, or its results. This commitment, however, is bigger than any one ṣulḥ process or event. But as it manifests in a case, the potential of ṣulḥ mobilizes witnesses of this commitment and creates a community of peace pursuers. In the coming chapters, my account of ṣulḥ as a rhetorical intervention that counters conflict and refashions subject positions is, therefore, consequential, for it taps into rhetoric's power to be—as Bradford Vivian would put it—"a precious aesthetic technology within this process" ("The Threshold of the Self" 316).

2

THE POWER OF SWEET PERSUASION

Cultural Inflections of Interpersonal Ṣulḥ Rhetorics

> Ṣulḥ *is good.*
> *C'mon let's reconcile.*
> Ṣulḥ *is good!*
> —*Excerpted from "al-ṣulḥ khayr" (Ṣulḥ is good)*

Living in Cairo in the 1990s, I was inundated by Nādiah Muṣṭafá's coaxing, playful call for reconciliation, which is largely captured in the first stanza quoted above.[1] I interpreted this song—"al-ṣulḥ khayr" (literally "conciliation is good")—as a romantically charged inducement to renounce hostility and embrace reconciliation. Little did I know that "al-ṣulḥ khayr" is a unique song: not only does it capture the emotive and interactional vocabulary of ṣulḥ's conciliatory "sweet persuasion" (Lang)—the power of using kind and sweet words to cool anger and reach out to reconciliation—but it also circulates moral and relational imperatives, imperatives to pursue reconciliation as a social and personal good.

In the late 1980s, Nādiah Muṣṭafá's song, which is approximately nine minutes long, was very popular, especially because of its happy, folkloric undertone. Her voice embodies a cajoling intervention, transforms a conflictive impasse into the possibility of peace, and makes a case for ṣulḥ as a worthy good. Her voice manifests the power of "sweet persuasion" to mediate the transition from hostility to peace. The lyrics written by Muṣṭafá al-Shandāwīlīy model "open hand" rhetoric (Corbett) used to invite others to pursue reconciliation, evoking the doctrinally driven call—*al-ṣulḥ khayr*. Interestingly, it is also a vernacular uptake of such morally and doctrinally charged relational good. Muṣṭafá's voice captures her relational investment in restoring relations with a loved one. Her voice echoes the voices of many women who negotiate and initiate ṣulḥ in private spaces, which are under the scholarly radar.[2] Yet ṣulḥ practices exceed the situation embodied by her voice and entail numerous rhetorical choices. Across the different meanings of ṣulḥ and positions of ṣulḥ pursuers, there is a conspicuous use of rhetoric that seeks reconciliation while reckoning with the relational and moral imperatives to make peace. This peacemaking rhetoric can be thought of as an invitational rhetoric that extends "an invitation to understanding as a means to create a relationship rooted in equality, immanent value [of human beings], and self-determination" (Foss and Griffin 5). Yet reconciliation is more than just an invitation. Accordingly, ṣulḥ rhetoric manifests an array of rhetorical practices that exceed invitational rhetoric, condenses a culturally inflected wisdom about the "labor of response"—borrowing Elizabeth Ellsworth's term—that accepts the uncertainty of initiating peace and the indeterminate rewards of peacemaking.

Shedding light on ṣulḥ practices mandates a nuanced and complex conceptualization of rhetoric that transcends a minimalist definition of rhetoric as persuasion. It is not surprising then that different forms of rhetoric are decisive to articulating claims of injustice, contending with retaliation/conflict resolution frames, and pursuing peacemaking. Rather than drawing on a minimalist definition of rhetoric, I draw on an expanded definition that includes internal rhetorics, functional silence, and (dys)functional rhetorics of listening and accountability, as detailed below. This expanded definition invokes ways of seeing rhetoric as deliberate(d), context-responsive action, whether expedient or prudent; as constituting pursuers of peace; and as a way to reknow those involved and their world. Put differently, rhetoric is a way of *doing*, *being*, *becoming*, and *knowing*.

This expanded definition of rhetoric is crucial especially because Abu-Nimer, Drieskens, Irani, Lang, and Smith provide ethnographic accounts of ṣulḥ, but there is no rhetorical study of ṣulḥ. Their cases help me exemplify different ways ṣulḥ is initiated by the wrongdoer, recipient of violence, or a third party. Together, they help chart the rhetorical and cultural nuances of ṣulḥ. In addition to underlining ṣulḥ types and processes, I draw on Abu-Nimer, Drieskens, Lang, and Smith to foreground external persuasion in transgressor-initiated ṣulḥ and mediation rhetorics; on Drieskens to foreground internal rhetorics; and on Ayoub to underline interpersonal, wronged-initiated ṣulḥ (postpunitive justice).

This chapter builds on chapter 1, which details ṣulḥ's axiological and doctrinal dimensions; it explicates the rhetorical dimensions and processual nature of ṣulḥ, which is energized by the recognition of responsibility. The chapter adds the dilemmas of real people who resorted to ṣulḥ as a cultural resource. But, more important, the selected ethnographic studies and historical references cover a long historical span, ranging from the Middle Ages to contemporary times. Geographically, these cases include a rural area in the 1960s where Lebanese villagers rely on the clan/tribe as a key organizing social force (Ayoub) and a case in an urban neighborhood in contemporary, late-1990s, Cairo (Drieskens). As I revisit ethnographic studies of ṣulḥ cases, I identify three main types of ṣulḥ and explicate how they are initiated. Turning to ṣulḥ's cultural inflections, I then show how the "logic" of violence is reversed by exploring the dynamic rhetorics of ṣulḥ pursuers. Their rhetoric manifests internal deliberation as well as external rhetorics like the rhetoric of recognition and apology, mediation, sweet persuasion, listening, and silence.

TYPES AND INITIATION OF ṢULḤ

Ethnographic accounts of ṣulḥ from Ayoub, Drieskens, Irani ("Islamic Meditation," "Acknowledgment"), Lang, and Smith, among others, outline its goals and processes. As a conciliation practice, ṣulḥ can be used to resolve different types of conflict (al-Bukhārīy).[3] Ṣulḥ can be used to resolve disputes over money or property, offenses, bodily injury, and even crimes that lead to death. The gravity and consequences of the offense partially determine whether the ṣulḥ process/ritual will be fully fledged or reduced and who will be invested in initiating reconciliation.[4] Ṣulḥ has a known default pattern, in which aggressors (or someone on their behalf) initiates ṣulḥ. There are two other patterns of ṣulḥ, which are less emphasized in the literature. They are initiated differently: in cases of multiparty conflict, a third party may initiate ṣulḥ to protect the community from endless cycles of revenge and to regain stability. The least recognized is wronged-initiated ṣulḥ, which is rare and more taxing. Despite differences in who initiates ṣulḥ, the process involves a series of arduous, interdependent steps that lead to conflict resolution.

In transgressor-initiated ṣulḥ, the initial phase doesn't necessarily begin by the transgressor coming forward to appease (if not apologize to) the recipients of violence. Rather, the process can begin when the transgressor requests a delegation of family members or community elders/notables to initiate reconciliation on her behalf. The delegation decides on a prompt meeting date to visit the attacked family; their visit seeks the family's acceptance of the delegation's mediation (Smith 388). The main task of the delegation is to bring about ṣulḥ, and in the case of a blood dispute, the delegation's main goal is to "persuade [the attacked family] that it is possible to 'wipe away the stain' on their *sharaf* (honor) with *sulha* rather than the blood of the killer or one of his kinsmen" (Lang 54). Thus, a cycle of vengeance and further victimization can be short-circuited. When the victim or the victim's family accepts the delegation's mediation to effect reconciliation, "they throw the whole burden [of mediation and conflict resolution] on [the delegation]" (Smith 388). Their (in)direct acceptance must be witnessed so the delegation's ruling is final. This witnessing acts as a public, self-binding commitment of the involved parties, a mode of participation that I refer to as *commissive witnessing.*

Ṣulḥ entails a period of truce referred to in Arabic as *hudnah* (Lang 54); agreeing to a truce implies that "the two families promise 'no revenge,' until [delegation members] are able to come to a ruling" (Smith 389). A truce agreement can be supported by an agreed-on amount of money, which is a symbolic compensation to address grievances, cover damages, and prove the aggressor's willingness to make amends. However, sometimes families refuse restitution. In these cases, their word guarantees their binding commitment to reconciliation, hence called "attwa of honour" (389) or a bond of honor. Either way, the period of truce allows the delegation to decide how to recognize and redress "rights and honour," which Smith considers the "two basic elements to the Sulha" (389). In addition, their decision must conform to a systematic enforcement/judgment of "the precedents and the coming" (390). Together, recognition of rights, honor, and precedent help realize ṣulḥ's relational and moral imperatives: rights and honor address personal and relational needs, whereas recognizing precedents confirms interests in systematic, enforceable justice and attends to the ethical imperative to heal the violated "moral tone" (Stovel) of the community.

In the second and third types of ṣulḥ, the process is not initiated by the transgressor. Rather, ṣulḥ is initiated by a third party or by those wronged. Third-party initiated ṣulḥ is often invoked in situations of multiple victimization in which immediately affected parties are unwilling to initiate ṣulḥ or in situations in which the transgressor is oblivious to damages incurred. Third-party-initiated ṣulḥ is touched on briefly by Lang and is a recurring situation, especially considering the relational worldview and investment of family/community members in the appeasement of conflicting parties. Type two is manifest in a case of medieval ṣulḥ that ended decades-long conflict between members of Yathrib. Prophet Muḥammad, who was a new emigrant to Yathrib, can be considered a third party. Well known for his trustworthiness and mediation skills, he assumed the role of a mediator to heal rifts between tribes of Yathrib. The communities agreed to end their strife and recorded their agreement. The original text of the agreement is lost, but there are trusted, detailed reports of this accord that demonstrate how this type of ṣulḥ can respond to communal needs and result in a formal, binding agreement (Hamidullah).

The third type is infrequent mainly because it is the reverse of what would be considered the default ṣulḥ, namely victim-initiated ṣulḥ. However, it is an enduring ṣulḥ type. The third manifestation of ṣulḥ is initiated by those wronged (i.e., directly involved parties) and is not apology-driven reconciliation. Sulḥ might be resorted to by those wronged because the situation comprises (or is anticipated to comprise) multiple victimization, the transgressor has a (callous) disregard for damages incurred, or initiators have claims of rights—including the right to amicable relations. This ṣulḥ dynamic is infrequent anḍ demanding, especially because it operates optimally when conciliatory discourses move away from notions of power-over (domination) to the power of togetherness. There are numerous cases to document this infrequent but inspiring form of ṣulḥ.

Ayoub documents an interpersonal contemporary case of this type of ṣulḥ, which took place in a Lebanese village during the 1960s. The events started more than two decades earlier when a piece of land was sold to someone who years later "laid claim to it again by attempting to plow it for himself. He may have reasoned that sufficient ambiguity existed in the original sale to make it worth a try. Mediation would get him something" (Ayoub 14), especially because he claimed that there were problems with the deed. At the time of the transaction "a simple statement affirming the sale was the only contract" (14). Often people record their transactions in this way. This continues to be the case in many places in the Arab world. Often, people ratify the legal status of such sales at a later date.

However, these kinsmen did not, which resulted twenty years later in the seller's attempt to regain the land, "claiming that the land had not belonged to him alone, but to his brothers as well" (15). The son of the current owner, a well-educated, young teacher, after initially approaching an intermediary, proposed that the original seller get in touch with his brothers, who were in Brazil at the time, and request that they confirm "they wanted the land back by granting him the power to speak and act for them" (15). Because, as Ayoub explains, the letter was never written and because the former owner "had been irresponsible in the disposal of land which they [the brothers], in fact, did hold jointly," the teacher decided to go to court to prove his rightful claim to the land. His father who generally was reclusive chose to step in without notifying the son, showing the contract to "eminent members of the clan. One of them, a village official at the time, concluded that the former owner did have a claim because his brothers' agreement to sell had not been obtained." When the son learned this, he consulted a lawyer in the capital, Beirut, who advised him "to needle the former owner into an attempt to taking the land," which eventually happened (15). The teacher explained to Ayoub that he resorted to litigation because he was convinced that mediators "will only try to find some way to make everyone satisfied." He preferred to "take it [to] court . . . and either lose the whole land or keep it all, rather than give him one-tenth of it [through mediation]" (15). So far, this seems like a typical case of litigation, which ended when the judge ruled against the former owner of the land.

What is crucial is that when Ayoub asked the teacher if he later resorted to mediation to "patch up differences," the teacher explained: "It had not been necessary. Sometime after, he visited the man in his home, quite unceremoniously. Apparently there was nothing for the loser to do but acknowledge the teacher's presence and to talk to him. It was an act of deference on the latter's part to be the first to make such a visit, doubly significant in that it was not gained through a formal effort at reconciliation" (15).

The teacher, who is rightly described as "a most unusual young man," underlines how he acted on his sense of accountability and initiated ṣulḥ "unceremoniously." Before he initiated ṣulḥ, he saw the importance of litigation for holding the former owner accountable. Considering the history of the former owner's irresponsible transactions and the tendency to reach a compromise, he felt that litigation was the preferable measure for accountability. Later, he felt that to be accountable is to initiate ṣulḥ. To many, the relational move to "patch up differences" may seem incompatible with litigation. However, initiating reconciliation "unceremoniously" actualizes the teacher's own accountability to relations with his kinsman. As he pursued litigation and ṣulḥ, the teacher embraced different forms of accountability. The former manifest through punitive and institutionalized forms of justice, whereas the latter manifest as a ṣulḥ practice informed by restorative justice.

When conflict is resolved, conflicting parties may have a ṣulḥ event. In a public space, a celebratory ritual—known as ṣulḥa (Lang 53)—brings together formerly belligerent parties. In the fullest realization of the ṣulḥ ritual, especially in rural communities where elders guide the process, community members might rely on symbolic, ritualized, performative rhetorics. For example, the transgressor may hold a white flag that symbolizes peace and to show "the problem has been cleansed" (Smith 390). Then the transgressor shakes the hands of lined-up family members (of the victim), and "when they put their hands together—the case is cancelled" (390).[5] This is all done under the close supervision, sponsorship, and protection of the delegation. Also, in a fully fledged, traditional, public ṣulḥ ritual, the ṣulḥ agreement is sealed in two ways. The first is a symbolic act of making one or more knots on the aforementioned flag, which is a sign of everybody's acceptance and ratification of the agreement. The second is a verbal declaration of the binding nature of ṣulḥ on present and future witnesses (Smith 390). Sometimes, short formal speeches are given at the end of the ceremony commending those involved for restoring peace (Abu-Nimer, *Nonviolence*). Finally, to symbolize forgiveness and the restoration of peaceful relations, the wrongdoer takes bitter coffee at the victim's house.[6] This ritual is typically followed by an invitation for the victim's family to have a meal at the wrongdoer's house (391). The exchange of visits facilitates "entering into a new mutually enriching relationship" (Assefa, "The Meaning"). Such enriching relations and healing can be underwritten by a cultural logic that is worthy of attention. In the following section, the subtle, cultural inflections of the rhetoric of ṣulḥ are explicated.

CULTURAL INFLECTIONS OF ṢULḤ'S RHETORICAL PRACTICES

Conflict and peacemaking are recurring rhetorical situations, and their recurrence can render their dimensions invisible. Indeed, culture is often a subtle resource and force. As such, it is worthy of attention. As Smith asserts, "If symbolic or 'ritualized' behaviour is essential to understanding a conflict more fully, then surely the resources for reconciliation must come from a more creative analysis of the symbolic cultural resources of the societies which are involved in the conflict itself" (386). Common parlance often focuses on and exaggerates cultural resources of violence. Rhetoric scholarship can help shed light on and nuance our understanding of cultural resources that underwrite peacemaking rhetoric across cultures. Ṣulḥ can be fully appreciated only in relation to its cultural context.

There are many venues for pursuing justice rhetorically, and in some sense, all would bring about peace even if limited. But when people resort to ṣulḥ, they are often pursuing more than simply (punitive) justice. They seek to realize a relational imperative in addition to the moral one, which punitive justice would address. For this reason, ṣulḥ is sought in tandem with the typical juridical system—as in the aforementioned case of interpersonal victim-initiated ṣulḥ—or as an extrajudicial "ritualization of peace-making" (Smith 394). It is in that sense that the use of healing words or "sweet persuasion" becomes paramount. To a great extent, the cultural inflections of ṣulḥ rhetoric can be condensed into what Lang refers to as the "main pillars"

(53) of ṣulḥ and the phrase *il-kilmah il-ḥilwah*, which Lang transliterates as "*elkelma elhelwa*" (Lang). The main pillars of ṣulḥ realize "performative open hand rhetoric," conspicuous in the performative acts of *muṣāfaḥah*, *muṣālaḥah*, and *mumālaḥah*—respectively, shaking hands, reconciliation, and eating together (Smith 391), which can be said to manifest and enable conciliation as a worthy relational good. The phrase il-kilmah il-ḥilwah (literally "sweet word" or "sweet persuasion") refers to an investment in words that heal or "cool the heart" of those wronged. In all cases of ṣulḥ that I have explored, il-kilmah il-ḥilwah works best when the timing is right for recipients of violence. But, this is not the only powerful moment for the initiation of ṣulḥ. When violence reaches its limits, a transgressor realizes the need to alter a reality defined by their violence and ensuing conflict. At this kairotic moment, they have the potential of becoming rhetorical agents whose deliberate(d) rhetorical choices counter violence they have initiated or participated in. As rhetorical agents, they harness the power of il-kilmah il-ḥilwah to "alter reality, not by the direct application of energy to objects, but by the creation of discourse which changes reality through the mediation of thought and action" (Bitzer 4). However, the rhetorical work of ṣulḥ necessitates the involvement of all involved parties.

Ṣulḥ is informed by a relational worldview, which values functional and meaningful relations, and invests continuously in individual needs and in a community's "moral tone" (Stovel).[7] In this relationally driven sphere, ṣulḥ pursuers can resort to functional modalities of interacting with self and other, attend to severed relations, and initiate conciliatory work to restore a community's moral tone, which, in turn, brings about healing and peace. The role different stakeholders (transgressor[s], those wronged, mediators, and third parties) play as they attend to the logic of violence addresses (dys)-functional relations, points to how they realize the relational and ethical imperatives of the community, and attains ṣulḥ. In what follows, therefore, I explicate the "logic" of violence or how power-over provides a rationalization for violence. Then I turn to the dynamic array of rhetorical acts used by ṣulḥ pursuers to reverse this logic, rebalance relations, and establish different relational terms, underlining the cultural inflections of their rhetoric.

The "Logic" of Violence

As a relational phenomenon, violence may be caused by the abuse of power-over. Daye, in *Political Forgiveness*, explains the implicit "logic" on which most acts of violence or violation are premised: "I [the wrongdoer] am essentially more important than you [the victim] are. It is acceptable for me to trample your dignity or rights because I am a more important person than you. . . . [Thus t]hose who wrong others demean them, while operating on the incorrect belief or assumption that their own value is high enough to warrant this treatment" (106).

These tacit justifications objectify the victim, dismiss their rights, and inflate the rights of the wrongdoer. These acts signify a relation, which in Buber's terms reduces the recipient of aggression to a thing; they become an *It*. "*I-It* [relation] can never be spoken with the whole being" (3). This is why such justifications support and result in an act of violence. To subvert this "logical" justification, ṣulḥ strives to attain—or rather reclaim—balance. This entails a dynamic array of rhetorical acts, which are referred to as a *rhetoric of balance* for short.

THE DYNAMIC RHETORICS OF ṢULḤ PURSUERS

The phrase *a rhetoric of balance* sheds light on the most decisive rhetorical dimensions of ṣulḥ: a rhetoric that seeks to counter violation/violence that has caused conflict and the "logic" that justifies, enables, and sustains it. A rhetoric of balance comprises patterns of rhetorical engagement, which are typically enabled by mediation. These patterns can be condensed using three terms: *recognition*, *labor of response*, and *accountability*. First, recognition acknowledges the presence of victims, who are rendered invisible by violation and violence, and acknowledges their rights and restorative needs. Second, ṣulḥ affords its participants ample chance to embrace the arduous "labor of response" (Ellsworth), especially on the part of the offender, and encourages reciprocity with reluctant—or rightly ambivalent—wronged ones. Third, ṣulḥ ensures accountability using mediation and commissive witnessing. However, ṣulḥ is more than just recognition, responsiveness, and accountability, for each has a constitutive potential. When ṣulḥ pursuers assume this work, they allow (and advocate) for *becoming* peace pursuers.

Ṣulḥ, like other restorative justice models, is premised on a rhetoric of recognition of the immanence of all human beings and their rights. To actualize this work of recognition, ṣulḥ pursuers engage in numerous deliberative acts and undertake the "labor of response" (Ellsworth) by listening rhetorically (Ratcliffe) and responding restoratively while, at best, recognizing the integration needs of the aggressor. This process implies that a transgressor acknowledges the presence of victims who are objectified, dismissed, and harmed. Then, they respond to the needs of those violated. These rhetorical acts initiate peacemaking, restore dignity, and balance power. To illustrate, a transgressor can initiate ṣulḥ using an other-oriented move, like apology, to recognize others and their rights. More important, this orientation toward the other reverses the logic of "I-It" relations, wherein a recipient of violence is objectified and then violated, and shifts to "I-Thou" relations (Buber), which recognize the immanence of another. This move means a change in the relation between recipients of violence and the transgressor. As such, ṣulḥ manifests an inventive and constitutive rhetorical potential that enables/is enabled by the rhetoric of recognition, responsiveness, and accountability. Together, they become a potent force geared toward co-authoring conflict resolution; reconstituting a subject position that can enact conflict resolution goals; and charting a road toward moral and relational responsibility.

Like other conciliatory practices that are informed by a relational world-view, ṣulḥ's (lasting) effectiveness hinges on the reciprocal, responsive, and responsible engagement of all involved parties. Many voices and speakers are engaged in ṣulḥ. These include transgressors, victims, their families, mediators, different stakeholders, and community members at large who sometimes weigh in as silent but often as vociferous participants. Ṣulḥ participants' engagement and the impact of their suasory moves reflect Herbert Simons's classification of suasive impact based on decoders' predispositions. For example, in a ṣulḥ process reported by Drieskens, which will be detailed later in the chapter, recipients' predispositions ranged from hostility toward the idea of ṣulḥ to agreement or strong agreement with the idea. Both are plausible predispositions that depend on a variety of variables, including people's degrees of hurt; exposure to and acceptance of cultural resources that promote conflict resolution; stakeholders' material conditions that allow for or inhibit resolution; and will(ingness) to change or adapt these material conditions. Dispositions addressed by ṣulḥ participants' suasory moves range from response shaping, to response reinforcing, to response changing (Simons 23–24).[8] Because of its embeddedness in a relational worldview and because of the varied dispositions of participants, ṣulḥ enlists a dynamic array of deliberative, suasory, and constitutive rhetorics wherein ṣulḥ participants are dissuaded from retaliatory aggression and persuaded of reconciliation. This array testifies to the dialogic nature of ṣulḥ. Though there are some monologic genres—like short speeches given to celebrate ṣulḥ—ṣulḥ tends to be a dialogic phenomenon. There are always tumultuous voices: expressions of pain, claims of grievances, negotiations of rights, compromise ruses, acknowledgment of harm, and atonement for violence. As these voices come together, we can see varied forms of deliberations.

Internal Deliberation

Ṣulḥ pursuers resort to both external and internal deliberation (e.g., Burks; Nienkamp). Typically, the focal point of rhetorical studies is external rhetoric and concomitantly external persuasion, which remains the exclusive domain of Western rhetoric since its inception in Europe in fifth-century BCE (Nienkamp xi). However, many formative moments that precede ṣulḥ initiation entail internal deliberation. Because of its invisibility and to follow the chronological development of a ṣulḥ case, internal deliberation is addressed and represented as a counterpart to external deliberations.

The tendency to emphasize external rhetoric eclipses internal persuasion, which can be simply defined as *inner dialogicality* (Bakhtin ctd. in Taylor 33) or a deliberation that one relies on (sub)consciously to engage the multitude of stances and voices that address conflict and conflict resolution. Put differently, it is a form of rhetorical deliberation that focuses on how "persuasion . . . [is] conceptualized as acting within a person" (Nienkamp xi). Though understudied, internal rhetoric can be rhetorically explored, especially since its impact can be traced in the words and actions of ṣulḥ stakeholders.[9] As such, internal rhetoric—as an analytical category—unveils this internal mode of deliberation and allows us to speculate about what happens before, for example, a transgressor initiates ṣulḥ or how a recipient of violence decides whether to pursue or reject ṣulḥ.

To date, there is no study of the internal rhetoric that precedes and enables ṣulḥ. Ethnographic research on ṣulḥ (e.g., Abu-Nimer, *"Nonviolence"*; Lang; Smith) is silent on what happens before the moment of initiation; ṣulḥ accounts typically begin with the transgressor seeking elders' intervention. Instead, current literature is vocal about two crucial aspects of their rhetorical engagement, namely manifest *intention* and *effect* (Nienkamp 127), which can point to a wrongdoer's internal deliberations. Literature on ṣulḥ touches on the importance of a genuine pursuit of ṣulḥ. This genuineness can be seen in a wrongdoer's deliberate and resolute appeal to elders, seeking their intervention. It is reasonable to assume that the exigencies and change between the moments of violation and the kairotic moment of ṣulḥ initiation are rhetorical—minimally as meaning-making and deliberate(d) doing. Ṣulḥ pursuers will need to find for themselves reasons *for* and *against* pursuing ṣulḥ. Ideally, "When a person is thinking, his mind would not be concerned with pleading or with seeking only those arguments that support a particular point of view, but would strive to assemble all arguments that seem to it to have some value, without suppressing any, and then, after weighing the pros and cons, would decide on what, to the best of its knowledge and belief, appears to be the most satisfactory solution" (Perelman and Olbrechts-Tyteca 41).

As rhetorical agents, wrongdoers weigh alternatives, which can lead to a deliberate, moral reasoning. Transgressors can be motivated to initiate ṣulḥ for varied reasons. They can be motivated by self-interest, which can be legible as the visceral fear of retaliation and/or hope of warding off retaliatory attempts, especially when/if prompted by ṣulḥ-seeking external deliberation; family elders/community notables can motivate a transgressor to redeem themselves in the community, apologize to recipients of their aggression or their kin, and make amends. Alternatively, their initiation of ṣulḥ can be a slow, at times faltering, but at best intentional, reorientation of the self toward the victim and their family.

Leading up to this moment, transgressors are likely to talk *with* and *against* vociferous, internal voices. These clamoring voices might address issues of violation and their consequences in general or ones that (are imagined to) respond to their acts of violence. When transgressors engage in an internalized mode of deliberation, they are making use of "a cultivated art, using language in ethical or unethical ways to make a decision or to incite desired actions or attitudes in the self" (Nienkamp 3). A transgressor's internal dialectic then manifests as moral agency when they choose to apologize or even approach elders seeking their intervention. Accordingly, what precedes the moment of initiation/reorientation is worthy of rhetorical attention, for it is probably indicative of and responsive to (1) external deliberations/persuasion, which results from interpersonal discourse or (2) internal deliberation/persuasion, which emerges through intrapersonal discourse. Whether external or internal, these forms of deliberation interrelate and lead to action. A transgressor uses these deliberations to survey aspects of their situation, weigh risks of (or lack of) intervention, and find alternatives to ward off retaliation or restore their standing in the community.

Like transgressors, recipients of aggression face the moral and social dilemma whether to reconcile or not to reconcile. Recipients of aggression, too, face a multitude of voices. Their internal deliberation, "takes up and reflects, modifies, or resists the various social languages that pervade . . . [them] and [their] environments" (126). Their internal deliberations at best realize their needs and at worst coopt their needs if/when they succumb to unfair communal pressure or ṣulḥ practices. In either case, their deliberations entail inconspicuous rhetorical work whose impact is crucial to and precedes their participation in or rejection of ṣulḥ initiation. Though current research mutes internal rhetoric that results in and precedes the assumption of moral agency, it reveals traces of manifest intention as moral agency and its effect.

In a case study of a Cairene ṣulḥ, Barbara Drieskens documents the wrongdoer and recipient of violence, arising moral agency and internal deliberations against the backdrop of ṣulḥ as a cultural resource for peacemaking and cultural logics of what is deemed a violation or face threat. Her ethnographic study analyzes a conflict in a suburb of Cairo caused by "a small disagreement about a price and about the way to address the client" (103). The dispute escalated to a fight; Mohsen, the brother-in-law of one of the disputants, intervened to resolve the dispute, only to find himself "attacked from behind" and injured (107). Soon after, he was hit by a member of the Bani Mohammed (literally, the house/family of Mohammed), the perpetrator(s) fled the scene, and Mohsen was taken to the hospital, where he received ten stitches (104). Mohsen was not just physically hurt; he felt violated. According to Drieskens, "He was touched in his honor (*sharaf*) . . . honor and traditions meant a lot to him and his family" (106). A crisis of honor, "caused by an injury or an insult directed at the 'blood, here both a physical substance and a social bond'" (107), makes people feel violated and threatened because "when a man [or any person] loses respect, people treat him [or them] with contempt" (108). The dynamic mix of these psychological and social forces mandated one of three responses: retaliation, reconciliation, or resorting to state law (Drieskens).

Both victim and transgressor knew these possibilities and their material consequences. Each had to make a choice. As Drieskens reports, the Bani Mohammed chose reconciliation. Their decision reflects their deliberations, which might have been mediated by values (like honor or the courage to admit one's faults) or fear of retaliation. Their rationalization was not part of Drieskens's focus; however, she notes its effect: to start, we see its effect in the transgressor choosing to approach elders and convince them to mediate and resolve the conflict on his behalf. The transgressors' appeals to the elders are significant; transgressors need to "beg" for elders' intervention, asserting their credibility and making a case for their genuine pursuit of ṣulḥ (Lang). Only then will elders agree to mediate. Another effect is conspicuous in Bani Mohammed's visit, which could mitigate the affront to Mohsen's honor (sharaf): "Three days after the fight, when Mohsen was still recovering from his wound, five men of the Bani Mohammed came to visit him at his mother's home. They came to ask for reconciliation, and Mohsen considered it to be a great honor that the Bani Mohammed had sent five older men. This showed their respect for Mohsen's family" (118).

Thus, the transgressor's internal deliberation as traced in his manifest intention and effect resulted in a stance of openness to consider diverse perspectives on the situation and reorient himself toward the victim. If the logic of victimization is embedded in I-It relations, where a recipient of violence is objectified then violated, the moves of Mohsen's aggressors imply a shift to I-Thou relations. This shift is evident when Drieskens refers to the recognition (i.e., manifest effect) afforded to Mohsen and his family by Bani Mohammed. Put differently, the wrongdoer's orientational change was noted, believed, and sponsored by elders, sparking ṣulḥ.

If deliberation has primed the transgressor to undertake ṣulḥ, a mirroring internal rhetoric (and external persuasion) enables Mohsen, the victim. Though Drieskens was neither interested in rhetoric nor its internal iterations, her ṣulḥ case study documents Mohsen's internal rhetoric. He weighed his alternatives. If the transgressor's internal dialectic wrangles with topoi—like retaliatory justice, vindication, and paying back; forces of shame and guilt; the logic of courage in upholding the truth; and standing up to the consequences of one's own actions—the diverse voices that *surround* and fight *within* a victim's mind are different. For Mohsen, "different logics were interwoven in his internalized discussion: there was the logic of honor, respect, and self-respect, on the one hand, and the logic of safety and continuity, on the other" (Drieskens 113). The commotion of values, alternatives, and risks entailed burdened him:

> Mohsen . . . was [indeed] of two minds. On the one hand, he preferred the money [blood money] because it was safer, but on the other hand, he felt that revenge would be more satisfying to his honor and self-respect. This situation also raised the question whether Mohsen had the option and the desire to remain in Bashtil [the same neighborhood where his attacker lived]. If he chose revenge, he would probably have to move elsewhere to avoid further hostilities, but if he accepted reconciliation he would need to enforce respect on the Bani Mohammed and the other men of the neighborhood. And then there was all the ambivalence of his attitude to this neighborhood. He had a nice flat there, but the area was not very pleasant, with garbage in the streets, crowded alleys and many social problems. He was tempted to leave the place anyhow, because it was the confusion of Bashtil that had put him in such a predicament. If he left, it would be better to leave the place honorably, following an act of revenge, rather than to accept some money and leave like a coward. (112)

Mohsen's "individual deliberation" (Burks 112) uncovers his self-persuasion that resulted in choosing and actualizing a conciliatory stance. Drieskens's script demonstrates that Mohsen's internal dialectic was fierce because he had a lot at stake: he had to weigh his and his family's safety, honor, and self-respect against the shame of cowardice. A wrong decision "would not only affect his honor and increase the risk of violence, but would also threaten the unity and reputation of the family" (Drieskens 112). The complexity of these psychological, ethical, and social concerns mandates intervention that addresses these issues while "cooling the heart" of those wronged.

Both Mohsen and his attacker deliberated *with* and *against* competing stances and alternative possibilities. Like them, many ṣulḥ pursuers deliberate *with* and *against*; their deliberations may be thorny and protracted, but often they lead to creative rhetorical invention. It is in this context of deliberation that the moral and relational awareness of ṣulḥ pursuers becomes acute and their agency arises. They deliberate with themselves and argue *with* and *against* other social voices, with varying degrees of consciousness, about the act of violation and its consequences. As they deliberate, they begin undertaking the work of recognition, response, and accountability.

External Rhetoric

External rhetoric takes the form of responsiveness, apology, recognition, and accountability; all signal the shift from I-It to I-Thou relations, enable stakeholders to engage in peacemaking, and set the scene for deliberations with others. To "cool the hearts" of those wronged, ṣulḥ encodes mechanisms that engender self- and other-oriented rhetorical stances, which can be recognized as the labor of response to one's violations. These mechanisms are (sometimes) distributed to involve participants and to balance their interactional rights—creating a space for openness and potentiality. This space brings together stakeholders to be held answerable to the different consequences of conflict/aggression. This role distribution necessitates an expansive rhetorical repertoire to negotiate moral and relational responsibility. This repertoire includes the rhetoric of recognition and apology, mediation, rhetorical listening and silence, and accountability rhetoric.[10]

Recognition and Apology

Though apology is often considered the moment of initiation of ṣulḥ or any reconciliation, recognition is actually the core force in all moves countering violation or oppression. The rhetoric of recognition, with its orientation toward the other, is what motivates apology and motivates one to assume an apologetic stance. The distinction between apology and apologetic stance is significant because apology is a speech act of acknowledgment or an expressive (Austin; Searle). By virtue of going to elders and seeking help, transgressors acknowledge and assume responsibility for offenses. These acts depend on transgressors recognizing violated parties. By addressing their offenses, they attend to the violated parties' "faces" and face needs (Goffman). This entails a shift from just an expression of regret, which I contend can be mainly encoder-oriented, to assuming an apologetic stance and addressing the needs of the recipient, which are decoder-oriented. The shift also entails work related to recognizing how the self and its rights are inflated. However, assuming this apologetic stance is neither automatic, easy, nor risk free.

Turning toward the other is demanding and risky, for it "involves meeting another person's position in its uniqueness, letting it have its impact" (Buber qtd. in Foss and Griffin 7). We often hear apologizers say, "I said I am sorry!" and realize that their statement has missed its sincerity condition, which entails their ability to recognize, genuinely own, and respond to an offense (i.e., an apology without an apologetic stance). In other words, an apology has to be perceived as genuine and believable to meet its sincerity condition (Malmkjaer 486–95); these features are realized when apologizers recognize others and their needs. These conditions—difficult as they are—become further convoluted by the presence of elders and community notables whose assistance is sought; the moment elders are addressed, their face needs must be recognized, too. Simply put, in order for a transgressor to enlist and guarantee their intervention, elders must be convinced of the sincerity of apology, pursuit of amends, and commitment to restoring peaceful relations. This is crucial rhetorical work that precedes ṣulḥ initiation.

Further, "meeting another person's position" entails confronting—as Ellsworth explains—"responsibility as an indeterminate, interminable labor of response" (29). As transgressors seek to reconcile, they recognize their wrongdoing, turn toward the other, earnestly pursue the intervention of a delegation of family elders or community notables, and plead for their mediation, which might not happen and not necessarily in this order. Assuming an apologetic stance is one of the early rhetorical moves manifesting a shift toward the other and I-Thou relations. Ideally, this stance culminates in an apology and is often the logical precursor to elders' intervention. In proposing apology (an expressive speech act) and committing to make amends (a commissive speech act)—speech acts explicit/implicit in a transgressor's approach of elders—the transgressor mobilizes self- and other-oriented reparative rhetorical moves: they "offer" an alternative perspective to retaliation; declare "social recognition of inappropriate, even wrong, behavior; personal failure; [and] injury" (Gronbeck); and do self-image reparative work, for an apology is also called for when "the rhetors believe their behaviors have caused people to consider them immoral or unethical" (Kruse 280). In recognizing their responsibility for wrongdoing, transgressors seek to repair their image, (re)claim their credibility, and offer an alternative to retaliation. This rhetorical work abounds with risk and hope.

The transgressor's reparative (self-oriented) and recognition (other-oriented) work is a fragile and unpredictable undertaking. The fragility and unpredictability of the labor of response can be illuminated using Foss and Griffin's explanation of offering. They distinguish between rhetoric that anticipates a particular end in mind (e.g., influencing action) and a rhetoric of offering whose goal is just to share a perspective: "Offering is not based on a dichotomy of cause and effect, an action done in the present to affect the future. Instead, as Johnson (1989) explains, the 'means are the ends: *how* we do something is *what* we get (35)'" (Johnson qtd. in Foss and Griffin 7).

The expectations of and need for recognition, apology, and (image) reparative work are typically high. Therefore, a transgressor's appeal for intervention needs to be prompt. However, often situations fester before intervention is seriously pursued. Sharon Lang's ethnographic study provides evidence for such delicate suasory, reparative rhetorical work that leads to elders' mediation. Lang recounts a transgressor's attempt to persuade elders to mediate on their behalf. She explains how the transgressor—as the elders elucidate—begs for the elders' intervention:

> According to them [*jaha* notables and other knowledgeable informants], within twenty-four hours of a killing, close male relatives of the aggressor go to the homes of influential notables in the village and surrounding to ask them—even *plead* with them—to form a committee of mediators to calm the aggrieved and enraged family and *induce* them to engage in the *sulha* process instead of taking revenge. The initiative is supposed to come from the aggressors who . . . voluntarily approach the *rijal kibar* ("big men") and, shedding their pride, stand before them *'ara'ya'* ("naked"), *rijal sighar* ("small men"). These humbled aggressors, according to the traditional account, employ set phrases, such as "I am in your house and you must help me; I am in serious trouble and I am in your hands." (56; emphasis added)

"Plead" and "induce" indicate the stakes and the goal-directed nature of a transgressor's advance; obviously, transgressors seek social cooperation to interrupt retaliation or plead for elders' intervention and sponsorship of ṣulḥ. Enlisting elders' help is a difficult process: when/if elders agree to work on the transgressor's behalf, elders will be the ones on the frontline, so to speak, of the pursuit of appeasement and conciliation. Though plead and induce point to the transgressor's goal of enlisting the help of elders and initiating ṣulḥ, a step toward the articulation of recognition and reconciliation, these terms also point to a more crucial, albeit inconspicuous and underexplicated, social function.

This social function is signaled by "humbled aggressor" in *al-jāhah*'s (elders) statement, which underlines yet another dimension of the rhetorical work that reverses the "logic" of violence; ṣulḥ, like other restorative justice models, uses two interdependent mechanisms to (re)balance power. The first recognizes victims by foregrounding their rights and using rhetorical moves like apology as noted earlier. The second involves esteem-lowering moves, which enable aggressors' responsiveness (Worthington 164). Esteem-lowering moves, in addition to decreasing (un)forgiveness of the wronged, counter the implicit "logic" of superiority that rationalizes wrongdoing. As stated earlier, the wrongdoer claims they are more important than victims and assumes they have the right to "trample [their] dignity or rights" (Daye 106). A transgressor's claim of superiority is replaced with a rhetorical stance of respons(a/i)bility or answerability—"accountability" in Ratcliffe's terms; recognition, responsiveness, and accountability rebalance power between involved parties. Victims are empowered since their acceptance/rejection of the initiative becomes a decisive factor in conflict resolution; this might be restorative to victims. As such, esteem-lowering acts are critical to changing the rhetorical stances of the transgressor, repairing their image, and potentially transforming the transgressor-victim relation.

Attending to and reversing power abuse is complex rhetorical work. Partly, this work is done using esteem-lowering moves, which counter power-over and facilitate responsiveness. However, responsiveness and accountability are typically taxing and often mandate mediation, which supports finding mutually acceptable resolution, enables healing, and models interactional patterns more consistent with peacemaking. As such, mediation charts a road for the labor of response, a response that would appease, if not heal, those violated.

Mediation

Venues to justice seek peace, albeit differently. When people resort to ṣulḥ, the process typically involves mediation, which is so crucial to ṣulḥ that Peters prioritizes it over who initiates ṣulḥ. Smith corroborates this statement, explaining that often community members recognize a dispute as resolved when they undertake mediation (394). Peters and Smith refer to mediation as humanistic endeavor that strives not just to reach a settlement. Rather, "a humanistic model of mediation is presented in order to more intentionally and consistently tap into the intrinsic transformative and healing potential of mediation" (Umbreit 201). This is the case simply because ṣulḥ mediation—like other restorative models—is dialogue-driven, and hence capable of realizing the relational imperative, which a regular juridical system (or a settlement-driven mediation, as Umbreit explains) does not address. As was noted in chapter 1, a case in front of a regular court focuses on vindicating a victim by punishing the violator; state authority punishes a transgressor and, accordingly, considers as excess the healing and rehabilitation needs of the victim and their family/community. By contrast, the process of mediation is a humanistic, dialogic, and context-sensitive model "geared not toward 'simple justice,' but social reintegration" (Smith 394).

Consequently, the mediator's role is multifaceted. Their rhetorical intervention is a delicate act or a balanced response to disputants, community, and precedent: "the mediator cannot rely primarily on rules but must construct an outcome in the light of the social and cultural context of the dispute, the full scope of the relations between the disputants and the perspectives from which they view the dispute" (Felstiner 74). Therefore, ṣulḥ mediation strives to recognize and balance the needs of all involved parties, which transcends punishment; heal victims by affirming their rights and enable the atonement/at-one-ment of the offender by holding them accountable to violation and reconciliation; restore the community's "moral tone" (Stovel); and facilitate conflict resolution and transformation. In order to attain all of these goals, ṣulḥ creates a parallel space for encounter.

A Parallel Space

As a conflict resolution mechanism, mediation offers a space, albeit a parallel one, where both parties can meet to confront one another, their fears of one another, and the throbbing presence of their hurt. However, the moment the ṣulḥ pursuers enter this space their interactions might change. This is akin to the transitional phase, betwixt and in between, that Victor Turner writes about. When ṣulḥ pursuers accept mediation, they separate themselves or freeze—even if momentarily—the act of aggression and dwell in a place/space that "has none of the attributes of the past or coming state" (235). Put differently, as they choose mediation they begin the process of potential "undoing" of aggression (i.e., their past), embrace a process that they do not fully know (i.e., the liminal process of mediation), and seek the transformative potential of ṣulḥ (i.e., their desired coming state).

Mediation—at best—holds this "between" space where I and Thou meet. Optimally, their mediated encounter enables restoration, realizes a relational good, and addresses reciprocal rights and needs. By holding space for an encounter and ushering the shift from an I-It to I-Thou relationship, the encounter is neither cheap nor easy; rather, it is bound to be messy, recursive, unleashing boundless possibilities, for as Buber asserts, "all real living is meeting" (11). Because ṣulḥ addresses the restorative needs, such as a better and peaceful life for all involved parties, this encounter is decisive: transgressor and victim can become partners in the co-invention of a mutually accepted resolution.

Scholars underline this potential and the decisive role of mediation (e.g., Peters; Smith). Because this encounter, which might not be face to face, at least in the early phases of ṣulḥ, provides a space where transgressor and victims' rights to justice are affirmed and their needs are acknowledged; structural reciprocity is a (minimum) requirement of this encounter. The mediator's role in facilitating the recognition of reciprocal rights and needs is asserted by Ifeanyi Peters: "The ritual of sulh does not necessarily emphasise either the victim or offender's role in initiating the process, but does emphasise using a third party to help facilitate the process. In this way, community relations are maintained and honour is preserved for both parties. Rituals, such as sulh, can be very powerful for acknowledging and resolving a grievance, and allow the victim and offender, and their families to resume some kind of relationship" (7–8).

Peters captures the potential of mediation to enable a forward-looking awakening. By fostering an encounter, mediation can create a space where "the relation to the other is *awakening* and *sobering up—that awakening is obligation*" (Lévinas 114; emphasis added). In other words, this encounter at best sobers pursuers to awaken to one another and foregrounds their obligation to respond *to* and recognize the face of the other. This accountability to the other is a "forward-looking [rhetorical stance] to address not just individual errors but also unearned privileges, which are grounded in the-past-that-is-always-present" (Ratcliffe 98).

As such, mediation's unique ability to facilitate an encounter, wherein the victim and transgressor acknowledge their needs and rights, makes mediation pervasive: "Mediation is employed widely to resolve disputes, however trivial or serious, between (and sometimes within) families" (Lang 53). The challenge and efficacy of this discourse mode, however, rests on mobilizing and distributing conciliatory moves. For example, in the regular justice model, only transgressors are asked/expected to be accountable because of their violations. Ṣulḥ mediation, as a restorative justice model, seeks the accountability of all involved parties: the transgressors are accountable to their apology, cessation of all acts of violence, and, more importantly, to making amends. The victim and/or their family's accountability implies withholding retaliation, upholding terms of truce, and accepting appropriate amends. The mediators, too, have a share, albeit different, in this accountability. Their role as rhetors is fraught with complexity. The mediators must be reflective about backward-looking, dysfunctional rhetoric and rhetorical stances. Not only do these stances derail or sabotage the process, they also short-circuit forward-looking, functional, rhetorical moves toward intra/interpersonal conciliatory engagement. An array of conciliatory-oriented rhetorics allows the rhetorical work of all these stakeholders to (e)merge as the "indeterminate, interminable labor of response" (Ellsworth 29). To persuade those aggrieved of the possibility of recovery and conflict resolution, this rhetorical work entails the use of il-kilmah il-ḥilwah as well as functional listening and silence.

Sweet Persuasion

Persuading victims (and/or their families) to accept reconciliation is often a tricky, reiterative, or cyclical process; it mandates savvy rhetorical performance, delicate evocation of shared values, and recognition of the decisiveness of time and timing. To illustrate, al-jāhah use persuasive adroitness to appease victims, decrease their unwillingness to forgive, and induce cooperation. This entails a rhetorical dexterity that relies partly on persuasive appeals but also on redeeming the victim's presence. For example, other than the esteem-lowering acts, there are esteem-enhancing acts that underline the elders' recognition of the victim: the delegation promptly visits the family of those violated after the transgressor assumes an apologetic stance. Their prompt visit draws on *musāyarah* (i.e., healing, accommodating rhetoric) and signals their empathy and understanding of the gravity of the matter (Smith 389). Additionally, their "oral performance comes to the fore: it is not merely who is speaking and what is said, but the *way* the jaha communicates—its skill in playing upon the *musayara* tradition of 'polite speech'—that is crucial" (Lang 57); musāyarah enables forgiveness and balances power. Musāyarah's rhetorical accommodations are conspicuous in *wāsṭah* (in Colloquial Egyptian Arabic) or "reversed patronage," and *shahāma* or "magnanimity" (Lang). Wāsṭah reverses the flow of authority. Typically, honor and authority flow from the patron to the client. However, in the case of ṣulḥ, there is an inversion of this typical flow: the honor resulting from assuming a stance of forgiveness, embracing the will to resolve conflict, and making the functional rhetorical moves of conciliation flows from the client (the family of those attacked) to the patron (community notables and elders). Wāsṭah is accentuated when the client is of limited economic or social resources in comparison to the patron or members of the delegation (Lang 56–57). Shahāmah indicates the victim's (or their family's) decision to undertake and be accountable to the work of forgiveness and reconciliation. Shahāmah is more than an alternative to retaliation; it is constitutive of an alternative subject position. Shahāmah is a deliberate(d) embrace of other-oriented acts, whereby those wronged willingly balance their interests with the needs of the transgressor to be forgiven and reintegrated into a community. The wronged party's magnanimity reintegrates the transgressor into the community and declares the transgressor is more than the act of wrongdoing. Reverse patronage and magnanimous articulations of forgiveness are esteem-enhancing moves that reaffirm the immanence of those violated. The mediators' ability to invoke shared values like magnanimity and forgiveness testifies to their ability to use il-kilmah il-ḥilwah, as reported by one of Lang's informants: "We [al-jāhah] make every effort to get the victim's family to agree. . . . We use the beautiful language (*hilwa*). We appeal to their sense of goodness and what is right, and we do not leave until the family agrees. But if they really refuse, we keep trying. We come back day after day. We speak to them each time with all the politeness and respect in the Arabic language. We beg them to be so kind, so honorable as to do us the favor, until finally they cannot refuse us" (57). However, it is important to note that besides the intervention and the impact of the mediators' suasive dexterity, other rhetorical forces are at play.

Participation in mediation does not mean that conciliatory rhetoric has exclusive dominion. Even if hushed, ṣulḥ pursuers live within communities that contend with the ramification of the act of aggression. This means that there are both rhetorics that look back at the moment of hurt and ones that can transcend it and look forward to reconciliation. The former manifests as blame/guilt rhetoric and denial apologies, whereas the latter results in the rhetorical stances of accountability and responsiveness. This means that a ṣulḥ process needs to comprise, yet control, its expressive dimension: a ṣulḥ process can enable the process of healing when people manage their hurt and anger. Alternatively, it can impede healing and productive conflict resolution when partners dismiss the discourse of grievance (i.e., absence of listening to the other) or resist (or deflect) actualizing responsibility (i.e., absence of accountability). Only when the expressive dimension is sufficiently controlled can a mediator remain goal oriented, focusing on the co-construction of a mutually acceptable solution. Defensiveness and blame/guilt rhetoric, even if allowed, are not the focal points since defensiveness and blame/guilt can short-circuit the rhetoric of accountability and the commitment to make amends. Therefore, to actualize the labor of response, the mediator and ṣulḥ pursuers need to reckon with their roles in functional listening and silence.

Listening and Silence

Mediation distinguishes itself from other conflict resolution mechanisms by providing a space where listening becomes possible. Only then can ṣulḥ pursuers listen to "excess narratives" (Ratcliffe). Unlike traditional juridical models that give primacy to the distant role of the judge who seeks only factual or forensic truth (Stovel 3), ṣulḥ (and other mediation-based conciliation models) affords a mediator proximity, which in turn enables recognition of excess narrative. Ideally, a mediator engages in rhetorical listening, which Ratcliffe defines as "a stance of openness that a person may assume in relation to any person, text or culture" (25). As a mediator assumes this openness, they listen to both parties; elicit their stories; and recognize their positions, grievances, and restorative needs. Listening here is a process that has the full power of rhetorical production, for it is deliberate, indicates agency, and seeks impact; mediators listen in order to resolve conflict and facilitate the initiation of healing. Listening, as such, allows and forefronts excess narratives, including grievances, apology, regret, justifications, and so forth. The process, ideally, enables stakeholders to recognize the subject positions of transgressor and victim and move toward realizing their reconciliation and healing. Rhetorical listening then, as Ratcliffe asserts, is "a trope for interpretive invention" (17).

During mediation, rhetorical listening enables ṣulḥ pursuers to attend both to *other-oriented acts* and *power-balancing acts*, which are crucial to reconciliation and reintegration of the community. Rhetorical listening enables this integrative potential because it operates within a reconciled logos.[11] Indeed, "within this more inclusive logos lies potential for personal and social justice" (Ratcliffe 25) because it recognizes both forensic and intersubjective truths. Ṣulḥ takes and promotes a stance whereby voice and ear are considered complementary and are balanced: In mediation, logos speaks *and* listens. Within an undivided logos, Ratcliffe asserts,

> [W]e choose to listen . . . for the exiled excess and contemplate its relation to our culture and our selves. Such listening does not presume a naïve, relativistic empathy, such as "I'm OK, you're OK" but rather an ethical

> responsibility to argue for what we deem fair and just while questioning that which we deem fair and just. Such listening . . . may help people invent, interpret, and ultimately judge differently in that perhaps we can hear things we cannot see. (25)

In the dire moments of conflict resolution, a mediator—a rhetor par excellence—employs this undivided logos to listen and invites others to follow suit. Through listening, ṣulḥ participants—aided and guided by a mediator—can engage one another in ways that make them pay attention to the possibility for coinventing conflict resolution or peace settlement; the process unites them in pursuit of their restorative goals and unites them against causes of divisiveness and violation. Thus, this rhetorical work integrates a conflict-stricken community, be it regional, communal, familial, or a community of interest.

However, it is important to note that rhetorical listening (when mediation starts) is enabled by functional silence (Glenn, *Unspoken*; Ratcliffe) and begins after/outside the blame/guilt discourse since its role starts after the admission of responsibility. Thus, listening, or at least the complementary acts of listening and silence, starts after the transgressor's recognition of the consequences of their deed and admission of guilt have taken place. Two factors allow for this shift from denial or defensiveness to accountability and rhetorical listening. The first is that silence (of the victims) ceases to be dysfunctional. Secondly, silence becomes a functional, deliberate, and strategic choice, and as such a crucial aspect of the traditionally observed features of ṣulḥ.

Before ṣulḥ initiation, the silence of those violated can be indicative of helplessness or disempowerment.[12] Silence, however, becomes functional when this coerced silence (caused by the act of aggression and violation) is transformed into a "voice" of grievance. This voice has a perlocutionary effect, which is conspicuous when the perpetrator acknowledges their responsibility and initiates mediation. The voice of those violated or injured is also conspicuous and valued when elders intervene. The initiation stage releases a space for listening. The delegation begins the process of listening to the victim or their families' acceptance or refusal of the delegation's intervention and appeal for reconciliation. The crucial work of reconciliation hinges on their response, their voice: "Once the victim accepts the reconciliation, the conflict is considered to be over and he renounces any right [if possible] to make an official complaint or to take revenge" (Drieskens 120). More importantly, when victims voice their acceptance of ṣulḥ, they allow for and take part in the co-construction of a parallel, alternative space, or in Foucault's terms, a heterotopic site (Foucault and Miskowiec), where peace is envisioned, negotiated, and enacted. This means that the voice of the violated/victim is listened to as asserting a claim of right. Therefore, silence after admission of culpability, if/when chosen, becomes functional and strategic.

Silence becomes a deliberately chosen act. It sanctions mediation, which mobilizes a forward orientation (toward reconstitution and healing) while being cognizant of the past (culpability and retribution needs/retributive possibility). This forward orientation depends on understanding conflict as a positive tension and as a generative force that can reset one's relational terms, rather than seeing conflict as intractable and insurmountable.[13] In addition, silence restrains the use of inflammatory discourse that might result in escalation and defensiveness; thus, it becomes instrumental in enabling listening, which in turn, as Ratcliffe explains, facilitates a serious and open engagement with both positive and negative terms (94–95). This engagement authorizes an exploration of what would otherwise be considered "excess." Accordingly, rhetorical listening affords the listeners "three different rhetorical stances—recognition, critique, and accountability" (96). This implies that rhetorical listening facilitates the processes of recognizing the other, their perspective, and their hurt; recognizing one's role in causing violation and its consequences; claiming responsibility for the violation committed; and making amends.

The Rhetoric of Accountability

Because a mediator listens to involved parties, recognizes their stories and restorative needs, and asks them to take account of and be accountable to each other, ṣulḥ can move closer toward healing and justice. Though Worthington states that the "the primary psychological effect of justice is to reduce unforgiveness, not to promote forgiveness," restorative justice can seek more when it takes into account excess narratives and invests in ṣulḥ's integrative function, which holds ṣulḥ pursuers accountable to one another and the community (169). This integrative potential is underlined by Felstiner, Smith, and Witty, who explain that mediation and the mediators', intimate knowledge (Felstiner) of the disputants help address not only the multidimensional and often subtle aspects of the conflict but more importantly reclaim communities' peace and harmony.

Rhetorical listening can attain this integrative function because it holds ṣulḥ pursuers accountable to each other's face needs. Simply, *face* (Brown and Levinson; Goffman) is a term that addresses an aspect of our social-psychological life. Face can be defined as conception or image of the self.

This conception entails desires or needs. Literature on face identifies different kind of needs. These include the desire for respect, acceptance, or approval (i.e., positive face needs) and the desire for autonomy, freedom from imposition, or freedom from being constrained by others' power (i.e., negative face needs). Acts of aggression lead to threats to honor—a dimension of face. Such a threat endangers one's sense of self (personal need) and social standing (social need), resulting in a crisis. The effectiveness and success of ṣulḥ hinges on the restoration of a victim's honor—a positive face need, as both Lang and Smith maintain. Restoring honor is a complex task as we have seen in Mohsen's case, which mandated attention to his own and his family's face concerns.

To be answerable to and to attempt to address such a crisis, one needs to listen, for a crisis in honor has both psychological and relational dimensions. Because of the intrapersonal and sociopolitical value of face and honor, "sulha is predicated on *sharaf* (honor)" (Lang 54), that is, predicated on functional attentiveness to positive face. Accordingly, attending to face needs, which entails both responsibility and response ability, is decisive. In a relational worldview, the self is connected. An act of aggression becomes also an affront to this connectedness. In a relational worldview "individuals are seen as both separate and connected, both individuated and similar. They are viewed as being to some degree autonomous, self aware, and self-interested but also to some degree connected, sensitive, and responsive to others" (Kuttner, "From Adversity," 931–32). This understanding of relations informs the conception of face, which is so crucial to a functional rhetorical conciliatory stance; it is one of the conditions of the possibility of ṣulḥ. By initiating reconciliation, a transgressor assumes moral responsibility and undertakes rhetorical work, and though stated earlier, is worth reiterating in this context: a transgressor recognizes the consequences of their act of violence; indicates a willingness to recognize the presence of an objectified other and their complex face needs, which also undoubtedly impacts a transgressor's positive face; and declares a willingness to undertake the risky and consequential work of beginnings (Doxtader, "Reconciliation"). As a transgressor embraces this work, they abide by the observed traditional process of ṣulḥ, which can be considered a response to the collective face need of the community or elders. As such, assuming the rhetorical stance of recognition and answerability to the positive face needs of those violated counters dysfunctional silence, which is premised on a guilt/blame logic.

A reflective rhetoric of accountability attends also to negative face needs. This is why ṣulḥ processes entail "esteem-lowering acts [performed] by perpetrators" (Worthington 164). These acts, though addressed earlier, deserve brief mention. Lang's informant points to how a transgressor's plea for intervention invokes a crucial act of self-humbling before elders: transgressors "voluntarily approach the *rijal kibar* ('big men') and, shed[ding] their pride, stand before them *'ara'ya'* ('naked'), *rijal sighar* ('small men')" (56). And by using statements like "I am in your house and you must help me; I am in serious trouble and I am in your hands," they allow magnanimity to flow from the elders to them, thus obligating themselves to the elders (Lang 56). Esteem-lowering acts have multiple goals. Though the most obvious is reversing the logic of superiority, which justifies and rationalizes acts of aggression, esteem-lowering acts help attend to negative face needs, namely the need to feel free from the imposition of the transgressor's domineering presence. In the literature on reconciliation, this last goal is addressed indirectly when esteem-lowering acts are explained as acts that help reduce the state of unforgiveness of the attacked/wronged family or community (Worthington 164). Esteem-lowering acts replace a perpetrator's claim of superiority with "the indeterminate, interminable labor of response" (Ellsworth 29); they attend to the negative face needs of those violated and empower victims, who have the final say in the process of mediation. In return, the process realizes the wrongdoer's positive face needs. For this reason, the initiation of ṣulḥ is much more than an apology. Had it been just a speech act of an apology (an expressive speech act), the wrongdoer would not have needed the intervention and mediation of community notables/elders. Rather, the plea for their mediation is embedded in a vested attempt to generate stances of responsiveness and accountability.

Restitution is another manifestation of this accountability to positive face needs. It surfaces in ṣulḥ rituals in the form of performative symbolism (Bourdieu 242). Money is often mentioned and offered as part of the ṣulḥ ritual. It is important to note that money for some has a literal significance, but for the majority offering money is a symbolic manifestation of apology and accountability. Not only can no amount of money fully compensate a wronged person, but also—as Ben Nefissa asserts—"accepting the [compensation] money would be a disgrace and a dishonour. It would imply that the family measures its dignity, prestige and honour in financial terms" (qtd. in Drieskens 119). This is the reason, in Drieskens's case study, for example, "the protagonists publicly proclaimed that an honorable family does not mention money; it is only as a result of its generosity that it decides to accept sulh" (119). Rather than a literal compensation, money should be read as part of the ritual manifestation of the rhetoric of accountability to, and recognition of, face needs. Often, as in Drieskens's case, positive face is affirmed through the generous decline of compensation.[14] Manifestations of the rhetoric of accountability realize ṣulḥ's two complementary goals: the transgressor recognizes the rights of and acknowledges their obligation to those wronged. This response ability mobilizes the forward-looking work of healing.

CODA: AL-ṢULḤ KHAYR

Ṣulḥ is rhetorically rich, and the process is complex, iterative, often messy, and demanding. Though depicting a simple and hopeful story, reality is often more complicated, taxing, and excoriating. We are typically undertrained in the rhetorical labor of response, which allows for the array of conciliatory acts surveyed here. Because power-over tends to be valorized, we have asymmetrical access to the rhetoric of warfare as opposed to the rhetoric of identification, peacemaking, and ṣulḥ. However, when we choose to release power-over, a core force energizing the "logic of violence," we can see others as equals. Buber, in *I and Thou*, sheds light on the moment of awakening to another as a worldview and an attitude. Buber explains that the primary words I-It and I-Thou are very different creations, and each does not refer to a thing but rather to a constitutive relation. Whenever a Thou is hailed, an I is constituted. Many centuries before Buber wrote about I-Thou relations, the evocative, axiologically charged al-ṣulḥ khayr underlined this potential labor of response. Many centuries later, Nādiah Muṣṭafá's coaxing, playful call for reconciliation echoes the call for ṣulḥ, a call for people to awaken to each other's restorative needs. Those who attend to the call have an intuition of ṣulḥ, a beginning.

3

WE THE RECONCILED

The Convergence of Ṣulḥ and Human Rights

Since the creation of the Universal Declaration of Human Rights (UDHR) in 1948, there has been renewed interest in the discourses of human rights, which by affirming rights, proactively prevent violence. But this interest in human rights is neither unprecedented nor is it likely to cease. Indeed, with the proliferation of discourses of rights in the Middle East, as manifest in the Arab Spring as well as "Black Lives Matter" slogan and the Occupy Movement in the United States and around the world, there has been a conspicuous uptake of the discourses of human, economic, civic, and political rights. Concomitantly, this rights momentum brings to the fore the premise, promise, and limitations of discourses of rights. Minimally, articulations of rights seek to counter violation of or outright denial of rights (i.e., acts of aggression). It is not surprising then to find articulations of rights folded into or catalyzing conflict resolution processes.

In an attempt to further understand the variegated nature of *ṣulḥ* discourses, I focus in this chapter on the Charter or Constitution of Medina (CM), a medieval document that ended conflict and addressed the individual and collective rights and responsibilities of citizens of Medina. As a historical text, the CM documents multiple, long ṣulḥ processes, which resulted in formal agreements between the contentious tribes of Medina (formerly known as Yathrib). These ṣulḥ agreements *by* and *between* the people of Medina resulted in a document recognized today as the Constitution of Medina, which is much more than ṣulḥ agreements combined. As it resolves the conflicts of the different tribes that lived in Medina, the CM relies on and affirmed the rights of peoples living in Medina. Recognized as the first written constitution in Islam (Arjomand; Khan; Rubin), the CM is also the first document that establishes Medina as a city-state. While calling forth a city-state, the CM interpellates a unified citizenry and provides the people of Medina with a collective imaginary of an emerging, unified city-state. The constitution of this confederation (Serjeant) of unified citizenry results from and is supported by a ṣulḥ practice and process that worked in tandem with the articulation of the equal rights and obligations of the people of Medina.

However, these conciliation agreements and affirmations of rights exceed their historical and local limitations because they constitute a conspicuous part of a bigger discourse of rights in Islam.[1] As such, the discourse of ṣulḥ intersects with the CM's iteration of the discourse of human rights. This discourse informs but exceeds the CM. As such, the study of the CM provides a different dimension of ṣulḥ as a process and practice, which blends with rhetorics of rights. To demonstrate this unique blend, the chapter explicates the CM's articulation of peacemaking and rights, whose convergence continues to have an inspirational and evocational quality; it is not surprising that the CM was invoked recently in debates about imaginaries of the state, transitional justice, and generative, efficacious, and actionable articulation of (minority) rights in the Arab world post-January 25, 2011 revolution.

Because the CM does not only reflect a culturally inflected conceptualization of human rights but also sheds light on the process and product of ṣulḥ, it contributes important insights to this book. Moreover, though the CM has been explored from a variety of disciplinary orientations including Middle Eastern studies, government and political science, sociology, history, and law, it has yet to be analyzed rhetorically. My rhetorical analysis of the CM attends to the dual goal of studying different uptakes of ṣulḥ while looking at how ṣulḥ interrelates with other justice-oriented discourses. To this end, the chapter moves to the medieval Arabian Peninsula and explores the rhetorics of conciliation and rights in the CM. The CM complicates the account presented thus far of ṣulḥ by shedding light on an exemplary moment in the history of charters, constitutions, and documents ratifying ṣulḥ processes at the communal level. Though ṣulḥ pursuers frequently ratify their ṣulḥ agreements, the CM is an atypical manifestation of ṣulḥ rhetoric as it *hinges on* and *affirms* discourses of human rights in today's terms. This means that in addition to providing us with another manifestation of ṣulḥ documents, the CM helps us understand better the conditions that are fostered and established by ṣulḥ processes. More important, this analysis contributes to our historical account of the discourses of human rights by shedding light on a seventh-century document affirming human rights in response to conflict and contentious blood disputes.[2] Put differently, the CM predates the Magna Carta (1215) and the UDHR (1948) by five and thirteen centuries, respectively. Further, this document assumes a formative impact. It has inspired further visions and articulations of (minority) rights, though it cannot be reduced to minority rights. The inspirational dimension of the charter lies partly in its context and partly in its impact: written in 622 CE, the CM affirms equal rights, countering the pervasiveness of a tribally driven logic of superiority and long-lasting animosity, conflict, and contentious blood money disputes. For example, "South Africa's Muslim Community is but one of the plethora of Muslim communities around the globe that have from time to time referred to the Medina Charter for their inspiration and guidance" (Haron, Cajeee, and Dangor 616). Because the CM exemplifies a convergence of ṣulḥ rhetoric and articulation of multiple human rights and the need for deliberate(d) communal investment to affirm and institutionalize rights, it proves to be a unique document. Because the CM continues to inspire articulations of rights, underlining how citizens are bound to one another by the dynamic interplay of rights and obligations, a rhetorical reading of the Medina Charter adds another dimension to our understanding of ṣulḥ as a model of conciliation and invites further rhetorical analysis of Arab-Islamic rights discourses.

While situating the CM in its historical context, in this chapter I analyze the intersection of the discourses of reconciliation, rights, as well as establishing a political community and interpellating a unified citizenry. I next focus on the discourse of conciliation that mandated the rise of Prophet Muḥammad to rhetorical leadership, a situation that implied both constraints on and exigence for intervention. To reconcile the different tribes of Medina, Prophet Muḥammad relied on mediation strategies like fractioning. I next address the articulation and nature of rights in the CM. I conclude the chapter with a discussion of the political discourse that establishes the community that benefits from and is held accountable to the CM's articulation of rights and the ṣulḥ agreements. This community comprises a unified citizenry that is interpellated in the CM and participates in the creation and actualization of a vision; this citizenry reimagines Medina and Medinians and agrees to be bound by the CM.

THE MULTIDIMENSIONAL NATURE OF THE CONSTITUTION OF MEDINA

Often dated 622 CE, the CM is a composite text. Scholars agree that the CM is a composite text though they differ in their analyses of the composite nature of the text. Serjeant contends that it is made up of eight different pacts, Yildirim insists that there are two main pacts, and Arjomand posits that there are three. These differences are significant because they point to the multidimensional nature of the document. On the one hand, the CM documents a series of conciliatory processes and agreements; on the other hand, the aggregate of these ṣulḥ processes and agreements had political, legal, and visionary features. As we receive it, the CM is a composite document that has forty-seven articles.

Recognized by some as a charter and by others as a constitution, the CM is a constitutive, legal, and deliberative document reflecting a formal, binding agreement between Muslims, Jews, Christians, and polytheists living in 622 CE in Medina. The charter recognizes the current sociopolitical order of the community by naming in detail tribes, clans, and religious communities and recognizing their established power networks. More important, the CM transcends a descriptive recognition of this sociopolitical dynamics by establishing an *in actu* political and administrative system and vision for an emerging city-state that binds all tribes, clans, and faith groups. As a political instrument, the CM establishes a pluralistic, free, safe city-state; manages power; establishes governing authority; and binds everyone to the city-state, affirming the religious and political rights and obligations of all its members. But the document is also recognized as a constitution because it articulates foundational laws that regulate and guide the lives of its people. These laws cover significant issues like channels and modes for the pursuit of justice, equality before the law, and sanctions for violating one's obligations to the political community.

In legal, political, and rhetorical terms, the CM is much more complex than this description implies. This is a seamless combination of both genres of reconciliation treaties/agreements and human rights declarations. As such, this document exemplifies one of the surprising features of ṣulḥ, namely that the conceptualization of ṣulḥ practices is not reducible to a culturally inflected model of conciliation discourse (negative peace) or—to put it differently—postconflict reconciliatory rhetoric. Rather, the CM demonstrates that ṣulḥ conceptualizes peacemaking as a proactive, *in actu* as well as preventive, discursively mediated, long-term investment in the life of the community. As such, revisiting the CM as a manifestation of conciliatory, rights-affirming practice in the Arab-Islamic world sheds light on the use of a rhetorically powerful discourse that can contribute to our explorations of human rights rhetoric and conciliation rhetoric as well as their intersection.

HISTORICAL BACKGROUND OF THE CONSTITUTION OF MEDINA

To fully grasp the social, political, and religious contexts that led to the writing and ratification of the CM, the history of Medina and Mecca must be addressed. Medina (literally "city") before the CM was known as Yathrib. It was not what we would consider a city-state as it had ill-defined boundaries and no "municipal organization." During *al-Jāhilīyah* (the pre-Islamic period), it had a population of 5,000–10,000 people (Hamidullah). The inhabitants were mainly Arab and Jewish tribes; the Arabs were pagan for the most part, and there were also Christian and polytheist minorities.[3] Across ethnic and religious differences, the tribe was the main sociopolitical organizing unit, and during the times of al-Jāhilīyah, tribal logic prevailed.

The tribe was the social unit, and Yathrib was diverse in both religious and tribal terms. Jewish tribes had lived for centuries and made up almost half of the population in Yathrib (Hamidullah 13). They were wealthy and had well-established business. For example, Banū Qaynuqā' had a lot of capital, and made and traded in arms and gold. The two other prominent tribes, Banū al-Naḍīr and Banū Qurayẓah, owned and planted the fertile land (Barakat 30). There were also Arab tribes, and the two prominent Arab tribes were al-Aws and al-Khazraj, who also owned and planted land in fertile Yathrib. However, life in Yathrib was not peaceful. Rather, tribes fought one another, seeking power and dominance. They made alliances, but the alliances often did not last, which further exacerbated conflict: "Hostility between these tribes had existed for generations and some sought power through military dominance over others, *regardless of religion.* This long history of aggression generated numerous prisoners of war in addition to contentious blood money claims, which greatly contributed to the hostilities" (Yildirim "The Medina," 440; emphasis added). The situation in Yathrib was further confounded by a wave of migration from Mecca.

At the time, Islam was a new religion faced with a great deal of hostility; Muslims were persecuted for years in Mecca. Muḥammad, after his prophetic revelations (610 CE), had converted many followers in Mecca. At the time, Mecca's population of different tribes was mainly pagan and polytheistic, and the rise of the new religion threatened leaders of Quraysh (one of the prominent tribes) and Mecca in numerous ways. Hamidullah explains that soon after Muḥammad's revelation, persecution increased:

sanctions sabotaged the businesses of wealthy traders, Muslim converts were held under siege, and laborers and enslaved converts like Bilāl ibn Rabāḥ were flogged and beaten. The leaders of Mecca persecuted the new converts "probably due to their fear that the Prophet Muḥammad would organize Muslims in rebellion against the leadership of the city" (Yildirim, "The Medina," 440).

This persecution eventually led to two waves of migration. The first migration of Muslims (615 CE) was to Abyssinia. Seven years later, because the persecution escalated, Prophet Muḥammad, who persisted in spreading his teachings, began to look for a community that would be willing to accept the migration of Muslims from Mecca to their land. A group of seven (six men and a woman) from al-Khazraj, one of the two prominent tribes that lived in Yathrib, accepted his teachings and shared them with the tribe. In Yathrib, the second prominent tribe, known as al-Aws, knew about and accepted Muḥammad's teachings. When Mecca's leaders heard of this and the potential alliance of al-Aws with Muḥammad, they unsuccessfully tried to dissuade them and warn them of the dangers of the rising religion.[4] In response to news about his impending assassination, and after seventy-five people from Yathrib converted to Islam, the Prophet Muḥammad emigrated to Yathrib in September of 622 CE.[5] The new immigrants were welcomed and supported by the native Muslims from the al-Aws and al-Khazraj tribes. For supporting and sponsoring emigrant Muslims, the native Muslims from al-Aws and al-Khazraj tribes came to be known as al-Anṣār (literally "the supporters").

Though many of al-Anṣār hosted the new emigrants, discontent simmered under the surface because of perceived economic competition. Many emigrants had no home and no trade. In Yathrib, emigrant men and women worked at developing new skill sets, mainly in agriculture, because competition over labor forced emigrants to buy and work new land. Those who did not have a home were allowed to live in the newly built mosque. Those who were wealthy traded and soon accumulated wealth, whereas those who were poor settled and were often supported by their fraternity (*ikhā'*) with al-Anṣār (Hamidullah). However, there was discontent concerning the economic burden caused by the new emigrants. There was another facet of discontent from the rich of Yathrib, who felt that the emigrants who accumulated wealth changed the economic stratification and life in Medina. But this discontent, driven by economic forces, was not the only force gnawing away at the peacefulness of Medina.

The political situation in Yathrib was also in dire need of intervention. Escalating hostility and tensions between the different peoples of Medina were met by key responses in 622 CE. "While some [tribes] sought external military assistance, which only exacerbated the conflicts, many were making preparations for the enthronement of 'Abd Allāh ibn Ubayy ibn Salūl" (Yildirim, "The Medina," 440), who was from the dominant Arab tribe al-Khazraj. In contending tribal communities, the rise to leadership of a member of one of the tribes would not necessarily lead to stability. However, Hamidullah, drawing on historic accounts, takes this move as an indication of how "the peace-loving parties were gaining preponderance in the city" (14). The road to stability was long especially because Yathrib was contending with a number of crucial and urgent political goals. These included "establish[ing] a political organization, creat[ing] a military defense for the city, reconcil[ing] tribal hostilities, defin[ing] local rights and obligations, and address[ing] the issues of the growing immigrant refugee population from Mecca" (Yildirim, "The Medina," 440). To attain all these goals all tribes of Medina needed to reconcile and work together. It is in this context that the discourse of conciliation and Muḥammad's expertise were crucial.

THE DISCOURSE OF CONCILIATION

Garnering a reputation as a prudent and trustworthy arbiter in Mecca, Muḥammad was chosen to serve as an arbiter for the pluralistic community now living in Medina, who together faced impending anarchy and chaos. From this historical account of life in Yathrib, we can reimagine the intricate conciliatory process needed to bring all of these tribes together to live amicably with one another, a process that involved dissuasion and persuasion.[6] Muḥammad, who was known for his arbitration and mediation skills, recognized that the current situation of turmoil, conflict, and instability was unsustainable. Within the context of religious turmoil and persecution in Mecca and chaos in Yathrib—years of escalating conflict between tribes in Yathrib; rising discontent because of the changes (especially economic ones) brought about by the new immigrants; and the desire for an alternative that would bring peace and stability to Yathrib—Muḥammad rose to leadership.

Rise to Rhetorical Leadership

The most dominant aspect of Muḥammad's rise to rhetorical leadership was playing the role of a mediator with its attendant investment in a discourse that could heal rifts, address injustice and sources of conflict, and provide all with a peacemaking alternative. After fleeing religious persecution and settling in Medina, Muḥammad took a few months to decide "to confront the situation in Yathrib and act as a third-party mediator to resolve the conflicts among the tribes" (Yildirim "Peace," 110). This role was neither unprecedented for a foreigner nor an atypical intervention for Prophet Muḥammad (Yildirim "The Medina," 442). Known as *al-amīn* ("Trustworthy"),[7] he was chosen as an arbiter and mediator, a trusted third party, a role that entails rhetorical leadership.[8] His intervention sought to (re)define Yathrib's political and social reality. The process of mediation—a humanistic, dialogue-driven, persuasive engagement—guides people's pursuits and co-construction of conflict resolution. As such, the CM exemplifies third-party mediation and arbitration, which anticipated and resulted in a binding agreement.

As a chosen leader and mediator, Muḥammad needed to affirm his ethos. Generally speaking, mediators affirm their ethos in rhetorical and extra-rhetorical ways. Regarding this ethos, Merry explains that mediators affirm "their authority to intervene from their positions in kinship networks, their wealth, their political power, their religious merit, and their past successes at mediation" (80–81). Though Muḥammad had distant family ties in Yathrib, it was his reputation as a mediator that was invoked in the city he migrated to, seeking refuge after the escalation of religious persecution in Mecca. Mediators affirm their (recognized) skills, which they use to dissuade stakeholders from acts of aggression and persuade them to coauthor a conflict resolution. To mediate between over twenty different tribes and clans is a tough task, for it involves no less than reframing issues of contention, providing an alternative perspective on the situation, showing new ways to realign and relate to others, and finding and sustaining buy-in to proposed solutions. In effect, a mediator "exert[s] influence and social pressure to persuade an intransigent party to accept some settlement" (Merry 83). In this context, Muḥammad's rhetorical leadership became conspicuous. Because the political milieu was characterized mainly by conflict caused by disputes over power and exacerbated by a leadership void (Yildirim, "Peace," 110–11), Muḥammad's rhetorical leadership sought to address both, and we can discern in his rhetorical leadership the prominent role that the discourse of conciliation and human rights played.

Constraints on and Exigences for His Rhetorical Leadership

In societies in which tribal logic prevails, dominance is sought after. The tribes of Yathrib sought power in different ways when they asserted military dominance, resorted to external military assistance, became allies of other tribes, and when some planned to enthrone leaders from their tribes. Each one of these strategies sought power and eventually exacerbated conflict between the tribes. Such a political context—as Hamidullah explains—results in double trouble: On the one hand, a leader (from one of the tribes) finds it difficult to transcend tribal allegiance and alliances, and members of other tribes find it difficult to accept their leadership. On the other hand, considering the protracted conflict between people of Yathrib and its changing circumstances, the stakes were high and the incoming leader needed to address urgent internal and external concerns. The former included defining rights and duties of all members of Yathrib, "rehabilitation of the Meccan refugees," as well as allaying the fears of and attaining an agreement with the non-Muslims of Yathrib. The latter included establishing a "political organization and military defence of the city" (15–16).

The CM documents Muḥammad's success at mediation and the ratification of agreements that sought to "establish a general basis of security" (Serjeant 7). Despite the leadership void and anticipated impasse, Muḥammad's leadership as both a mediator and a conflict resolution resource/authority for future disputes was recognized: CM ratified everyone's agreement on Muḥammad holding such authority. As a mediator, Muḥammad was a rhetor par excellence who could bring together and unite tribe members as a unified citizenry: as citizens Medinians were united, transcended tribal and religious divisions, and agreed to be governed by a constitution that provided collective protection, affirmed rights, and bound community members to one another and to their city-state.

Fractioning, Reframing Issues, and Rewriting Power

The process leading to this transformation is conspicuous in the CM. The mediation process that was successful in bringing conflicting groups together to deliberate and agree on the ṣulḥ treaties, relied on Muḥammad's use of three interdependent conciliation strategies, which are fractioning, reframing, and rewriting power (Yildirim "The Medina Charter").

Fractioning is one of the conspicuous conflict resolution features in the CM, as Yildirim rightly explicates.[9] Fractioning is a process that disentangles problems and conflicts and addresses them as manageable issues. By fractioning conflict into discrete, manageable problems, each could be named and addressed. Through numerous discussions and dialogues among the different groups in Medina, the CM "was drawn up in the form of a non-aggression pact" (Yildirim, "The Medina," 441). In its final form, the CM is made up of a preamble and what can be considered two major sections; each separates and addresses interrelated issues. The first mainly addresses the needs of emigrant and native Muslims of Medina (articles 3–23), and the second addresses the needs of the Jewish community (articles 24–46).[10] The first pact was between the emigrants and al-Anṣār, and it included Jews and polytheist groups who were in alliance with either al-Aws or al-Khazraj, the two main Arab tribes. The Jews were referenced in the first ṣulḥ treaty as political allies of al-Anṣār (Serjeant). The treaty aimed chiefly at bringing together all members of this group into a confederation.

In specific terms, this confederation treaty (1) sought to create a peaceful alliance between al-Anṣār and *al-Muhājirūn* (emigrants), affirming the rights of the new emigrants, their equal standing, and peaceful relations with al-Anṣār.[11] In addition, the confederation treaty (2) addressed turmoil and conflict in Medina caused by bloodwite or blood money (restitution for those killed or fatally injured). The long history of war and contention had resulted in blood money disputes, a thorn in the flesh of Medinans that would hamper amicable coexistence. The first pact, therefore, outlined the right and obligation to fair pursuit of justice practices as opposed to tribal warfare (Hamidullah; Yildirim). To illustrate, one of the main goals for al-Aws and al-Khazraj was resolving disputes about bloodwite and bringing home prisoners of war. Accordingly, the interrelated problems of cycles of revenge and lack of recognition of the rights of victims were isolated and clearly identified; the involved tribes were named and their immediate concerns (i.e., settling bloodwite disputes) were addressed. Further, fractioning enabled the emergence of the accountability of all stakeholders: the entities entering the agreement (e.g., Banū 'Awf), the conflict resolution measure under consideration (e.g., paying bloodwite and redeeming prisoners), and the conditions that bound parties of the agreement (i.e., "with the kindness and justice common among believers") were clearly identified. As such, Muḥammad did not only utilize fractioning to isolate problems, for he also translated a problem into a discrete, conciliatory, and binding agreement, thus satisfying process and content goals.[12] As a mediator, Muḥammad could address the need to resolve blood money disputes, which was one of the imminent and immediate concerns for people in Yathrib.

The second treaty, focused chiefly on the Jewish tribes and sought to enhance the relation between the Jewish tribes and the confederation. We can clearly identify in the second section of the CM three interrelated goals, which respond to three main problems facing the nascent community. First, it was important for Muḥammad and the immigrants to have a reconciliation pact and an alliance with the Jews of Medina. Citing Al-Tabari, Serjeant explains "that Muhammad 'when he arrived in Medina, had made an agreement with its Jews that they should not aid (*yu'īnu*) anyone against him, and that if any enemy made an unexpected treacherous attack on him (*dahimahu*) they would support him'" (25–26). The Muslims, especially immigrants, were concerned about being attacked by Meccans—a fear that materialized—and wanted to create safety in Medina, goals that necessitated a peace treaty with the Jewish tribes of Medina. "Through the peace (*ṣulḥ*) which took place between them and the Mu'minūn are like a jamā'ah (collective body) of them, their word and hands being one" (Serjeant 26). This is asserted in article 25, which states that "the Jews of Banu'Auf are one community with the believers" (CM 25). Second, the treaty extends to associates of the Jewish tribes, including clients of Jewish tribes like Tha'labah. In other words, people who had formed alliances or protection arrangements were considered as part of the Jewish community (regardless of whether they were Jewish or not). Third, the section includes "a declaration intended to allay Jewish apprehensions about their security" (Serjeant 32). Accordingly, the section affirms a reciprocal obligation of the signatories of the CM to support one another against attacks and to provide one another with "mutual advice and consultation" (CM 37). Each one of these goals counters a problem; without fractionation, reaching an efficacious resolution would not have been possible. More important, put together the three goals allay fears, establish security, and unify the people of Medina. Rightly then, scholars consider the CM to be an enduring and relevant example of conciliatory Arab-Islamic practices (Serjeant; Yildirim).

THE CONVERGENCE OF ṢULḤ AND HUMAN RIGHTS

My account of the conciliatory discourses that anticipated and were ratified in the CM signals that the conciliation processes were responsive to Medina's history of conflict. But the CM also shows that the ṣulḥ treaties were forward looking, and that at the time they were received as affirmations of rights and obligations. Though there is no detailed typological account of the conciliatory and mediation practices that intersect with human rights discourses in medieval Arab-Islamic literature, the affinities between the discourses of conciliation and rights cannot be missed. The pursuit of justice is a common topos in both human rights and conciliation discourses. Ideally, both seek to affirm the dignity and rights of all involved parties. In affirming the rights of people, mediation and ṣulḥ practices can indeed resolve a conflict at hand, which can be considered ṣulḥ's immediate goal. However, ṣulḥ can also proactively seek to decrease hostility and rights violation by creating precedents and a new, transformative, relational framework. In medieval Arabia, there was indeed a need for both the responsive and proactive dimensions of conflict resolution.

Historical accounts of the nature of conflict, tribal allegiance, and justice practices in communities in Arabia in the times of al-Jāhilīyah show us that long, contentious conflict fostered deep-seated animosity among the people of Yathrib. As noted earlier, to face conflict and struggle for dominance, tribes and clans formed alliances, which created a power structure that sometimes exacerbated conflict. In addition, because the tribe—the central social unit—maintained hierarchies, the right to exercise justice was asymmetrically distributed: those who were more powerful were often less accountable. However, justice was a valued pursuit, and arbitration and mediation were recognized as conflict resolution methods in the Arabian Peninsula (Rafeeq 113). In this regard, the interplay of fractioning and affirmation of rights, which at first might seem to be dissimilar moves, was crucial. The discourse of conciliation, as noted earlier, utilized fractioning, a conflict resolution method that helps focus on, isolate, and address issues, to resolve contentious disputes. Conciliation discourses, however, seem to be more effective when they address rights, power asymmetries, and the interests of stakeholders (Ury, Brett, and Goldberg); all exceed just settling a specific dispute.

Because ṣulḥ manifests in the form of written, legally binding contracts, affirming rights while also asserting obligations, it proved to be a useful conflict resolution resource. As a mode of restorative justice, ṣulḥ also reverses the grounds that enable aggression (like assumptions of superiority, affirmations of privilege, and denial of others' rights) and affirms values like justice (*'adl*), equality (*musāwāh*), and immanence of human life, values consistent with the conception of human rights manifest in the CM. Accordingly, both the mediation process and the resulting agreement respond to the need to affirm communities and individuals' right to pursue punitive or restorative justice and rearticulate power relations in a way that enables people to recognize their equality and interdependence.

What is unique about the CM is that its reactive and proactive functions discursively realize a relational imperative. This relational imperative, which balances self and other's rights and obligations, is not just a cornerstone of restorative justice and ṣulḥ but is also consistent with, if not conducive to, human rights discourse. In situations of conflict, violence is often justified and rationalized relying on privilege and power. Therefore, ṣulḥ—as a restorative reconciliation model with the imperative to rebalance power and heal relations—was resorted to and became a constitutive dimension of the CM. Relational goals are relevant to (human) rights discourse: in a relational worldview, conflict severs relations and violates a community's moral code. Even if relations are deemed less important after conflict, the relational needs of those involved remain, for they need to reclaim their sense of self in their community (positive face needs) while also affirming their right to freedom from imposition (negative face needs). Relational goals spell out how a conciliation pursuer "wants to be treated by others and the amount of interdependence they desire" (Yaldrin, "Medina Charter," 113). The CM addressed the relational goals of the community, which were linked to the community's different rights. For example, the right to justice addressed both positive and negative face needs. As a reconciliation method, the CM sought to affirm the rights of all members of the community. Additionally, to counter the logic of violence and rearticulate power relations, the CM regulated the relations between the different tribes, their collective relation to the governing terms and authority created by the CM, and their relations to others as the following sections will demonstrate. More important, because the mediation process aimed for a reorientation of all members of the community, it had to also seek a proactive intervention to address not just the disputes but also the sources of conflict by affirming the rights and obligations of all community members.

THE DISCOURSE OF RIGHTS

The CM affirms numerous rights at one and the same time. These include the rights to (1) equal protection of and accountability to the law regardless of social standing or power status; (2) fairness and nondiscrimination based on race, ethnicity, or origin; and (3) religious freedom (Bassiouni 24). As such, the CM "outlined the rights and duties of citizens, provided collective protections for all citizens of Medina including both Muslims [natives and emigrants] and non-Muslims, and implemented the first means of seeking justice through law and community as opposed to tribal military actions" (Yildirim, "The Medina," 439). By affirming the rights and obligations of community members, the CM transforms life in Medina at a time when tribal conflicts and decades-long hostilities were typical. However, the CM's articulation of rights as goals and grounds for action by a reconciled, unified citizenry is part of a larger discourse on rights in Islam, which deserves brief mention.

Human Rights in Islam and the Constitution of Medina

The study of human rights in Islam is beyond the scope of this chapter. However, shedding light briefly on articulations and grounds of the mandate to affirm human rights and rights in general is indispensable.[13] The term *human rights* in the post-UDHR world has consequences that are sometimes underrecognized. The expectation of the use and circulation of the exact equivalent of human rights as indicated in the UDHR eclipses the history of (human) rights discourses; the variegated nature of the discourse of rights, which differs greatly when informed by an individualist vs. relational worldview (Lyon), and its social constructedness (Gregg); and the processes of internalization and particularization of human rights discourses and their consequences (Hauser; Tagiliarina). But more important, a universal reading of human rights eclipses more expansive paradigms of rights that comprise human rights as well as other nonhuman rights. A paradigm of rights, affirming the individual and collective rights of all creatures, is more consistent with the discourse of rights in Islam. Put differently, the discourse of rights in Islam covers humans, vegetation and animal life, for example. In the Islamic tradition, *ḥuqūq al-'ibād* (the rights of people) include basic human rights (like the right to life), the rights of citizens, and the rights of enemies at war.

Articulations of human rights in Islam draw heavily on the Qur'ān and *Ḥadīth*. Together, they articulate a belief system informed by justice, right, and truth. This belief system is captured well by Said, who explains that "it is a belief system predicated fully upon *Haqq*, which is the Arabic word for right. But *Haqq* is also truth. It is justice. It is duty. It is the word of the Divine. [Al-]*Haqq* is God. The essential characteristic of human rights in Islam is that they constitute obligations connected with the Divine and derive their force from this connection" (63). More important, "in Islam human rights have been conferred by God, no legislative assembly in the world, or any government on earth has the right or authority to make any amendment or change in the rights conferred by God" (Mawdūdīy 12).

The discourses of rights in Islam refer to a bundle of rights that at times intersect. Scholarship on discourses of rights in Islam provides two informative taxonomies. The first taxonomy groups rights into two interdependent rights, namely *ḥuqūq Allāh* (the rights of God) and ḥuqūq al-'ibād. Only the second is focused on here because it addresses the rights of people, the subject of human rights discourse. Ḥuqūq al-'ibād are further elaborated using another taxonomy, which subcategorizes these rights into basic human rights, rights of citizens, and rights of people at war. Basic human rights include the rights to life, safety, a basic standard of living, freedom, justice, equality, the choice to cooperate or not cooperate, and respect of chastity. As to the rights of citizens, Islam recognizes personal, civic, and political rights; protects life and property, honor, personal freedom, freedoms of expression, conscience and conviction, and the sanctity of private life; and affirms the rights to protest against tyranny, avoid sin, enjoy the basic necessities of life, be treated equally before the law (including accountability of rulers), participate in state affairs, and be protected from arbitrary imprisonment (Mawdūdīy). Finally, the law of war and peace in

Islam recognizes two main categories of rights, those of combatants and noncombatants during and after war, and regulates the relation between people at war. Such rights protects noncombatant women, children, and the elderly; monks in monasteries; and people in places of worship. The rights of combatants include prohibition against torture, sanctity of the dead body, and repatriation of those killed during combat (Mawdūdīy). As to property, the law of war and peace prohibits pillage, looting, and destruction of public and private property; obligates Muslims to honor treaties; and regulates the declaration of war.[14]

Rights to Religious Freedom, Equality, and Life and Justice

The CM's forty-seven articles assume and affirm many of the aforementioned rights. It is true that the CM's primary goal was to reconcile the combative tribes in Medina, which led to the creation of a political community, but the establishment of this political community also hinged on other crucial questions. These included the question of religious pluralism, especially since al-Muhājirūn suffered from a prolonged period of religious persecution in Mecca. Also, there was the question of the changing dynamics in the standing of non-Muslims as well as the question of the standing of the non-natives who became residents of Medina. Within the interpellated and constituted political community, concerns about economic and social competition and questions of rights and obligations were deliberated, resolved, and documented. The rights affirmed by the CM include rights to religious freedom, refuge, equality, and justice.

Typically, human rights are defined as "moral rights that all human beings are entitled to, just by virtue of being human. Such rights are ascribed 'naturally,' which means that they are not earned and cannot be denied on the basis of race, creed, ethnicity, or gender" (Maiese). However, these human and natural rights are never affirmed or realized in a political vacuum, so it is important to situate the articulation of (human) rights in its political context, which in turn provides institutional support for their realization. As such, "these [human] rights are advanced as legal rights and protected by the rule of law. However, they are distinct from and prior to law" (Maiese). Accordingly, the aforementioned rights articulated in the CM became legal rights; the CM offered an institutional mechanism that supported the realization of these inalienable rights and sought to regulate vertically distributed power that sometimes resulted in rights violations and conflict. Now, I shed some light on the rights affirmed by the charter, namely the rights to religious freedom, equality (of immigrant and native Medinians, people of all confessions, all Jews, and all Muslims).

Religious Freedom

The charter explicitly affirms the religious freedom of Muslims and Jews, asserting that "the Jews have their religion and the Muslims have theirs" (CM 25). The same applies to all religious groups in Medina. Moreover, the CM neither restricts nor regulates religious freedoms (or practices) for any of the different tribes or clans of Medina. Arjomand asserts that "the lasting effect and significance of the CM . . . stems from its laying the foundations of the classic Muslim system of religious pluralism" (556). In affirming religious freedom, the CM is consistent with the "principal idea of spiritual freedom to practice one's religion as one believes it: 'to you be your Way, and to me mine' [(Qur'ān al-Kāfirūn: 6)]" (Khan 6).

Equality

The CM affirms equality and regulates alliances and political rights entailed. Equality is affirmed for everyone *within* and *across* the different groups. Muslims are equals; Jews are equals; all religious groups are equals. This equality is clearly articulated in the preamble; all groups make "one community (*umma*) to the exclusion of all men" (CM 2): the reference here is to a unified political community. The CM also addresses in different parts of the document the equality between immigrant and native Muslims, the equality of Muslims and Jews, and the equality of all the Jewish tribes.[15]

The equality of all Muslims is made clear in the first section of the charter. Muslims in Yathrib were natives and immigrants. The CM, therefore, addresses the immigrant Muslims from Mecca and native Muslims of Medina, who make up the "community of believers." Eight tribes of Yathrib natives are explicitly referenced in the CM, namely Banū 'Awf, Banū al-Ḥārith, Banū Sā'idah, Banū Jusham, Banū al-Najjār, Banū 'Amr ibn 'Awf, Banū al-Nabīt, and Banū al-Aws. In addition to these native tribes, the CM addresses a small group of one hundred immigrants from Mecca who were from Quraysh. Together, the Muslims of Mecca and Medina made up the community of believers. As Khan explains,

> Conceptually, the Constitution establishes the concept of the community of believers (ummat-al mummunin). The community of believers treats all Muslims with equal respect and dignity. It dissolves the distinction between natives and immigrants, offering principles of equality and justice to all Muslims, regardless of their origin of birth, nationality, tribe, or any other ethnic or racial background. It does not allow natives to have superiority over immigrants or vice versa. The Islamic Free State

is therefore not exclusively identified with one tribe or culture but is expanded to include immigrants with diverse dialects, cultures, and social habits. (3)

The equality between emigrant and native Muslims transcends all their differences as Khan explains. In addition to affirming the equality of Medina Muslims, the CM affirms the equality of all the Jews of Medina. Here it is important to clarify the sociopolitical dynamics that explain how the Jews are referenced in the second part of the CM. The second part, as noted earlier, is driven by the goal to unite Muslim and Jewish communities of Medina. Arab tribes who migrated from the south of Arabia (Yemen) comprised the two prominent groups, al-Aws and al-Khazraj, whereas the main Jewish tribes were al-Naḍīr, Qurayẓah, and Qaynuqā', who migrated from the north. There were also smaller Jewish communities who lived in different parts of Medina but didn't have a specific tribal affinity. "The fact that these groups do not have any definite tribal affinity of their own seems to indicate that for some reason they lost their separate tribal organization, and unlike the greater Jewish tribes they became closely associated with various Arab tribes among whom they dwelt" (Rubin 7). Scholars refer to *aḥlāf* (alliances) between Jewish groups and Arabs. These Jewish groups became the clients of the Arab tribes and were known as the Jews of that tribe. These aḥlāf predate Islam (Arjomand; Rubin) and had become crucial to the emerging community, for "the Jews who had such *ḥilf* . . . relations with Arab clans seem to have been almost affiliated into the Arab tribes whose *ḥaîlfs* they became" (9) But more important, such an alliance meant that the Jewish aḥlāf dwelt in the same territory and were called by the name of the Arab tribe. This type of alliance was not just a political arrangement. Rather it was in a relational matrix that is well represented by Rubin (8) as "an alliance (*ḥilf*), fraternity *(ikhâ') and* friendship *(wudd)*."

Because Muḥammad wanted to establish unity for all the inhabitants of the fertile valley, the CM focuses mainly on two Jewish groups. The first group is referenced in general terms (*yahūd* and *al-yahūd* or "Jews" and "the Jews," respectively). Though scholars do not explicate the categorical reference to "the Jews" in articles 24, 35, 37, and 38, they do tend to reference the second group. The second group was made up of people who lived together with the Arab tribes and were their clients in Yathrib, so they were referenced as the Jews of—(name of Arab tribe). I agree with Rubin that one of "the direct aim[s] of this document was confined to determining the position of the Arab tribes of Medina in relation to those Jewish groups who shared in their territory" (10).[16] However, the use of two different forms of reference to the general Jews, as well as the Jewish clients of Arab tribes, invites a reading that includes the three main prominent tribes (al-Naḍīr, Qurayẓah, and Qaynuqā‘) who also resided in Yathrib—this is a reading that is not acknowledged by Barakat, Hamidullah, and Rubin. Despite disagreements, this sociopolitical situation implies that there was an exigence for the alliance and a history of agreements between the Jewish communities, or at least some of them, and the Arab ones.

The complex situation in Medina in 622 introduced some new variables. These included a change in demographic structure because of the advent of the immigrants from Mecca, and their relations with al-Anṣār, based on what can be described as fraternal sponsorship. This demographic change might be seen as strength for the Arab communities. However, in a number of ways, this change was a source of economic and political vulnerability. Within the framework of ikhā’, al-Anṣār split or shared possessions with the emigrants who fled Mecca because of religious persecution. Yet, there was always fear of attacks from Mecca, which happened later in the history of Medina, mainly because of—comparatively speaking—the Meccans' ability to overpower them. Within this complex sociopolitical reality, there was a need to allay the concerns of both the Arab and Jewish communities, to rebalance power, and to affirm everyone's rights. This is why the CM affirms the equality of all Jewish tribes, equality between Muslim and Jewish groups as well as their autonomy, sovereignty, and religious freedom.

Accordingly, the CM represents all Jewish tribes and clans as equals, naming clearly the different tribes and affirming their equality. It is worth noting here that the Jewish community was represented in the CM neither as a monolithic community nor as reducible to one entity (Khan). This deliberate representation of the Jewish tribes recognizes their differences, the history of contention between the tribes and their former alliances (among themselves and with Arab tribes). For this reason, the CM goes into great length to refer to the Jews' alliance with the Arab tribes by name: the Jews of Banū ‘Awf (CM 25), the Jews of Banū al-Najjār, the Jews of Banū al-Ḥārith, the Jews of Banū Sā‘idah, the Jews of Banū Jusham, the Jews of Banū al-Aws, the Jews of Banū Tha‘labah, the Jews of Jafnah (a clan of the Banū Tha‘labah), and Banū al-Shuṭaybah (CM 26–35). Khan underlines this deliberate representation as both recognition and affirmation of the equality of the different tribes, explaining that "this comprehensive recognition of each distinct Jewish group in a separate Article of the Constitution bestows equal dignity and respect upon all Jewish tribes with whom the social contract was made, rejecting the concept that some Jews are superior to others" (4). The CM as such neither tokenizes the Jewish community, representing them as one tribe, nor affirms the Jewish tribes' hierarchical power. Rather, it recognizes and honors the differences between the tribes and their sociopolitical alliance (ḥilf) with the Arab tribes and affirms their rights to freedom of religious belief and practice and autonomy. The CM clearly stipulates that "the Jews have their religion and the Muslims have theirs" (CM 25).

The CM also affirms the equality of all the people of Medina regardless of religious and tribal affiliation. Accordingly, it affirms that Jews and Muslims are equals. This affirmation of equality was crucial in a context where Muslim immigrants were a minority. But, with the rise of Islam as a religion and with the increasing rise of the political power of Muslims, there was a need to affirm the equality of all, regardless of their religious or political power. It is in relation to these two aspects of the life of Medinians that the CM recognizes and affirms the rights of Jews in a variety of ways. In addition to affirming the equality and equal standing of all Jewish tribes and their freedmen (*muwālin*), the CM affirms the equality of Jews and Muslims: "The Jews of Banū 'Awf are one community with the Believers. (The Jews have their religion and the Muslims have theirs), their freedmen and their persons except those who act unjustly and sinfully, for they hurt but themselves and their families" (CM 25). Their equal rights range from financial independence, to solidarity, to the right to form political alliances, to the right to religious belief and practice. For example, the protection of religious rights is represented as an obligation. As indigenous Muslims of Medina were obligated to protect the rights of Muslim immigrants, all Muslims were obligated to recognize and protect the rights of other religious groups. This obligation is categorically stated in article 16: "To the Jew who follows us belong help and equality."[17] Then article 25 specifically underlines the right to belief and practice of religion, precisely asserting that "Jews have their religion and the Muslims have theirs." However, these religious rights are not the only rights affirmed. The political right to form (external/internal) alliances that are respected by others is pronounced by article 35, which states that "the close friends of the Jews are as themselves." This assertion complements the stipulation that the enemies of the Jews will not be aided, which is articulated in the second half of the aforementioned article 16: "He [the Jew] shall not be wronged nor shall his enemies be aided" (CM 16). These rights underline the equality of Medinians.

The Rights to Life and Justice

In addition to the right to equality and freedom of religion, the CM addresses the rights to life and justice. Medina's conflicts left its tribes—as noted earlier—with serious concerns about safety, protection, and the pursuit of justice, especially since there were so many contentious blood money disputes. Such a history of prolonged conflict mandated the affirmation of two distinct rights. The first, which is assumed, is the right to life and its complementary right to safety. The second is the right to justice. However, only the second is explicitly stated and institutionalized in the CM. The former deserves a brief mention only because it provides the context of the CM's articulation of the latter.

Typically, in Qur'ān and Ḥadīth, the word *nafs* (soul) refers to the subject protected by the right to life. Nafs is the unmarked reference to human, but not in the way we make use of marked/unmarked in common parlance to hide privilege. Rather, nafs "has been used in general terms without any distinction and particularization" (Mawdūdīy 15) to affirm the undeniability of such a right and to make the right conferred by God.[18] The injunction to protect the nafs obligates those signing the document to, on the one hand, abstain from killing any soul regardless of their "citizenship" status, creed, religious affiliation, race, or class, while, on the other hand, it obligates them to protect the safety of their life. This obligation covers, minimally, acts undertaken to ward off the threat of death or destruction caused by injury, illness, or starvation.

Within this framework of reference, the right to life and the pursuit of justice are addressed together. To affirm the right to justice and the sanctity of life, the CM regulates the pursuit of justice (in general and in relation to bloodwite) while addressing community members' responsibility for peace, rising against offences and treachery, punishing murderers, and supporting one another in their pursuit of justice. This is why numerous articles underline the right to pursue justice. "Articles 19, 21, 22, and 40 established the course of law for Yathrib" (Yildirim, "The Medina," 443) and affirmed everyone's equality before the law. For this reason, article 13, for example, states that "the God-fearing believers shall be against the rebellious or him who seeks to spread injustice, or sin or animosity, or corruption between believers; the hand of every man shall be against him even if he be a son of one of them." Rightly, Hamidullah explains that " in . . . the administration of justice, none would be permitted to take sides or show any favouritism to one's relations or even to save one's own son from the course of law" (28). Of particular importance are justice measures pertaining to blood money disputes, which were prevalent, and are more pertinent to the right to life. The CM addresses this concern in a number of articles: for example, article 21 affirms the right to seek justice (*qiṣāṣ*)—implying punitive justice—or conciliation (via *diyah*): "Whoever is convicted of killing a believer without good reason shall be subject to retaliation unless the next of kin is satisfied (with blood money), and the believers shall be against him as one man, and they are bound to take action against him."

All the rights addressed here respond to problems faced by the community, including derailed pursuit of justice or resolution of bloodwite disputes because of power differentials among tribe members or across tribal membership. The discourse of rights clearly overlaps with the discourse of conciliation. However, three conspicuous features characterize this articulation of rights because of its rootedness in a context that mandated a particular cultural responsiveness that had clear moral and relational grounds.

The Nature of the Discourse of Human Rights in the Constitution of Medina

Though the CM does not represent the different discourses that address human rights in Islam, it points to three central features of what unifies these discourses: immanent value of human beings and life; equality of all people (regardless of race, ethnicity, color, tribal affiliation, sociopolitical standing, wealth, native/immigrant status, and religion); and the right to be a responsible member of a community. My analysis of human rights recognizes a central difference between human rights as conceived of in the CM and as conceived of and critiqued by studies of human rights rhetorics (Doxtader "The Rhetorical Question"; Hauser "The Moral Vernacular"). Because this scholarship is written in the context of the UDHR, it is to a great extent informed by rights in relation to citizens whose rights are affirmed and realized in relation *to* and *against* the state. In this context, the state operates as a political authority that can sponsor/impede rights' realization or regulate punitive measures of rights' violators/withholders. The CM is indeed a unique document, a document coauthored by all its signatories—in many ways—to resist tribal law, the authority that underwrites rights in medieval Arabia. However, tribal law was notorious for rights violations; the mighty and powerful within tribes casually denied the rights of others. Indeed tribal law stood still and in effect advocated numerous rights violations. For example, the right to life and the right to social and economic justice were continuously denied by practices like female infanticide, overworking and underpaying the poor, false contractual practices and usury that resulted in enslavement and forced prostitution. Tribal logic was part of a dominant worldview that casually denied the humanity of many (Esposito). It is within this context that the discourse of rights that resulted in the CM affirms and seeks to realize rights. Because there was no "institution" to affirm and actualize rights as well as to offer punitive measures for rights' violators, the CM had to simultaneously envision an alternative worldview where people are equally valued and where their lives is protected and nourished while creating a system that has the stamina to undertake the burden of actualizing and maintaining this vision.

A crucial part of the enactment of this vision is obligation clauses. Though in Islam God confers rights, they are casually violated by humans. Though the ultimate obligation is to God, a central premise of the discourse of rights is the human-to-human obligation to honor all life. Violating this obligation often results in attempts to actualize rights as conditional and secondary. Rather, I contend that when one chooses to coauthor a legal document, a document that humans generate to regulate their accountability to one another, they chose to give precedence to what each is accountable to honor and protect. This results in the need to textualize rights as obligations, which are universally applicable to all members of the community. Therefore, an actualization statement is a textual trace of a bigger discourse that sought to affirm rights in a context when rights were violated casually and for years, as evidenced by the religious persecution of Muslims in Mecca. In this way, the document combines a resistive and visionary force that grounds itself in a political nascent creation.

DISCOURSE INTERPELLATING A UNIFIED CITIZENRY

As noted earlier the long ṣulḥ process resulted in and was ratified by a legally binding discourse. In addition to articulating rights, this discourse assumes political functions as it identifies a political community, names a territorial jurisdiction, sovereignty, and a jurisprudential power that regulates power dynamics and pursuit of justice. Human rights, whether defined as moral or natural rights, are never affirmed or realized in a political vacuum. Therefore, it is important to read the articulation of (human) rights in relation to the political context, which in turn provides institutional support for their realization when "these [human] rights are advanced as legal rights and protected by the rule of law" (Maiese). The articulation of rights and calling forth Medina as a city-state worked in tandem. The following section demonstrates how the interpellation of a unified citizenry is essential to the process of actualization of rights.

Establishing a Political Community

The CM clearly names one *ummah* (nation or community), identifying its members. By identifying the tribes and clans of Medina, the CM established Medina as a city-state with territorial bounds—the jurisdictional function of the CM. This political work is significant: earlier, the tribe was the recognized social unit, which was driven by a tribal logic that often asserts the self mainly in opposition to others; this dynamics made dominance and assertions of power crucial. Contending tribes tended to affirm their dominance and act as sponsors of smaller tribes, which meant that in Medina there was indeed a notable vertical distribution of power. As Medina became a city-state, all tribes needed to be seen as having equal political and legal rights and responsibilities as well as equal right to religious freedom. Accordingly, the charter spells out legally binding terms that regulate the groups' relations to one another and the city-state, which is the jurisprudential dimension of the CM. These legally binding terms were ṣulḥ instruments that sought to resolve eminent conflict and proactively ward off others (e.g., power struggles over leadership and tribal dominion and escalations of bloodwite disputes). The establishment of a political community, which identifies its people and claims jurisdictional and jurisprudential power, does not only respond to eminent conflict but also proactively provides an "institutional" frame for the rights discourse. It was in this newly constituted political community that rights were affirmed. The affirmation of a unified citizenry, then, worked in tandem with and as an institutional manifestation of rights. But what are the textual/rhetorical features of the CM that signal this moral, sociopolitical work? To address this question, I begin by explicating how the CM claims jurisdiction and jurisprudential power and then turn to interpellation of a unified citizenry.

Muḥammad wanted to establish a "territorial unity." This goal might be dismissed as unimportant or irrelevant, but it is a crucial component of the interpellation of a community because, as noted earlier, the affirmation of rights is never exercised in a political vacuum. With a claim to territory, claims for sovereignty can arise. In Mecca, Muslim converts could not ward off religious persecution because their sovereignty (i.e., their ability to control their affairs, including the rights to religious belief and practice and freedom from the imposition of others) was undermined. Establishing territory, and its attendant affirmation of sovereignty, enabled the affirmation of religious freedom and collective and organized resistance against impending danger from the powerful, who had earlier persecuted Muslims, a small minority in Mecca, mainly because the Muslims were perceived as a threat to the dominion of Quraysh. Within the context of discursively establishing a political community, the CM articulates the rights to equality (of all Jewish tribes and between Muslim and Jewish groups), autonomy, sovereignty, and religious freedom.

The preamble names the parties involved in the agreement/charter and constitutes them as a unified citizenry (Yildirim) that determines its own affairs and relations with others (i.e., internal and external sovereignty) and that is distinct from other peoples: "This is a document from Muḥammad the prophet (governing the relations) between the believers and Muslims and Yathrib and those who followed them and joined them and labored with them. They are one community (*ummah*) to the exclusion of all men" (CM). What united these citizens—despite the fact that until then they had tended to define themselves as tribes, a typical characteristic of tribal communities—is a form of an *in actu* sociopolitical contract. As Khan, a law scholar, explains, this contract is "an actual agreement among real people of diverse ethnic and religious groups. This reality based social contract is not even a theory or an inspirational constitution to be implemented in the future. The Constitution of Medina offered social contract in real time, in real space, to real people through a real agreement, hundreds of years before the theory of social contract gained widespread approval, mostly in the West" (3). The social contract is a result of a multidimensional conciliation that recognizes the identity, rights, and interests of different groups while affirming the qualities of interdependence, brotherhood, and obligation that can bind them as a political community. By affirming these qualities, the charter interpellates and recategorizes the parties involved as a community of united citizens. But how can people recategorize themselves as citizens of Medina rather than as members of their tribe or ḥilf?

Drawing on Harvey Sacks's sociolinguistic work on categorization of membership and Maurice Charland's constitutive rhetoric, both of whom address the constitution of subjects to maximize cooperation, I foreground the constitution of an alternative subject position in the CM. Together, Sacks's and Charland's work helps explain how communities are discursively (re)imagined and refashioned by embracing a new membership in addition to choices and actions that support this new membership, hence constituting their subject positions. Recategorization of membership can create a new subject position that transcends tribal, ethnic, and religious polarization, hence creating a viable possibility for the emergence of a sovereign city-state.

The process begins when people enter a rhetorical situation wherein they are addressed, albeit differently. When they recognize that they are addressed or hailed, which is the meaning of the French *interpellé* from which the term *interpellated* is derived, a new subject position is envisioned. "Interpellation occurs at the moment one enters into a rhetorical situation, that is, as soon as an individual recognizes and acknowledges being addressed. An interpellated subject participates in the discourse that addressed him. . . for the acknowledgment of an address entails an acceptance of an imputed self-understanding which can form the basis for an appeal" (Charland 217). The unified citizens are interpellated in a number of places in the document. For example, at the very beginning, all involved parties are represented as "one community (*umma*) to the exclusion of all men" (CM 2).

Then, the interpellated subjects need to be mobilized. Charland explains that interpellation hinges on socialization (217). One aspect of this socialization is naming their group membership. Typically, as Sacks explains, "membership categorization devices" are used in text and talk to identify with or separate from others ("The Baby Cried"; "Invitations"). These membership categorization devices can be as simple as *us* (vs. *them*), which can be traced in the CM's preamble "one community (*ummah*) to the exclusion of all men." Membership categorization devices are always qualified and attached to value systems like loyalty and treachery (CM 37 and 46), and invite actions that maintain membership. Work done to maintain membership is another aspect of socialization. Interpellating and constituting a unified citizenry involves choices and acts consistent with the new subject position. Making and actualizing these choices result in "social [and political] category maintenance work [that] is accomplished through social identity contrasts observable in the form and structure of language in use" (Nilan 71). Put differently, besides categorization devices (i.e., interpellating a unified citizenry using references like ummah), the charter clearly invokes category-bound activities, which are acts that manifest or perform membership (Sacks, "Invitations"). The CM manifests social, political, and moral acts.

Through the processes of mediation and ṣulḥ, the interpellated subjects agreed to goal-oriented choices and acts, which can be considered aspects of the contractual rites. These choices indicate their category-bound acts, which include recognizing their interdependence, consulting with one another, being loyal to one another, and supporting refugees (i.e., social, political, and moral acts). The roles and expectations of this interpellated and unified citizenry are further explained in the CM when their perfect obligation to protect their autonomy and sovereignty is underlined, indicating an awareness of aspects of both internal and external sovereignty (Brahm; Philpott; Schooley). Internal sovereignty (protecting the rights of citizens) is clear when the CM addresses dispute resolution in article 42: "If any dispute or controversy likely to cause trouble should arise it must be referred to God and to Muḥammad the apostle of God. God accepts what is nearest to piety and goodness in this document."[19] This article gives precedence to the autonomy of communities to resolve their conflicts using their own dispute-resolution mechanisms. Only when they fail to do so are they supported by other authority, namely divine law and their chosen arbiter, Muḥammad, to help them resolve conflicts. External sovereignty (the responsibility to protect against external attack and to regulate access to their territories) is asserted in relation to warding off threats and granting refuge. Potential external threats (e.g., from Quraysh, the most prominent tribe in Mecca) are addressed in two complementary articles. The first mentions internal threat caused by treachery or temptations to be disloyal, situations that weaken the internal front, if you will; this kind of threat can be countered by strengthened unity and interdependence. The groups' interdependence is underlined in the article that urges them to attain these goals: "They must seek mutual advice and consultation, and [their] loyalty [to one another] is a protection against treachery [by outside forces or the temptation to be disloyal]" (CM 37).[20] United efforts toward external threat are again highlighted in article 44, which complements internal threat with explicit reference to external threat: "The contracting parties are bound to help one another against any attack on Yathrib" (CM 44). Sovereignty also implies the right and obligation to offer refuge and equality (in terms of rights and responsibilities) to strangers which is clearly articulated in articles 39–40: "Yathrib shall be a sanctuary for the people of this document. A stranger under protection shall be as his host doing no harm and committing no crime." The category-bound acts of uniting to ward off threats, regulate refuge, and support community members implies internal/external sovereignty work, a manifestation of the work of being interpellated as citizens, who rightly undertake socially, morally, and politically grounded acts. All of these category-bound acts are consistent with the charter's relational and communal conceptions of (human) rights. As a sovereign body, Medina's pluralistic community is defined both internally and externally, invoking their (social, legal, and political) rights and obligations.

If ṣulḥ—as a mediation and agreement document—is the backbone and the force behind the document as we now have it, the CM is also a charter in the sense that it is a founding, guiding, and regulatory document that "spells out in detail the rights and duties" of the Medina tribes (stakeholders) and names the "powers and mechanisms for good . . . governance" and peacemaking (Haron, Cajee, and Dangor 619). Besides identifying powers and governance mechanisms, the CM interpellates those bound by the charter as citizens, identifying the territory that geographically and spatially binds them together. Moreover, the CM enlists constitutional power when the text articulates laws that both establish justice in a community and articulate the limits of the governing authority. As such, the Medina Charter is a political document par excellence, for it names its subjects and binds them legally and politically to one another and to a city-state that has both jurisdictional and jurisprudential power. However, a key component in creating a community is the provision of measures that help actualize these legal and political visions.

Actualizing a Political Reality

The CM sheds light on aspects of the political and legal work done to actualize these category-bound acts and support a community committed to respecting and affirming rights. These include underlining (1) mechanisms for managing power abuse, righting wrong, pursuing justice, and affirming intracommunal organization and agency resources; (2) identifying an accepted intervening authority; and (3) articulating guiding values/principles.

In its attempt to establish a system of governance, the CM resorts to dispute resolution resources already in place; these mechanisms for managing power abuse and righting wrongs were crucial for the transformation of Medina. Accordingly, the CM affirms the internal sovereignty and worth of the tribe as a noncompetitive institution and as an authority that can be resorted to. In this regard, two articles illustrate the way the CM establishes a mechanism that counters conflict and affirms justice pursuits and rights. For example, article 3, in addition to recognizing the different tribes or associations by name, recognizes their resources for the pursuit of justice and affirms their right to their *shara'i'* (i.e., customary blood money practices): "The Quraysh emigrants according to their present customs shall pay the bloodwit within their number." Rather than elide their differences or assimilate them into a uniform, idealized representation of justice customs, in recognizing their distinctiveness, the CM affirms their cultural resources.

Moreover, part of good governance is proactive provision of mechanisms for recovering from setbacks. The capacity to provide such mechanisms explains why the CM complements the aforementioned customary practices (i.e., internal sovereignty) with a provision of an accepted intervening authority. This intervening authority sustains the pursuit of justice when it is impeded in article 42. Though quoted earlier, it's worth quoting again: "If any dispute or controversy likely to cause trouble should arise it must be referred to God and to Muhammad the apostle of God. God accepts what is nearest to piety and goodness in this document." This article underlines the autonomy of communities to resolve their conflicts using their own dispute-resolution mechanisms, identifies another resource/authority that can support their pursuit of justice. Only when communities fail to resolve their own conflicts are they supported by divine law and their chosen arbiter, Muḥammad, who can help them resolve conflicts. However, naming an arbiter/judge/mediator and identifying the limits of their intervention is not enough. It is hard for a community to thrive without shared responsibility. It is this conundrum of authority and responsibility that points to the constitutional/jurisprudential dimension of the CM.

The text also has constitutional power: it represents principles and values (like equal rights to safety, security, justice, and solidarity) that guide laws; these principles and values become the third measure of actualization. Against the backdrop of these values/principles, the CM regulates relations between the different communities, establishes justice as a worthy good in the community, and articulates the limits of the governing authority. Because these values/principles entail complex pursuits, the articles cover a broad range of interrelated goals (like establishing justice as a worthy good), and each of the laws/contractual agreements become potential measures of actualization, addressing one of the underlying values or principles. Safety is another value or principle that authorizes and calls forth their collective intervention. In communities suffering from conflict/impending conflict, societal safety, solidarity, and interdependence become crucial to the lives of individuals and groups. For example, articles 12a through 19 underline the tribes' interdependence and collective responsibility to maintain societal safety.

As a case in point, the charter seeks to first regulate tribal-driven alliances that pitted the interests of Muslims and people of another faith against each other. This regulation enhances solidarity among the members of the different tribes of Medina, which is addressed in article 14: "A believer shall not slay a believer for the sake of an unbeliever, nor shall he aid an unbeliever against a believer."[21] The CM also seeks to enhance solidarity and the shared responsibility of all members of the community. When the CM obligates them in article 19 to "avenge the blood of one another shed in the way of God." This article obligates people to pursue justice and upholds the moral codes of the community by supporting others in the pursuit of justice. Moreover, it extends their sociopolitical responsibilities to a form of economic justice. The CM obligates them in article 12a to offer financial support: "Believers shall not leave anyone destitute among them by not paying his redemption money or bloodwit in kindness." Believers are also obligated by article 15 to provide shelter and refuge to one another: "God's protection is one, the least of them may give protection to a stranger on their behalf. Believers are friends one to the other to the exclusion of outsiders." Furthermore, to establish a community based on security and justice, they are enjoined to pursue justice and honor their agreements. Regardless of tribal and familial ties, in article 13, everyone is enjoined to uphold justice and stand "against the rebellious or him who seeks to spread injustice, or sin or animosity, or corruption between believers; the hand of every man shall be against him even if he be a son of one of them." They are also enjoined to honor their binding agreements in articles 16 and 17, wherein they are asked not to make separate peace, a practice that would undermine the unity of the community, and to honor their allies and other citizens, a practice that enhances their moral integrity: "To the Jew who follows us belong help and equality. He shall not be wronged nor shall his enemies be aided." Accordingly, based on the aforementioned values and principles, the charter spells out legally binding terms that regulate the groups' relations to one another and the city-state, which is the jurisprudential dimension of the CM. These legally binding terms resolve imminent conflict and proactively ward off others (e.g., power struggles over leadership and tribal dominion, economic competition, escalations of bloodwite disputes).

These actualization measures respond to the community's need for justice, safety, and security; obligates people to respond to the needs of others and affirm others' rights to such measures. This is why the measures cover justice, economic, and humanitarian issues, issues that Medina could not shrug off in its pursuit of reconciliation and healing. These actualization measures enlist the help of a new subject, a citizen who is invested in and benefits from a reconciled city-state. Within this coauthored sociopolitical and moral universe, the CM articulates the equality of Medinians. This equality looms large in the different articles, and manifests in statements of rights and responsibility. The interdependent nature of statements of rights and responsibility provides actualization measures of a reconciled city-state.

A VISION FOR PEACE

As a peaceful, rhetorical mode of conciliation, ṣulḥ is indeed rich, for it can be initiated in different ways—by the transgressor, by the recipient of injustice/aggression, or by a third party. The CM exemplifies yet another type of ṣulḥ in which a third party initiates it. Muḥammad's third-party intervention as mediator and the communities' dialogues resulted in the CM, but Muḥammad was also one of the immigrants, a stakeholder. This typological detail, however, recedes into the background, for what looms large is a document that in the seventh century could not only establish Medina as a city-state, but also could bring together tribes that had fought for decades. As the unified citizens affirmed each other's rights and established a system of reciprocal rights and obligations, they were able to transcend the tribal logic and tribal law that often denied rights, foregrounding tribal privileges and status. The CM exemplifies a successful convergence of mediation, the interpellation of a new subject (cornerstones of ṣulḥ), and discourses of rights.

The CM is much more than a complex text that interweaves political, legal, and social visions for a nascent community. It has an evocative power, which continues to inspire political (re)visions for different communities and across vivid ideological divides. Not only was the CM seen as an inspiring vision and model for the Muslim community in South Africa (Haron, Cajee, and Dangor), where Muslims are a minority but also Islamists as well as liberals in Egypt (Muslims make up the religious majority) following the January 25 Revolution. Surprisingly, before and during the drafting of the 2012 Egyptian constitution, numerous scholars and public figures brought up the Constitution of Medina as an exemplar of a conciliatory constitution that addresses the varied, and at times conflicting, needs of a pluralistic society. Numerous panels sponsored by political parties and movements in Cairo as well as TV political shows addressed the CM. Dr. Muḥammad Salīm Al-ʻAwā—an Egyptian presidential candidate in the 2012 elections, a lawyer, and a writer specializing in Islamic law and arbitration—at different points during the election year spoke about the CM as an exemplary constitution, establishing and supporting a civilian state. This was a crucial part of his argument to partly explain the political constructedness of "Islamic state" and its lack of historical accuracy. However, his explanation also was probably meant to allay fears of an "Islamic State" especially in relation to minority rights. Though al-ʻAwā is right in his statement, it was clear that he was using the CM to construct an image of himself as a proponent of a civil state, while to many he was yet another Islamist candidate.

What is curious about this point is not just his uptake of the CM, but that clips of his talks were shared with me when I was invited to talk to Hizb al-Dustūr (al-Dustūr Party), a nascent liberal, revolutionary party established in the wake of the January 25 Revolution, about my analysis of the same text, also to affirm the rights of all in a pluralistic society. Had I given the talk, I would have generally agreed with the five-minute clip of al-ʻAwā's talk; however, the panel did not convene. The process of deliberating the value of historical precedence was thwarted when former president Mohammed Morsi issued a Constitutional Declaration in November 2012. In effect, he unilaterally granted and decreed for himself unprecedented and noncontestable authorities while constraining the judicial system, a key promoter of rights and accountability. The stark contrast between the converging aspirations of Medinians who could write in the seventh century the first constitution in the Arab-Islamic world and Cairo in 2012 testifies to the inspirational and evocational power of the CM. These rich debates also addressed international peace treaties suggesting that we need to reexamine our distant past iterations of peacemaking like the CM and more recent ones like Camp David.

4

FROM THE EGYPTIAN PEOPLE'S ASSEMBLY TO THE ISRAELI KNESSET

al-Sādāt's Knesset Address, Ṣulḥ, and Diplomacy

> Those who like us are shouldering the responsibilities entrusted to us are the first who should have the courage to make determining decisions that are [commensurate] with the magnitude of the circumstances. We must all rise above all forms of obsolete theories of superiority.
>
> —*Muḥammad Anwar al-Sādāt,* "Speech to the Knesset"

In late November 1977, Muḥammad Anwar al-Sādāt undertook a risky and highly visible trip across the Egyptian-Israeli border to visit with the Knesset. The epigraph above comes from his Knesset address (hereafter KA) and sums up its overall goal, which sought to enable deliberation commensurate with the gravity of a series of wars and to attain peace. al-Sādāt's KA interrupted and transformed a prolonged diplomatic stalemate, resuscitated peace talks, and eventually led to the Camp David Treaty. The KA and texts it deliberates *with* and *against* are the focal point of this chapter.

This chapter offers a bidimensional reading of *ṣulḥ* discourse, underlining how al-Sādāt's diplomatic deliberations resuscitated Egyptian-Israeli peace talks in 1977 by drawing on a long tradition of public, formal ṣulḥ in addition to the three main features of ṣulḥ, namely initiating peace through commitment; mobilizing witnesses; and creating a community, political structure included, of peace pursuers. As such, this chapter provides yet another case where the three main features of ṣulḥ are conspicuous. I contend that these features of ṣulḥ are crucial to understanding al-Sādāt's 1977 peace initiative and that they are the backbone of the address. However, ṣulḥ continues to be invisible in scholarship on al-Sādāt's initiative. It is important to note that in this case ṣulḥ expresses itself in relation to other discourses that also seek to create transformative encounters, namely diplomatic discourse, border crossing, war/peace epideictic rhetoric, and policy articulations at moments of crises. In this mix, ṣulḥ can be forgotten unless we deliberately tease out its manifestation in both the symbolic and procedural dimensions of peacemaking.[1]

Because the KA is complex and rich, I focus on explicating its symbolic and procedural dimensions; the former mainly focuses on perceptual and relational transformation, whereas the latter addresses institutional response. The analysis draws mainly on the KA while contextualizing it in reference to other texts.[2] These include an earlier speech to the Egyptian People's Assembly (Maji el-Sha'b; EPA) and Security Council resolutions (SCR), for example. To underline the rhetorical work of ṣulḥ, I draw on a number of rhetorical and linguistic analytical categories including speech acts, rhetorical narrative, and epideictic, deliberative, and constitutive rhetoric, identifying how al-Sādāt's peacemaking rhetoric manifests the critique *against* war and *for* peace, a general characteristic of peacemaking rhetoric, as well as initiating peace through commitment, mobilizing witnesses, and creating a community that deliberates and seeks peace, all of which are features of ṣulḥ.

The analysis starts by focusing on epideictic rhetoric, which underwrites al-Sādāt's critique *against* war and critique *for* peace and energizes the symbolic dimension of his peace initiative: I demonstrate how epideictic rhetoric is used to articulate the logic that orchestrates peacemaking efforts and underwrites self- and other-oriented peacemaking moves. To underline self- and other-oriented moves, I draw on speech acts and rhetorical listening. Speech acts of promise (i.e., commissives) are encoder oriented since they bind encoders to fulfill their promise. al-Sādāt initiated and committed to the peace process publicly in both the EPA and Knesset addresses. Alternatively, moves toward the other in terms of recognizing their grievances and needs are traced using rhetorical listening and representations of locution. Additionally, the analysis demonstrates how al-Sādāt discursively constituted a deliberative community of peace pursuers, a prominent feature of ṣulḥ, drawing on both constitutive rhetoric and categorization of membership. Finally, the analysis focuses on the procedural dimension of the KA by drawing on insights from diplomacy concerning public declarations, for example, and insights from rhetorical studies concerning exigences and constraints at moments of crisis. Ṣulḥ informs the reasons al-Sādāt engages the needs of the self and other to foster functional prenegotiation deliberations that can help stakeholders address and resolve the crisis. This rhetorical work entails naming central questions, foregrounding the urgent need for a viable (re)solution, proposing a workable framework that meets stakeholders' varied expectations, and underlining the accountability of the international community, and the United Nations especially, to their (re) solutions, which are probed using question-answer and problem-solution organizational patterns.[3]

In broad strokes, the chapter first situates the KA historically, politically, and diplomatically. Second, the chapter explicates how al-Sādāt rewrote the spheres of contact and reimagined possibilities: stalled peace negotiations mandated the rewriting of the spheres of contact to enable the coming together of belligerent parties and to transform their relations from hostility to peacemaking. This rewriting constitutes a holding space, where three spheres of contact intersect, namely ṣulḥ, diplomacy and international relations, and border crossing. Third, the chapter addresses how al-Sādāt reversed intractability by responding to deliberating voices, which he worked *with* and *against*. This sets the stage for the analysis of the KA, which demonstrates how al-Sādāt's ṣulḥ manifests as epideictic and deliberative rhetoric that underwrites self- and other-oriented peacemaking moves and articulates deliberative possibilities.

A BRIEF HISTORICAL ACCOUNT

al-Sādāt's peace initiative needs to be read against the backdrop of wars and peace efforts. As to the wars, Egypt, other Arab states, and Israel have lived a state of belligerence for years, which go as far back as 1948 (the year of *al-nakbah* or disaster) or three decades earlier with the Balfour Declaration. Historically, Egypt and Israel were engaged in military confrontation in four different wars, namely 1948, 1956, 1967, and 1973. Memoirs and multidisciplinary scholarship reflecting on these wars, their root causes, and possible solutions have been published by Arab, American, and Israeli scholars for decades (e.g., 'Abd al-Salām; al-Sādāt, *In Search of Identity*; Ben-Ami; J. Carter; Kamel; Fahmy Quandt). What is intriguing is that the political momentum between the 1967 and 1973 wars was inconsistent with peace efforts. Shlomo Ben-Ami, a historian and former minister of foreign affairs of Israel, chronicled this when he wrote that "the interval between the two wars—1967 and the Yom Kippur War—emphasized once again a central feature of the Arab-Israeli conflict. Israel's military victories and the Arabs' humiliating defeat could never be the prelude to peace" (116). al-Sādāt knew this too well, but this was glaringly obvious especially after Hāfiz Ismā'īl's, al-Sādāt's national security adviser, meeting with Kissinger in Paris in February of 1973: "The drift of what Kissinger said to Ismail was that the United States regrettably could do nothing to help so long as we [Egypt] were the defeated party and Israel maintained her superiority" (*In Search of Identity* 238). Ironically, the 1973 war was a partial prelude to peace.

Ben-Ami quotes Usāma al-Bāz—an Egyptian diplomat who helped al-Sādāt with his visit to the Knesset when his Minister of Foreign Affairs at the time resigned—and writes about the necessary change in power dynamics that the 1973 war enabled:

> "The spirit of October," as Osama El-Baz, President Sadat's national security adviser, defined it, meant that the illusion of the Israelis about their invincible military prowess was shattered. "We have proven ourselves their equals, both intellectually and practically," he wrote in *Al-Ahram*'s weekly magazine on the twenty-fifth anniversary of the war. Having "restored its honour," as Sadat explained in a speech in the middle of the war, Egypt was now ready for peace. Sadat's strategic war put Israel off balance and destroyed the famous "conception" whereby time was in her favour. Now, Israel was forced to consider making peace not on the basis of her unchallenged supremacy, but on that of the most profound crisis of confidence ever known by the Jewish state, a crisis triggered in its turn by the most traumatic setback ever suffered by its legendary defence forces, Israel's military power—and this was a message to the Americans as well—could no longer ensure regional stability. By an act of force Egypt had asserted her own agenda and compelled Israel to enter a peace process with the now more than ever vital purpose of getting Egypt out of the war cycle in the Middle East. (147–48)

As to peace efforts, the 1977 peace initiative is preceded by a long and invisible history of failed peace initiatives. These include the February 4, 1971, peace initiative, which was announced in the EPA (al-Sādāt, *In Search of Identity*, 219). Historically, the 1971 peace agreement was followed by two other peace initiatives. One of these initiatives preceded the October 6 war and took place in February of 1973, whereas the second took place ten days after the war began on October 16. The former was dismissed quickly; however, documents pertaining to this failed peace initiative were released to the public and studied by Bar Joseph in his article "Last Chance to Avoid War: Sadat's Peace Initiative of February 1973 and Its Failure." The latter is referred to in al-Sādāt's KA. al-Sādāt's 1977 peace initiative and his numerous references to the 1973 war must be read in this context of military confrontation, failed peacemaking efforts, lost opportunities for peace mainly caused by the imbalance of power, which has been addressed by many writers. All these variables mandated a daring rewriting of possibility.

REWRITING SPHERES OF CONTACT AND POSSIBILITY

As a rhetor, al-Sādāt had to confront the realities of this long history of wars and their (inter)national ramifications and harness a possibility for peace. This task was unfathomably difficult given the deep distrust and ever-fresh wounds on both sides of the Egyptian-Israeli border. In 1977, many grievances were fresh in individual and collective memories. War atrocities and civilian and military losses left none above pain. Additionally, dangers were continuously looming, undermining stability and prosperity and indicating an impending war. In this context, entertaining the possibility of peace is difficult. However, to reverse the resultant intractability, al-Sādāt had to hold a space for contact and for possibility.

When we study al-Sādāt's public rhetoric at that time, it becomes obvious that he created a liminal, diplomatic space for a potentially transformative encounter across international borders. In calling for and creating a space for encounter, his discourse fostered conditions for a functional "intellectual contact" (Perelman and Olbrechts-Tyteca 14) geared toward peace. This discourse of possibility can be traced in both the EPA and Knesset addresses, which encoded "a vision and time apart amid the ticking bombs" (Hatch "Beyond Apologia" 205) and threats of an impending war. It's not an exaggeration to say that the EPA and Knesset addresses tightly knit a discourse of possibility at once epideictic and problem solving—exhibiting powerful features of deliberative and constitutive rhetoric. To end the stalemate, al-Sādāt rewrote potential spheres of activity and contact, namely ṣulḥ, border crossing, and political and diplomatic deliberation.

Ṣulḥ is invisible. Border crossing and diplomacy are the most visible in the sense that the former got a lot of media attention and the latter is the focal point of scholarly attention. There is a tendency to read the speech through the lens of international diplomacy. Ṣulḥ is, therefore, sandwiched between the other spheres and can easily be missed, especially since all these spheres of contact converge in their goal to make peace. Accordingly, this chapter sheds light on ṣulḥ as not only a crucial cultural resource that informs and is traceable in the text but one that is crucial to understand the spheres of contact enabled.

The first sphere of contact is ṣulḥ, which is one of the initiative's cultural and historical dimensions. To recap, ṣulḥ is a forward-looking, interceptive, problem-solving, and constitutive mode of conflict resolution that brings stakeholders together to end conflict. In this case, ṣulḥ is used in the international domain to mobilize stakeholders to make peace. Its three central features (i.e., initiation using commitment, mobilization of commissive witnesses, and reconstitution of a community of peace pursuers) are conspicuous in this case of public, international ṣulḥ, too. In this case, stakeholders include publics, politicians, national leaders, and international institutions. Though the key players are different, for they include both publics and political elite, ṣulḥ here invites (in)directly affected people to the "table" since they incur the consequences of war and benefits of peace. The preceding chapters illustrate how ṣulḥ becomes an *occasion* and a *condition* for functional contact of those who become othered in conflict and enables cooperation to reach a mutually acceptable conflict resolution. In this case, too, ṣulḥ underwrites al-Sādāt's interpellation of a community of peace pursuers.

Besides the relational transformation implied by the interpellation of a community of peace pursuers, ṣulḥ has yet another crucial dimension. As noted earlier, ṣulḥ entails processes and ceremonial rituals, which manifest its customary, public, and performative dimensions. In its formal manifestation, ṣulḥ is characterized by technical, formal, and goal-directed (Irani, "Islamic Mediation") discourse. Public ṣulḥ often results in a formal, binding agreement that regulates relations between ṣulḥ pursuers and spells out conditions promoting peace. Peace treaties/pacts are a special kind of this formal ṣulḥ, and the historical record abounds with ṣulḥ treaties. According to Jordanian judge Muhammad Abu Hassan, "Public sulh is similar to a peace treaty between two countries. It usually takes place as a result of conflicts between two or more tribes which result in death and destruction affecting all parties involved" (qtd. in Irani 12, "Islamic Mediation").

Not only does al-Sādāt's KA articulate a vision for a bilateral peace in which responsibility for the attainment of peace is distributed among the different stakeholders, but he also articulates a framework for an ethically and politically binding agreement. In addition, he refers to Ṣalāḥ al-Dīn (or Saladin) and 'Umar ibn al-Khaṭṭāb: both are known for issuing and implementing peace treaties and for protecting religious freedoms, tolerance, and recognition of rights. This tradition and the socially, ethically, and legally binding contractual nature of ṣulḥ is underscored in legal scholar Cherif Bassiouni's compilation of Islamic instruments affirming or guaranteeing human rights. This tradition of formal, public ṣulḥ treaties comprises bilateral agreements (e.g., Ṣulḥ al-Ḥudaybīyah), multilateral agreements (e.g., Ṣaḥīfat al-Medīnah or the Charter of Medina) (Bassiouni 27; see also chapter 3 in this volume), and unilateral commitments (Ṣulḥ al-Quds).[4] This tradition is important as a historical collective memory, precedent, and cultural resource. al-Sādāt draws on this collective memory as he entreats, "Instead of reviving the precedent of the Crusades, we should revive the

Spirit of ‘Omar [ibn al-Khaṭṭāb] and [Ṣalāḥ al-Dīn], namely the spirit of tolerance and respect for right[s].” ‘Umar ibn al-Khaṭṭāb’s peace pact guaranteeing religious freedom is an example of public ṣulḥ, which had a prominent procedural component, organizing religious institutions and affirming the right to belief and practice. Similarly, Ṣalāḥ al-Dīn is also known for Ṣulḥ al-Ramlah (or the ṣulḥ at Ramlah) with King Richard the Lionheart in 1192, which included territorial partitioning and the freedom to go on a pilgrimage to the holy lands in Jerusalem.

Ṣulḥ as a historical event and legal/political record is not just referenced in the speech: as a conciliatory model, it is a key frame of reference in the speech. Numerous features of public ṣulḥ are conspicuous. These comprise interpellating a community that deliberates on *what* can be agreed upon/done to promote rights and underscore obligations and *how* to formalize these rights/obligations in terms of an agreement—even if a preliminary one. These features are addressed below. As a framework, ṣulḥ happens to overlap with other frames (i.e., border crossing and political deliberation and diplomacy) that result in the deliberative dimension of the KA. Intriguingly, these features of public ṣulḥ neatly dovetail with both border crossing and political deliberation and diplomacy.

The second sphere of contact is enabled by border crossing, which is a crucial part of the social, psychological, and symbolic context of al-Sādāt’s peace initiative. In transnational literature, border crossing implies movement between source and destination points, networks of migrating people (Hesford and Schell; Waldinger and Fitzgerald), policy interarticulations (Dingo), networks of “imagined communities,” and citizenship that transcends geopolitical boundaries (Sassen, “Repositioning”; “Local Actors”). al-Sādāt’s border crossing embodied and modeled a different form of contact: al-Sādāt crossed the Egyptian-Israeli geopolitical border, which was still considered a frontline. Thus, he materialized the peacemaking quest across borders. However, the circulation and/or movement of people, ideas, policies, and goods across national borders do not just connote possibility and transformation; they also connote risk (Vertovec).

Political deliberation and diplomacy together make the third sphere of contact. As a political actor, al-Sādāt’s visit to Jerusalem was a diplomatic encounter with a multiplicity of goals, for al-Sādāt clearly mobilized both regular diplomacy and public diplomacy, which can be traced in his discourse in November of 1977: al-Sādāt sought to influence political bodies and publics. This is why his KA has numerous features of both regular diplomacy and public diplomacy. I first address regular diplomacy. al-Sādāt’s fourth peace initiative carried traits of regular diplomacy as a community of practice, which seeks to realize the mandates of diplomacy and international relations. Both the EPA and the Knesset addresses opened public channels for diplomatic players to meet and resuscitate the peace process. Like border crossing and ṣulḥ, diplomacy implies and promotes functional contact. In this case, functional contact resulted in deliberations about (external) policy formulation. Also, in diplomatic parlance, a diplomatic solution "gives priority to negotiation rather than the threat or use of force" (Berridge and James). As such, it is a goal-oriented, functional encounter of diplomatic players who coordinate action to excise violence, establish communities of shared interests, and promote peace. In diplomatic encounters, interlocutors (track-one or track-two political bodies) negotiate and deliberate rights, concerns, visions, or policies, which implies routine deliberations as well as those at moments of crisis (hence the terms *routine diplomacy* and *crisis diplomacy*, respectively). These features converge with ṣulḥ, and especially public ṣulḥ, and this convergence offers a partial explanation for the invisibility of ṣulḥ, which was briefly addressed in the introduction.

Second, al-Sādāt engaged what is known as *public diplomacy*, which refers to a discourse seeking to impact perception or action across borders. Nicolas Cull explains that "at its best, public diplomacy is a two-way street: a process of mutual influence whereby a state (or other international player) facilitates engagement between publics or tunes its own policies to the map of foreign public opinion" ("Public Diplomacy: Seven Lessons" 12). Though the EPA speech mainly addressed Egyptian MPs, it also addressed the Egyptian general public, Israeli political leadership, and the international community. Once in the Knesset, al-Sādāt addressed the Israeli public, not just members of the Knesset, hence mobilizing both regular and public diplomacy (Cull, "Public Diplomacy before Guillon").

al-Sādāt's peace initiative sought to engage and impact, in addition to his primary addressees, the political elite and Israeli (and worldwide) public opinion, creating a community that devalues war and appreciates peace, thus defying the logic of separation and confrontation encoded in international borders and a frontline. If ṣulḥ seeks to mobilize and commit stakeholders and witnesses to the pursuit of peace, public diplomacy, which harnesses the political power of different constituencies and publics, certainly encodes a consistent goal. As Cull puts it, "In the ideal case, public diplomacy treats the foreign public as an active participant—not just as a flock of sheep waiting to be ideologically shorn" (12).

Regular and public diplomacy are complementary: besides the exigence for preparing the public for and resuscitating diplomatic prenegotiation, there was the need to attend to procedural reconciliation—substantive issues concerning policies, measures, and institutions that counter conflict—which complements the relational, symbolic dimension addressed by public diplomacy. Though some scholars differentiate between symbolic and procedural reconciliation, many see them as complementary. Together they can create a vision and institutional framework for change. As rhetors seize such visions, they can effectively take up procedural/symbolic reconciliation, which can lead to articulating an agenda to realize peace. This agenda can respond to and be informed by cultural practices—like ṣulḥ—that act as precedents, guides, and frameworks for peace.

Like ṣulḥ, diplomatic discourse abounds with possibilities and transformative influence as well as risks. Optimally, diplomatic deliberative encounters coordinate action between international political bodies, whereas public diplomacy seeks to mobilize public support. Like ṣulḥ, the rhetoric of diplomacy as potential community-building sociopolitical construct/practice enables a functional intellectual contact that makes use of discourse as an alternative to (physical) violence/conflict. However, its potential doesn't eliminate risk.

In this case, the stakes were high because in addition to the present complexities of negotiating peace, al-Sādāt had to contend with a difficult history. On the one hand, there was a state of belligerence and internecine military confrontation, which entailed polyvocal grievances, a present caught up in the vicissitudes of contestations, and an uncertain future.[5] On the other hand, there was the aforementioned history of failed initiatives as well as public criticism of the Geneva Convention itself.[6] Despite its ability to bring stakeholders together, signaling an investment in peacemaking and providing a legitimate forum for Arab-Israeli negotiations (Berridge 37), the Geneva Convention did not really generate an articulation of a framework. Considering this history, al-Sādāt faced a high-risk situation. Failure in diplomatic deliberations, public diplomacy, or procedural reconciliation risks loss of time and resources at best or exacerbates tension at worst. Certain conditions exist that hamper/enhance possibilities of diplomatic encounters. If left unmet, these conditions become liabilities. For example, there was the risk of being read as selling out or settling for diplomatic ventures that promise limited rewards. Such history of contestation and failed diplomacy highlighted the need to resuscitate prenegotiation deliberations to end the crisis and increase the possibility of transformation. It also mandated strong and firm leadership that firmly articulated grievances and charted a workable solution.

To illustrate, in moments of crisis—like a diplomatic stalemate—national leaders need to exude power and strength both at home and abroad.[7] Political leaders, as decision makers and rhetors, must demonstrate "strong leadership qualities" (Kuypers 2), navigate the tricky and high-risk tasks of allaying their compatriots' fears, manage their compatriots' expectations, and "communicate to various constituents that a certain development is critical and to . . . [promote] . . . a certain course of action to remedy the critical situation" (Kiewe xvii). In addition, policies framed as workable and advisable must be more than goal-directed responses to the crisis faced. They also must create a coherent image of meaningful and efficacious decision making guided by "precedent, tradition, and expediency" (Kuypers). The perils and potentials of crisis rhetoric are captured by Amos Kiewe, who explains that "such discourse is expected to offer quick solutions, preserve the strength and integrity of the nation and its leadership, justify necessary action, garner support for action, correct misperceptions and recover from setbacks. Crises, then offer unique challenges to those managing them. They can be seen as opportunities to mold images beyond the usual practices of political discourse, but they can also be seen as threats to the decision maker's overall standing in the public eyes" (xviii).

The three converging spheres of contact meant both opportunity and risk. They hinged on seizing possibility and mandating transformation. All imply a crossing from one state to the other, and these processes of transformation are mediated by a rhetoric of possibility (Kirkwood; Poulakos) that underlines opportunity, hope, risk, and obligation. A rhetoric of possibility engages interlocutors "in terms of their capacity to *become* what they are not, and brings to their attention things that they do not already feel, know, or understand. Further, it invites them to abandon their familiar modes of thought by challenging their current values and beliefs" (Poulakos 223–24; emphasis added). Put together, ṣulḥ, diplomatic discourse, and border crossing provide spheres of contact for interlocutors to engage the realities of war, reconsider the viability and feasibility of peace, and share frames and narratives that "disclos[e] creative possibilities of thought and action" (Kirkwood 30). Accordingly, these spheres provide a context wherein a discourse of possible peacemaking emerges.

REVERSING INTRACTABILITY, DELIBERATING VOICES, AND BORDER CROSSING FOR PEACE

Peace processes involve many telling behind-the-scenes conversations, events, and correspondences: each provides a window into deliberating voices and the confluence of exigence that prepare political actors and stakeholders for a change in the dialectics of conflict and conflict resolution.

The first voice can be traced in a correspondence between presidents Jimmy Carter and al-Sādāt that points to al-Sādāt's commitment to peace and a perception that the moment is opportune; the second relates to the emergence and dismissal of iterations of collective action in favor of a solo trip to Jerusalem; the third relates to Menachem Begin's response to al-Sādāt declaring his readiness to go to Jerusalem and address the Knesset. Each can be considered a formative, deliberating voice that responds to the escalation of conflict, political impasse, and impending war and envisions transformative, albeit different, encounters. As such, these voices constitute crucial layers of (minimally) the context of the production of the speech. Moreover, they weave a pattern of "call and response" that gestures toward the dialogic nature of peacemaking rhetorics in general and the dialogic dimension of al-Sādāt's peace initiative. Conversing *with* and *against* these voices, al-Sādāt engaged intractability, harnessed the power of peacemaking as he charted different ways to move forward. A study of these deliberating voices explicates how al-Sādāt reversed intractability and uncovered his deliberat(iv)e decisions to create a liminal space where stakeholders could engage the peacemaking ritual and discourse.

President Carter wrote a letter to al-Sādāt on October 21, 1977, when diplomacy failed and war seemed impending. While recognizing and responding to the Arabs' reservations about the American working paper, Carter called for public endorsement of the paper. More important, he touched on al-Sādāt's commitment to the peace process, manifest since 1971.

> When we met privately in the White House, I was deeply impressed and grateful for *your promise to me that, at a crucial moment, I could count on your support when obstacles arose in our common search for peace in the Middle East.*
>
> . . .
>
> The time has now come to move forward, and your early public endorsement of our approach is extremely important—perhaps vital—in advancing all parties to Geneva. (Quandt 139; emphasis added)[8]

Carter's call for al-Sādāt to publicly endorse the American working paper charted a possible route for action to resume preparation for the Geneva Convention. Carter's letter was one among many voices that al-Sādāt worked with and against.

Ḥasan Tuhāmī was another deliberating voice backing the idea of a civil march to Jerusalem. In 1977, as the deputy prime minister, president's adviser, and envoy, Tuhāmī had a series of secret meetings concerning peace possibilities with Israel's foreign minister, Moshe Dayan. According to Tuhāmī's account—as reported by Zahid—the Tuhāmī-Dayan meetings ended well when "the Israelis . . . had agreed to withdraw their forces from all occupied territories in return for peace" (65). After the meetings, Tuhāmī revived the idea of a civil march: "The idea was to gather three million Muslims from all over the Islamic world in Jordan and then begin a civil march on Arab Jerusalem in order to regain it from Israeli control" (66). The revival of the idea sought to optimize this "good news"—Tuhāmī's description—and called for demonstrating strength and collective action, while arguing against al-Sādāt's meeting secretly with Begin (Zahid).

Because "Sadat became convinced that some *preliminary contact* with the Israelis was essential" (Zahid 65; emphasis added), he wanted a high-stakes step to push the peace process forward, anticipating that the Geneva Conference would fail in this regard. Accordingly, Tuhāmī (qtd. in Zahid 66) advised al-Sādāt, "Go to Jerusalem. Let us go to Jerusalem—our land, our holy place, center of the world and center of the problem. . . . From there we will declare our demands and let the world hear and know in a last attempt for true peace. We shall see if they have the courage to go along with us in the same way." Going to Jerusalem was on al-Sādāt's mind in September as the pre-Geneva negotiations stalled. Later, when the political impasse became imminent, the idea of a trip to Jerusalem, albeit contested, accrued force and morphed gradually into a solo journey and a summit meeting.

Ismail Fahmy, the Egyptian minister of foreign affairs at the time, suggested that al-Sādāt respond to Carter's letter by preparing for a summit meeting including heads of Arab states. His suggestion opposed a high-risk, solo trip by al-Sādāt, which he rightly anticipated would be divisive to Arabs.

> When Carter's letter arrived, Sadat was already considering telling Carter that he was planning a trip to Jerusalem. At this point, Fahmy put his foot down and told Sadat that such a trip would not only scuttle Geneva but that the Israelis would trap Sadat into making a separate peace if he went alone. When Sadat insisted, Fahmy made an alternative suggestion. He advised that if Sadat was determined to do something dramatic in Jerusalem, he should propose a summit meeting in that city to include the heads of state of the United States, the Soviet Union, Britain, France, China, Israel, and the involved Arab states—as well as Yasir Arafat. (Zahid 67)

Carter, however, did not respond favorably to the idea of the summit. By the end of October, threats of war amassed and possibilities for a successful

Geneva Convention were frittered away. This political accretion intensified the need for a prenegotiation intervention. "All of this left Sadat once more brooding over the prospects for success at Geneva. He turned again to thoughts of a solo journey to Jerusalem" (67).

al-Sādāt forcefully and publicly shifted the discourse of intractability to one of possibility by initiating peace talks in his address to the EPA on November 9. His address covers many issues, including foreign affairs and a commitment to reinvigorate the Arab-Israeli peace talks considering the dwindling possibility of the Geneva Convention reconvening before the end of the year (i.e., within fifty-two days). Situating his commitment in relation to his peace initiatives before and after the 1973 war, he sets the stage for his fourth peace initiative.

As he commits to realizing peace, al-Sādāt asserts the need to prepare rigorously for the convention, addresses dysfunctional stances impeding the move forward, and declares his readiness to go to Israel in order to change the prospect of the Geneva Convention from *negligible* to *possible*. He explains, "Such preparations should lead us to achieve a peaceful, just and overall settlement within a reasonable time and prevent the conference from becoming an oratory platform or an arena for exchanging accusations and putting on record positions for propaganda purposes" (EPA 39–40). Peace negotiations continued to stumble because of distrust that made parties wary of the possibility and feasibility of "a peaceful, just and overall settlement." This political distrust had reproduced the rhetoric of conflict that takes over when peace talks are reduced to empty oratory and propaganda tactics. By pointing to his diplomatic efforts and continued interest in the efficacy of the Geneva Convention, al-Sādāt counters discourses of looming, ineluctable war and endless, fruitless peace negotiations, renews interest, and foregrounds conditions that resume stalled negotiations and facilitate the attainment of peace.

More important, he assumes a high-risk, self-commissive stance with no guarantees of reciprocity. To begin, he avows that he is not only ready to prepare to go to Geneva, but also to participate "despite all procedural impediments," asserting his commitment to the peace process and reclaiming the territories occupied in 1967:

> Let me state clearly before our people, the Arab nation and the world at large that we are ready to go to Geneva and to sit for the peace talks, despite all the procedural impediments raised by Israel to deprive us of the opportunity by irritating us so that we will say "No" as we used to

> do in the past. To say "no, we will not go," so that it can appear as the advocate of peace before the world.
>
> I agree to all procedural matters. In the final analysis, when we go to Geneva, Israel cannot prevent me from claiming the territories occupied in 1967, Arab territories . . . (EPA 50)

Then, he declares his readiness to go to the Knesset: "You must have heard me say that I would go to the end of the world to spare an injury to one of our men, much more the death of one. *Israel must be greatly surprised to hear me say that I am even ready to go to the Knesset and discuss with them*" (51; emphasis added). At the time, there were no diplomatic relations between Egypt and other Arab countries and Israel. A diplomatic visit by an Arab leader was not only an unprecedented move but was also risky. Thus, al-Sādāt's internationally visible, voluntary, self-binding declaration of his willingness to visit and discuss with members of the Knesset ways to end the "no war no peace" stagnation and to bring peace to both countries was unprecedented and noteworthy. And he did keep his word.

Tacit in al-Sādāt's self-binding commissive is a call for a reciprocal commitment, a diplomatic response. His call to the Israeli officials elicited a positive response from Prime Minister Menachem Begin who addressed the Egyptian public on November 11; Begin accepted al-Sādāt's indirect request for an invitation, thus providing yet another crucial piece of the rising exigence and pursuit of conflict resolution. Begin's address was crucial for a variety of reasons. He addressed the Egyptian public for the first time, using referential terms like "neighbors," "real friends," and "allies" (1). He also responded to al-Sādāt's November 9 peace initiative by acknowledging rifts and losses on both sides and underlining possibility:

> Your President said, two days ago, that he will be ready to come to Jerusalem, to our Parliament—the Knesset—in order to prevent one Egyptian soldier from being wounded. It is a good statement. I have already welcomed it, and it will be a pleasure to welcome and receive your President with the traditional hospitality you and we have inherited from our common father, Abraham. And I for my part, will, of course, be ready to come to your capitol, Cairo, for the same purpose: No more wars—peace—a real peace, and for ever. (Begin 1)

Begin refers to a shared history, recognizing what unites Egyptians and Israelis in the pursuit of peace and al-Sādāt's initiative: he actually names ṣulḥ later in his address when he declares, "It is in this spirit of our common belief in God, in Divine Providence, in right and in justice, in all the great human values . . . it is in this human spirit that I say to you with all my heart: Shalom. It means Sulh" (2).

al-Sādāt's voluntary, public commitment to peace worked *with* and *against* these deliberating voices. The public endorsement Carter called for neither entailed nor identified border crossing to visit a country with which Egypt had no diplomatic relations. The idea of the march deflected attention from the risk of crossing national borders and frontlines. The idea of a solo trip contended with the risk of being denied the request for a visit, crossing the safety of one's national borders, and becoming alienated from all Arab leaders. However, al-Sādāt accepted all these risks and publicly initiated peace talks in his EPA address, which sought to reverse intractability and mobilize a discourse of ṣulḥ, but ṣulḥ—like other mutually constructed conciliation discourses—begins with a proposal to be followed by coherent action and agreement.

In keeping with his self-binding commitment to peace, al-Sādāt made public statements, offering a rough outline of his itinerary and reiterating his commitment to peace and a comprehensive solution to the Arab-Israeli conflict. Unless there is an agreement to undertake the arduous work of peacemaking, or a sufficient response to the call, the discourse ceases to be. Carter's letter, the idea of the Jerusalem march, al-Sadat's EPA speech, and Begin's response converged, gesturing toward a readiness—even if it was still to materialize—for the pursuit of peace. But gestures weren't considered enough by al-Sādāt, who felt the need to fulfill his commissive to go to Israel if and when the need arose, an action that entailed hope and risk. Among the acts he undertook to actualize his commitment, al-Sādāt choose to go on a solo trip to Jerusalem. This actualization of peace ushered a monumental shift.

Arnold Lewis, an anthropologist then working at Tel Aviv University, recognized that al-Sādāt's initiative morphed into an intricate ritualized rhetoric of peace.[9] He succinctly underlined the consequences of al-Sādāt's peace initiative, trip to Jerusalem, and KA. He explained that "through these activities, a shift in the constellation of Israeli opinions regarding Israeli-Egyptian relations was articulated, fostering compromise and agreement on a new framework of relations between Israel and Egypt at Camp David" (702). Lewis's reflections on the visit underline its impact, a noteworthy feat considering the stability of the Camp David agreement.

al-Sādāt mobilized his ritual of peace when he traveled to Jerusalem (November 19 and 20, 1977) and addressed the Knesset. Viewed from the vantage point of the present, his border crossing can be dismissed. However, at the time, his trip was polysemic and signaled a momentous shift enabled by a peace rhetoric that responded to and countered conflict-enticing forces. Border crossing had physical, symbolic, institutional, and relational dimensions. Literally, al-Sādāt, a military leader, crossed a frontline and geopolitical border separating two belligerent nations whose conflictive history had spread across three decades and culminated in four wars. However, I contend that border crossing happened symbolically on November 9, 1977 (i.e., ten days before the physical border crossing). Despite political assessment at the time (and scholars' political assessment later) of the limited success potential of the Geneva Convention (e.g., Lewis 688), al-Sādāt proactively addressed the EPA, responding to the rapidly deteriorating situation. He voluntarily declared and committed publicly to peace, overcoming procedural impediments that thwarted hopes for peace talks in Geneva, crossing the geopolitical borders and addressing the Israeli Knesset (EPA 50).

More important, al-Sādāt—an embodiment of the Egyptian national self—symbolically crossed into a transnational self, embraced public diplomacy, and addressed common values of peace, stability, and security. This was a crucial step, for the border also separated identities partially defined in opposition to the other. Thus, he crossed a geopolitical and a "psychological barrier," al-Sādāt's term, underscoring a deep mistrust and fear of an enemy on the other side of the border with whom the national self was in an intractable conflict, this stance mandated alienation and war, which in turn led to staunch opposition involving antagonistic discursive practices, military hostilities, grave human losses, and grievances on both sides.[10] All were coupled with and sustained distrust and fear. Moreover, this bidimensional crossing of geopolitical borders and diplomatic conventions overlapped with ṣulḥ ritual and practice, which allow ṣulḥ participants in both micro and macro social domains to cross over barriers—frontlines of hostility, fear, and distrust—to reach a common ground where they can deliberate means and ends. Until October 1977 (i.e., four years after the October 1973 war), threats of war were made on both sides (Lewis 688), and borders continued to connote danger, vulnerability, and potential for grave altercation if not grave losses. Yet these borders were crossed peacefully.

In transnational literature, border crossing is fraught, often accompanied by risk and hope, and may result in a complex rearticulation of membership (Vertovec 4). al-Sādāt journeyed from Cairo to Jerusalem to address Israeli politicians and people, a novel and risky diplomatic endeavor at the time, according to the assessment of numerous political analysts and international relations scholars (e.g., Kelman; Long and Brecke; Moaz and Felsenthal). Worldwide, "high officials cracked jokes about the matter, and considered Sadat's offer to be purely rhetorical" (Shoufani 3). Those who did not laugh it off accused him of betrayal. al-Sādāt was certainly aware of this reception of his peace initiative. In his memoir and speech to the Knesset, he reflects on his deliberate decision to break away from institutional practices or diplomatic conventions between belligerent parties:

> I have chosen to set aside all precedents and traditions known by warring countries. In spite of the fact that occupation of Arab territories is still there, the declaration of my readiness to proceed to Israel came as a great surprise that stirred many feelings and confounded many minds. Some of them even doubted its intent.
>
> Despite all that, the decision was inspired by all the clarity and purity of belief and with all the true passions of my people's will and intentions. I have chosen this road, considered by many to be the most difficult road. (KA 18)

al-Sādāt was aware of the risks entailed, which included powerful opposition from heads of state and Ismail Fahmy who was his own minister of foreign affairs (al-Sādāt, *Al-Bahth* 323), loss of the support of Arab states, and threats to his life. The risk materialized in his and Egypt's alienation, for "other political leaders reacted bitterly to what they considered betrayal of Arab brotherhood and the Palestinians" (Long and Brecke 88; Jiryis). To date, this continues to be the case for many. However, despite ridicule and charges of betrayal and being deluded by power, al-Sādāt rearticulated his commitment when he "repeated his offer on November twelfth before a visiting delegation of US Members of Congress, the same day on which Begin made a response to Sadat's statements in a televised address" (Shoufani 4), which was referenced earlier.

Crossing geopolitical borders, breaking away from diplomatic conventions, al-Sādāt crossed the typical frontline and shattered the psychological barrier (of fear and distrust) separating belligerent parties. This is how al-Sādāt confronted the fear and distrust that impeded the process of reconciliation. Public, self-binding commitments are considered confidence-building measures, and border crossing is another gesture establishing trust. His visit in effect built bridges and called for reciprocal trust measures, thus enabling others to move forward. But how did al-Sādāt attain this end discursively?

Three features converged to underscore and increase the possibility of peacemaking. First, peace was consistently positively valued as an honorable and expedient goal, while war was negatively evaluated and its consequences foregrounded. Using epideictic rhetoric, I demonstrate how common values—like the pursuit of peace—created a discourse that celebrated peace as a choice that could unite Egyptians and Israelis. Second, belligerent parties were reconstituted as peace pursuers. To explicate the interpellation of this new subject position, I draw on constitutive rhetoric, categorization of membership, and category-bound acts, which were also used to explicate the interpellation of Medinians. Constitutive rhetoric is complemented by two interrelated terms from sociolinguistics: *categorization of membership* and *category-bound acts*. These analytical categories are geared toward showing how a new subject position of peace pursuers is rhetorically constructed. Third, there is a clear distribution and negotiation of roles and responsibilities to establish peace. al-Sādāt assumed accountability and called for reciprocity, which are traced using the complementary self-oriented (underlining one's responsibilities) and other-oriented (demonstrating one's recognition of and responsibility toward the other) rhetorical strategies, including narrative, rhetorical listening, and speech acts of promise. Each one of these rhetorical features "disclose[d] possibilities" (Kirkwood 31–32) for peace: they articulated and shared a balanced vision of peacemaking, reconstituted participants' positions, and called for reciprocal commitment to peacemaking.

CRITIQUING WAR, EMBRACING PEACE: EPIDEICTIC RHETORIC AND A NEW MORAL ORDER

Epideictic rhetoric functions in complex ways in al-Sādāt's Knesset address. Generally speaking, it is the backbone of the speech: it articulates the critique *against* war and the critique *for* peace, which in turn authorizes self- and other-oriented moves. This epideictic force—interwoven with deliberative rhetoric—can be seen throughout the speech but is more prominent in the first half. What follows explicates how the epideictic—in both functions—"speaks to the recurring, [and] experientially 'permanent' [and] chronic issues" (Walker 8) of war and peace, representing the possibility of peace as a transhistorical and transnational concern.

Characteristically, epideictic rhetoric centers on the noble/ignoble and on people's "moral goodness or badness" (Corbett 152; see also Aristotle; Arnhart).[11] However, in modern times, articulations of moral goodness/badness are often not just intrinsically valued. Rather, they are goal oriented in three ways: they are instructional domains that (1) "have . . . a visionary quality," (2) catalyze individual and communal critical reflection, and (3) impact deliberation (e.g., S. Carter 327; Sheard; Walker 8). Because epideictic rhetoric creates an "instructional" space where communal values are (re)defined and related to a worldview, it can refashion constituencies:

their membership can transcend spatial and temporal boundaries, for the "epideictic is definable, in larger terms, as argument directed toward the establishment, reconfirmation, or revision of general values and beliefs" (Walker 7). Because the epideictic's evaluative nature models the *honorable* and *preferable*, "epideictic argument belongs, in sum, to the domain of theory, and it invites its listener/'spectator' (or *theoros*, as Aristotle says) to an act of contemplation, evaluation, and judgment" (8). This judgment implies accountability, for "in praising a great man [or a deed], he [the orator] was suggesting, indirectly at least, that his audience go and do likewise" (Corbett 152). Accordingly, epideictic rhetoric leads to judgment and decision making and has a constitutive potential.

In his KA, al-Sādāt uses an epideictic thread in which peace is consistently praised, whereas war is negatively evaluated. This praise/blame binary is mapped onto another binary in which those who seek peace are praised, whereas those who seek war are negatively evaluated. The war/peace epideictic thread, woven throughout the text, is foregrounded in the first half of the speech and generally backgrounded in the second until it surfaces again toward the end of the speech. The power of epideictic rhetoric is invoked as soon as al-Sādāt greets his audience using the typical Arab greeting: "Peace be upon you," a greeting and prayer for peace. al-Sādāt's greeting is conspicuously long as it incorporates an elaborate prayer for peace. After the typical, formal greeting, he proclaims:

> Peace and the mercy of God Almighty be upon you and peace be with us all, of the Arab lands and in Israel, as well as in every part of the big world, which is so beset by conflicts, perturbed by its deep contradictions, menaced now and then by destructive wars launched by man to annihilate his fellowmen.
>
> Finally, amidst the ruins of what man has built, among the remains of the victims of mankind there emerges neither victor nor vanquished. The only vanquished remains always a man, God's most sublime creation. Man whom God has created, as Gandhi, the apostle of peace puts it, to forge ahead, to mold the way of life and to worship God. (KA 17)

His prayer underlines the humanizing force of peace and animates the war/peace epideictic. This cross-cultural commonplace conjures a scene of destruction, suffering, and loss that spares none and is infused with powerful details later in the speech, foregrounding images of torn families, widowed wives, and "innocent children who are deprived of the care and compassion of their parents" (KA 17). These images are evocative: to active listeners they "communicate meaning and emotions . . . [and] evoke scenes"

(Tannen 135). al-Sādāt's detailed images, therefore, materialize the negative consequences of war and recognize the grievances of many on both sides of the border. Moreover, depiction of destruction, widowed spouses, and orphaned children seeks to involve his audience in the problem and make them more inclined to contemplate the significance of this historical moment in which peace can be deliberated and realized.

The counterpart to the imagery-rich war scene is a scene of peace, which represents its imminent rewards. The scene is enlivened by a doctrinally charged image of coexistence: "We all love this land, the land of God, we all Moslems, Christians and Jews, all worship God" (KA 17). al-Sādāt continues to underline shared divine teachings and commandments, asserting that we all live under God; "God's teachings and commandments are . . . love, sincerity, purity and peace" (17). If these doctrinally charged values argue for peace's intrinsic worth, its pragmatic ones are also asserted in numerous places in the speech. To illustrate, its benefits are enumerated when al-Sādāt underlines how peace protects "the lives of sons and brothers" and "afford[s] our communities the opportunity to work for the progress and happiness of man" (17). The detailed imagery used highlights the difference between war and peace as social realities.

Further, al-Sādāt juxtaposes war and peace as moral orders, which correspond and inform these sociopolitical realities. Because of epideictic rhetoric's positive evaluation, peace becomes the meaningful alternative moral order to war and a condition for possibility. As an alternative moral order, peace offers an explanatory frame for the preferable and honorable, which has a symbiotic relationship with the material world. This explanatory frame underwrites al-Sādāt's own actions as well as his calls for transformation and interpellation of a new subject position whose actions are consistent with peacemaking. The rhetorical work of interpellating a new subject position hinges on the establishment of a meaningful moral order. As Jayyusi explains, "In examining the ways in which persons are described and the ways in which such descriptions are used to accomplish various practical tasks—e.g., to deliver judgments, warrant further inferences, ascribe actions, project possible events, explain prior events, account for behaviour, etc.—it becomes clear that categorization work is embedded in a moral order, how that occurs and how that moral order operates practically and pervasively within social life. Indeed one can explicate in detail how it is that the social order is a moral one" (qtd. in Nilan 92). The connection between peace as a moral order, recategorization discursive work, and category-bound acts is best illustrated in al-Sādāt's call for transformation, which was used as the epigraph for this chapter and is quoted again here:

"Those who like us are shouldering the responsibilities entrusted to us are the first who should have the courage to make determining decisions that are [commensurate] with the magnitude of the circumstances. We must all rise above all forms of obsolete theories of superiority, and the most important thing is never to forget that infallibility is the prerogative of God alone" (KA 17). To a great extent, this quote sums up the rhetorical work authorized by the peace epideictic, the call for accountability, and the ways al-Sādāt's KA orchestrates self- and other-oriented moves.

Self-Oriented Moves

The counterpart to inviting others' accountability is to establish one's own accountability and to set its record. This is why al-Sādāt reiterates his voluntary, self-binding declarations, recounts the history of his peace initiatives, and underlines his accountability stance, especially because his commitment materialized when he travelled to Jerusalem and addressed the Knesset. All are self-oriented acts, which are probed in the following section using speech acts of promise and rhetorical narratives.

Commissives

As noted earlier in the chapter, al-Sādāt voluntarily and publicly committed to the peace process. To highlight the rhetorical dimension of this work, I draw on commissives, or speech acts of promise, that voluntarily commit interlocutors to taking a particular course of action.[12] al-Sādāt's commissives cannot be dismissed: not only can commissives play a role in peacemaking as they invite trust and signal openness to change, but commissives also uniquely characterize ṣulḥ. Previous chapters demonstrate the centrality of commissives to ṣulḥ. The long ṣulḥ process can be initiated by a wrongdoer, a victim, or a third party. Acting on a conciliatory exigence and commitment to peace, which entails using symbolic and procedural peacemaking measures, initiators seek the intervention/mediation of family or community elders, make amends, and reconcile. Like apology- and forgiveness-driven reconciliation, a commissive can provide "conditions preliminary to the contact of minds" (Perelman and Olbrechts-Tyteca 17). Commissives can hold an alternative space for conflicting, polarized participants to meet and find a mutually acceptable peaceful resolution. Commissives can be especially generative in situations of contested histories and double victimization. In specific terms, self-binding commitments can confront issues of distrust that can impede the creation of spaces of functional encounter and contact of minds, thus providing an alternative to violence.[13]

Commissives are crucial to al-Sādāt's peacemaking initiative. Despite his previous failed diplomatic interventions and a looming war, he undertakes voluntary, public, self-binding acts, indicates a change in subject position, and names and mobilizes witnesses, albeit commissive witnesses. These acts bind him to actualize his commitments. His commissive speech acts recur, and can be first noticed in his EPA address. To illustrate, as he addressed the EPA, presidential aides, the Egyptian public, and Israel, al-Sādāt avows to "go to the end of the world," visit the Knesset, and undertake necessary measures to end war and save lives (EPA 51). His unambiguous, public, voluntary, and self-binding message comprises both future action and an assertion to act on this promise. Commissives have necessary and sufficient conditions, that is, variables that facilitate their achievement (Malmkjær 490–91). In speech act theory, the former (future action) corresponds to the propositional-content rule, whereas the latter (a specific assertion of how one plans to act on a promise) fulfills the sincerity condition (Malmkjær 492). al-Sādāt repeatedly affirmed his commitment. When asked by politicians and journalists about his response to an invitation to address the Knesset—a question that recognizes the obligation to keep his promise (i.e., fulfill the conditions)—al-Sādāt affirmed: "For sure, for sure I'm serious and whenever I shall be receiving the invitation, I shall be making all the preparations needed and visit the Knesset there, and discuss with them the whole problem" ("Interview with Sadat").

al-Sādāt's reiterated voluntary, self-binding act implies a shift in subject position and underlines a stance of accountability, especially because his commitment materialized when he travelled to Jerusalem and addressed the Knesset. Yet he needed to sustain the momentum of his peace initiative, affirm the genuineness of his commitment, and invite his audience to reciprocate. A sustainable, meaningful, and effective peace hinges on a reiterative (Long and Brecke) and reciprocated commitment. To prove that his commitment to peace was genuine, al-Sādāt recounted a rhetorical narrative that transcends its recapitulative function (Simpson 116) and "serves as an interpretive lens"—to borrow a phrase from John Louis Lucaites and Celeste Michelle Condit (94).

Rhetorical Narratives

al-Sādāt infuses his KA with narrative episodes, which weave a compelling story of his peace pursuit: the narrative poignantly recapitulates and reflectively analyzes his decision-making processes, motivations, and fortitude. al-Sādāt knew the political impasse was partially related to distrust. He wrote in his memoir, titled *In Search of Identity*, that he wanted to "break the vicious circle [of distrust] within which [Arabs and Israelis] had been caught up for years." Countering distrust hinges on changing the perception of his audience (members of the Knesset and Israeli public). The narrative episodes do this by not only supporting but also unveiling the deep internal motivations of his commissives. As the following analysis demonstrates, al-Sādāt uses narrative to (1) vocalize his internal dialectic, tracing some of the voices he worked *with* and *against* as he committed to peace; (2) narrate his previous peacemaking endeavors and initiatives; and (3) situates his current quest for peace. All foreground his self-binding, irrevocable, and public pursuit of peace. In the KA, these functions overlap and recur in the text to forge a new persona that counters that of the "enemy" whom war is/should be waged against and creates a sense of trust consistent with his commissive.

al-Sādāt begins the narrative by declaring his goal: "I come to you today on solid ground to shape a new life and to establish peace" (KA 17). Then he underlines the risk of his irrevocable, public, performative, self-commissive act to meet those who until recently were labeled the enemy. To modern readers, the risk may be lost, but to his immediate audience, the risk was readily recognizable, even if not fully, especially since most risks materialized later. These risks included loss of support of the Egyptian and Arab publics and leadership as well as the risks' attendant political and economic ramifications. al-Sādāt's reflections also acknowledge the surprise and logic of opposition to his plan to address the Knesset. To illustrate, he surmises, "No one could have ever conceived that the President of the biggest Arab state, . . . should declare his readiness to go to the land of the adversary while we were still in a state of war" (KA 17). Because imminent war and decades-long bereavement complicate the expression and reception of his commitment to peace, al-Sādāt complements his recognition of opposition with a condensed articulation of his internal dialectic, clarifying how his internal deliberation resulted in and sustained his decision to go anywhere in the world and "put before the people of Israel all the facts" (KA 17) and pursue peace—despite escalating opposition.

More important, this stance of openness leads him to uncover important information: al-Sādāt narrativizes his calls for peace initiatives and agreements from 1971 to the moment he addressed the Knesset, which are now recognized as historical facts:

> I have shouldered the prerequisites of the historic responsibility and therefore I declared on Feb. 4, 1971, that I was willing to sign a peace agreement with Israel. This was the first declaration made by a responsible Arab official since the outbreak of the Arab-Israeli conflict. Motivated by

all these factors dictated by the responsibilities of leadership, on Oct. 16, 1973, before the Egyptian People's Assembly, I called for an International conference to establish permanent peace based on justice. I was not heard.

> I was [not] in the position of man pleading for peace or asking for a cease-fire, motivated by the duties of history and leadership, I signed the first disengagement agreement, followed by the second disengagement agreement in Sinai.
>
> Then we proceeded, trying both open and closed doors in a bid to find a certain road leading to a durable and just peace.
>
> We opened our heart to the peoples of the entire world to make them understand our motivations and objectives and actually to convince them once of the fact that we are advocates of justice and peacemakers. (KA 17)

These narrative episodes shed light on historical precedents (i.e., peace initiatives, peace agreements, or ceasefires), which had started six years earlier in 1971.

To many, al-Sādāt's rhetorical narrative changed the timeline of his staunch and perseverant advocacy for peace especially since he shed light on some failed initiatives that have only been recognized recently (e.g., Bar-Joseph) as wasted moments as noted earlier. Thus, he contextualizes his commissive, proving that it is neither isolated nor unprecedented—even if the readiness to address the Knesset is. This recontextualization is multidimensional: first, al-Sādāt's peace initiative and visit are situated in relation to a six-year long investment and a series of peace initiatives. The decision to unveil failed peace initiatives asserts the fidelity and plausibility of his pursuit for peace and foregrounds a different ethos, one based on responsibility and accountability to peace. Second, his initiative is related to an inescapable need for a responsible, forward-looking, proactive response to war, which binds conflictive parties in their grave losses and death. Third, it is related to a common goal, that is, the pursuit of security and prosperity, and a preferable moral order, detailed earlier: al-Sādāt articulates his overall goal in a way that demonstrates its consistency with Israelis' concern over their security, a divisive force in the negotiations. His goal—to spare Egyptians, Arabs, and Israelis further injury and death—extends to Israelis and people around the world, for "Any life that is lost in war is a human life, be it that of an Arab or an Israeli" (KA 17). al-Sādāt's rhetorical narrative underscores his commitment to peace, the history of his peace initiatives and ceasefire agreements, the shared losses to war, and the benefits of peace. All increase the rhetorical force of his commitment and make it recognizable to Israeli publics and political elites. Rhetorical narratives and commissives are self-oriented moves that underscore al-Sādāt's peacemaking efforts. I now address how accountability *of* and *to* the other is discursively communicated.

Other-Oriented Moves

Besides refashioning himself as a trustworthy partner in the pursuit of peace, al-Sādāt needed to refashion the Arab/Egyptian-Israeli relationship, a process that hinged on addressing grievances and restorative needs. He also needed to expand the circles of accountability to enhance the possibilities of negotiation. I now turn to these goals by attending to other-oriented rhetorical peacemaking moves, which address the restorative needs of the other, acknowledge them as stakeholders, and develop a shared accountability to the peace process. To study other-oriented moves, I draw on rhetorical listening and representation of locution, interpellation and (re)categorization of membership, and commissive witnessing (i.e., the mobilization of witnesses of al-Sādāt's commissives). Each other-oriented move contributes to the discourse of accountability.

Listening Rhetorically

The refashioning of others called for rhetorical listening to voiced grievances, which in turn uncovered the limitations of the current situation and invited accountability. Simply put, rhetorical listening—as described by Krista Ratcliffe—is an interpretive invention, a deliberate, reflective, and consistent choice to embrace a stance of openness (25). In her words, "Its purpose is to cultivate conscious identifications in ways that promote productive communication, especially but not solely cross-culturally" (25). al-Sādāt assumes, models, and asks for this stance of openness in which people can use their capacity and will(ingness) to listen.

In the narrative section of the KA, al-Sādāt acknowledges first dimensions of conflict when he points to the "walls of separation," "psychological warfare" (his terms), distrust, and Israelis' contribution to the problem and then turns to acknowledge the Arabs' role by representing and responding affirmatively to Israeli grievances:

> You want to live with us [in this] part of the world.
>
> In all sincerity I tell you we welcome you among us with full security and safety. This in itself is a tremendous turning point, one of the landmarks of a decisive historical change. *We used to reject you.* We had our reasons and our fears, yes.
>
> *We refused to meet with you, anywhere*, yes.

> *We were together in international conferences and organizations and our representatives did not, and still do not, exchange greetings with you.* Yes. This has happened and is still happening.
>
> It is also true that *we used to set as a precondition for any negotiation with you [that] a mediator . . . would meet separately with each party.*
>
> Yes. Through this procedure, the talks of the first and second disengagement agreements took place.
>
> *Our delegates met in the first Geneva conference without exchanging a direct word*, yes, this has happened. (KA 17–18)

al-Sādāt rearticulates Israeli grievances (italicized) concerning recognition. In rearticulating the grievances, he names acts inconsistent with peacemaking—acknowledging responsibility—and embraces rhetorical listening in two conspicuous ways.

A variety of forms can acknowledge responsibility, and these do not necessarily entail reproducing the locution of grievances. Uniquely, al-Sādāt's representation of Israeli grievances avoids what could have been reproduced as "You said, I said." Rather, he reiterates acknowledgment and accountability utterances while narrativizing the grievance using declarative structures (i.e., "We refused . . .," "We used . . ."); *yes* signals these projections of locution (Halliday and Matthiessen; Thompson). In reiterating grievance locutions and incorporating them into his speech, al-Sādāt signifies that he is listening/has listened to the question "Didn't you reject us?" But, he chooses not to repeat each grievance locution, its attendant emotions, and conflictive interactional roles. Instead, he acknowledges the grievance and enacts responsiveness and accountability using a declarative structure that recognizes and assumes responsibility for each grievance, noting interactional patterns that deterred functional peacemaking endeavors. Thus, he reiterates grievance locutions in a way that short-circuits regression to blame-guilt discourse and shifts the direction of discourse: blame-guilt discourse tends to be—as Ratcliffe explains—backward-looking, whereas accountability is forward-looking.

al-Sādāt's choices demonstrate listening and responsiveness. However, in situations of prolonged, double victimization, listening must go both ways. Otherwise, listening leads neither to reconciliation nor to sustainable results: al-Sādāt, therefore, voices Arab grievances, which becomes an indirect call for reciprocal listening and accountability. As al-Sādāt acknowledges the problems of conflict, psychological warfare, and distrust, he underlines Israeli's contribution: "There was a huge wall between us

[Arabs, Egyptians, and Israelis] which *you* tried to build over a quarter of a century, but it was destroyed in 1973. It was a wall of an implacable and escalating psychological warfare" (KA 18; emphasis added). He elaborates by narrativizing threat locutions, which makes the articulated grievances less adversarial in tone: "It was a wall of fear of the force that could sweep the entire Arab nation from one end to another. It was a wall of propaganda that we [Arab nation] were a nation reduced to immobility" (KA 18). Dare I add that it is a wall that still exists for the Palestinians, which all Arabs witness on a daily basis?

As al-Sādāt embraces and calls for reciprocal rhetorical listening, an other-oriented move, he recognizes grievances and acknowledges responsibility. al-Sādāt, therefore, establishes a multidimensional discourse of accountability. Now I turn to another crucial dimension of this accountability discourse, which is manifest in his interpellation of peace pursuers and commissive witnesses.

Naming Commissive Witnesses, Interpellating Peace Pursuers

al-Sādāt's self-binding declarations, narratives, and rhetorical listening underline his commitment, refashion him as a pursuer of peace, and indirectly call for reciprocity. This reciprocity depends on a shared commitment and desire for peace, whose terms are set by epideictic rhetoric. These terms—in addition to underwriting al-Sādāt's commitment to peace—invite his audience to be witnesses to his commissives and interpellate his audience as peace pursuers. They are also invited to reflect on whether their actions realize the peace potential. As such, their interpellation foregrounds a forward-looking discourse of accountability, which redefines their relation to the events from observer to participant. I now turn to explicating how al-Sādāt names his commissive witnesses, then focus on his interpellation of peace pursuers.

al-Sādāt, in the EPA and Knesset addresses, identifies audiences to his (fulfilled) commitment as commissive witnesses. To recap, commissive witnessing is a crucial feature of ṣulḥ since the counterpart to a refashioned self who makes a self-binding commitment is a commissive witness who shares accountability to the pursuit of peace. al-Sādāt does not address only Egyptians and Israelis (using the general deicitic terms you and Israel) but he goes a step further and expands the circle of commissive witnesses to include the international community. For example, he asserts to the EPA: "Let me state clearly before *our people*, *the Arab nation* and *the world at large* that we are ready to go to Geneva and to sit for the peace talks, despite all the procedural impediments" (50; emphasis added).

Naming witnesses has two main functions: both inform the accountability discourse. First, by naming witnesses to his voluntary commitment, al-Sādāt heightens the risk of failing to observe the sincerity and essential conditions of his promise as well as his implied subject-position change. Failure to observe the conditions of al-Sādāt's self-binding, public commitment would have exacerbated internal political and economic turmoil, undermined his legitimacy as a leader of other Arab nations, weakened or foiled Egypt and Arab nations' negotiating power, and left Egypt vulnerable among her neighboring states. Internationally, failure to observe the sincerity and essential conditions would have ruined beyond easy repair al-Sādāt's credibility in rallying international players to further his peace pursuit. Second, members of the expanded circle of commissive witnesses are not just addressed, they are also refashioned and mobilized to participate in the peace process. This is conspicuous in the following excerpt:

> Let us be frank with each other . . . as we answer this important question:
>
> How can we achieve permanent peace based on justice? Well, I have come to *you* carrying my clear and frank answer to this big question, so that *the people in Israel* as well as *the entire world* may hear it. All those devoted prayers ring in my ears, pleading to God Almighty that this historic meeting may eventually lead to the result aspired to by millions. (KA 17; emphasis added)

al-Sādāt weaves together his commissive witnessing and statements that seek to redefine the witnesses' relation to the events from observers to participants: the call for listening implies acting on his call to participate in the pursuit of peace.

Rather than being just observers, they are invited/mobilized to pursue peace. The rhetorical work that refashions them as participants is traced using deictic terms (Green), juxtaposition that expresses the epideictic's moral order, and category-bound acts. This rhetorical work is conspicuous as early as al-Sādāt's Knesset greeting, which is atypically long. His extended greeting, wishing all parties to be blessed with peace, seeks to reverse the feelings and attitudes of conflicting parties textually traceable in "us/them" deictic reference and the resulting polarizing rhetoric, which entices/sustains conflict discourse.[14] If categorization of membership—along the lines of "us/them"—leads to violence and conflict, recategorization of membership using proximal deictic terms like *we* and *us* is a viable way to deescalate and resolve conflict and optimally create peace. Recategorization of membership could create a new "social contract" for Medinians. Likewise, recategorization's rhetorical work in al-Sādāt's peace initiative seeks to create a new subject position that transcends polarization and offers new possibilities for foreign policy. al-Sādāt's greeting speaks to this potential collective self that would maximize cooperation.

Transcending polarizing rhetoric, al-Sādāt sets the stage for a community of peace pursuers by repeatedly highlighting the commonality of their experiences and by using proximal deictic terms. al-Sādāt first highlights the commonality of loss to war of people on both sides of the border and beyond. He accordingly articulates a shared incentive to pursue peace as a common goal (i.e., a general category-bound act). As such, al-Sādāt's greeting brings Egyptians, Arabs, Israelis, and the international community together in suffering and gain, a bond signaled by deictic terms like *vanquished* and *victor*: everyone at war is represented as "vanquished" whether, militarily or politically, they define themselves as "victors" or more powerful. This universal loss mandates al-Sādāt's pursuit of peace and invites those named to participate in this noble pursuit (i.e., the epideictic positive term), for as discourse analysts explain, "categorizing" groups, in this case into the categories of vanquished and victor, "is normally done to accomplish something other than just categorizing" (Hausendorf qtd. in Leudar, Marsland, and Nekvapil 244).

The mandate to counter the subject position "vanquished" is stated and reiterated several times in the KA to invite people to embrace an alternative membership and its category-bound acts so they will become participants (not spectators). To this end, al-Sādāt underlines the first category-bound activity and sets the tone for the speech when he explains that he has come "on solid ground to shape a new life and to establish peace" (KA 17). al-Sādāt has realized his commitment to cross (symbolic and literal) borders and advocate for peace, and the goal—"to shape a new life and to establish peace"—becomes peace pursuers' general category-bound act. This act, in Kenneth Burke's terms, invites "ultimate identification" (*Rhetoric of Motives* 163, 328), which transcends "divisive individual or class interests and concerns. This identity transcends the limitations of the individual body and will" (Charland 222): transcending their divisive relations as belligerent parties—which have led to intractability—Egyptians, Arabs, and Israelis are addressed as a group that witnesses and is called to build a new life and establish peace.

This alternative, discursively constructed subjectivity (i.e., one that shares a perspective and a goal [Charland]) shifts away from intractability and toward a discourse of possibility. The new subject stands in solidarity with others and pursues a mutually accepted conflict resolution. Deictic terms usher this rhetorical recategorization of membership, which holds space for functional encounter; category-bound acts help these subjects actualize and assess accountability to their newly formed membership. To illustrate, al-Sādāt invites his audience to consider alternative routes that would end the state of war and initiate peace when he entreats, "Why don't we stretch our hands with faith and sincerity so that we might destroy th[is] [psychological] barrier [of fear and distrust]?" (KA 18). More important, juxtaposing the moral orders of war and peace, al-Sādāt reclaims the role of the warrior/leader in times of war and establishes category-bound acts that support and sustain the valued moral order. No longer is the hero just the typical soldier at war. Instead, heroes courageously and bravely confront the logic of dominance (i.e., power-over), which fuels war. Accordingly, al-Sādāt summons the warrior, asserting, "Those who like us are shouldering the responsibilities entrusted to us are the first who should have the courage to make determining decisions that are [commensurate] with the magnitude of the circumstances. We must all rise above all forms of obsolete theories of superiority" (KA 17). After decoupling courage and power from dominance, al-Sādāt relates them to cooperation, explicating the transformative, category-bound acts that realize a just and lasting peace. These include the call to seek a noble goal and to build an edifice of peace, "an edifice that builds and does not destroy. An edifice that serves as a beacon for generations to come with the human message for construction, development and the dignity of man" (18). Finally, these invitations to embrace category-bound acts of the reclaimed hero are grounded in and informed by collective spiritual memory. After inviting everyone to remember "the wisdom of God conveyed to us by the wisdom of the [P]roverbs of Solomon" and the Psalms of David (18), al-Sādāt quotes the following "Deceit is in the hearts of those who devise evil, But counselors of peace have joy" (Proverbs 12:20); "Better is a dry morsel and quietness with it than an house full of feasting with strife" (Proverbs 17:1); "To You, O Lord, I call; . . . Hear the voice of my supplications when I cry to You for help, When I lift up my hands toward Your holy sanctuary. Do not drag me away with the wicked And with those who work iniquity, Who speak peace with their neighbors, While evil is in their hearts. Requite them according to their work and according to the evil of their practices; Requite them according to the deeds of their hands; Repay them their recompense" (Psalm 28:1–4).[15] Collective spiritual memory and authority are evident in his reference to Prophets Solomon and David: they commended and prayed for peace, promised peace pursuers earthly happiness and heavenly reward (i.e., epideictic's praise), and condemned those who seek or fuel conflict and war (i.e., epideictic's blame).

Category-bound acts address the Israeli public, too, and then Israeli officials, underlining peacemaking endeavors consistent with both their action and effect domains. The Israeli public is mobilized as an agent who can impact policymakers. In this capacity, they are urged to "encourage your leadership to struggle for peace" and to "Let all endeavors be channeled towards building a huge stronghold for peace" as the following excerpt demonstrates:

> Allow me to address my call from this rostrum to the people of Israel. I pledge myself with true and sincere words to every man, woman and child in Israel. I tell them, from the Egyptian people who bless this sacred mission of peace, I convey to you the message of peace of the Egyptian people, who do not harbor fanaticism and whose sons, Moslems, Christian and Jews, live together in a state of cordiality, love and tolerance.
>
> This is Egypt, whose people have entrusted me with their sacred message. A message of security, safety and peace . . . To every man, woman and child in Israel, I say, encourage your leadership to struggle for peace. Let all endeavors be channeled towards building a huge stronghold for peace instead of building destructive rockets. (18)

As the president of the Egyptian state, al-Sādāt addressed the Knesset members, but he clearly was invested in the Israeli public who could embrace the subject position of peace pursuers. al-Sādāt actually later asks them to introduce and model to the whole world the image of the "new [hu]man," a peace pursuer; the emerging collectivity of peace pursuers is "positioned and constrained" (Charland 223–24) through assuming peacemaking stances and seizing their ability to impact decision making.

As such, al-Sādāt calls forth a deliberative community across geopolitical borders. In addition to the Israeli public, al-Sādāt addresses Israeli officials as well as international organizations as potential peace pursuers, pinpointing acts and dispositions that manifest their commitment (i.e., category-bound acts). The acts include confronting the psychological barrier (of animosity, distrust, suspicion, fear, deception, hidden motives, and betrayal) that impedes such a pursuit, whereas the dispositional shift hinges on courage and daring to critically imagine, believe, and invest in the potential of peace (KA 18). The dispositional shift and category-bound acts are geared toward creating "an edifice [of peace] that builds and does not destroy. An edifice that serves as a beacon for generations to come" (18). Further, peacemaking category-bound acts extend to the United Nations (UN) in its official capacity as an international entity that attempts to balance power, monitors and regulates the (excessive) exercise of power, and guarantees the rights/obligations of nations in relation to one another and the international community at large. The role the UN can perform as a key player in this deliberative community is tacitly and explicitly articulated in numerous places. Among its other roles, which will be addressed more extensively later in the chapter, is the promotion of a culture of peace whose membership extends to people around the globe, mobilizing their ability to shape and transform public opinion. This culture necessitates peace-making category-bound acts, which can manifest in publics choosing to exert a formative influence on policy choices, for example. This is tacitly and explicitly articulated in many places in the KA, but the clearest articulation is quoted below: "The call for permanent and just peace based on respect of the UN resolutions has now become the call of the entire world. It has become the expression of the will of the international community, whether in official capitals where policies are made and decisions taken, or at the level of world public opinion, which influences policymaking and decision-taking" (17). A rhetorically constituted collectivity of peace pursuers, which extends beyond the national borders of both national leaders and publics to include publics and leaders around the globe, is presented as being made up of members of one and the same group losing to war, hence mandating their solidarity in the pursuit of peace. This collectivity's potential impact hinges on *committing* to undertaking policies and actions that support and sustain peace. The construction of a community that gravitates toward positively valued peace and embraces accountability is central to ṣulḥ. Members of this community—as judges—choose and support peace within their institutional capacities.

DELIBERATIVE POSSIBILITIES

al-Sādāt's initiative shared some features with other deliberative texts. Typically, members of a deliberative community pore over matters of public, political, and governing interests, and as judges of critical and uncertain matters, they seek the good, possible, and advantageous (Aristotle 1359a, 1359b; Arnhart). However, the initiative uniquely carried the footprints of international relations, diplomacy, and reconciliation discourses. Capitalizing on the peacemaking momentum energized by the critique against war and for peace, al-Sādāt called on interlocutors—weak and strong publics—to act as judges who prudently discuss ways to end the Arab-Israeli conflict and to enable policies consistent with peace—matters related to international war and peace: the activity and effect domains of their deliberations were, therefore, the world of national and international politics. But this deliberative community was atypical in the sense that their membership to the community hinged on their recognition of the stakes of waging war and value of *committing* to and *promoting* policies and actions that support peace endeavors. Hence, the initiated deliberations addressed (1) the conditions consistent with reinitiating prenegotiation, (2) central questions to the Arab-Israeli peace talks, and (3) articulating a framework for peace. In what follows, therefore, I turn to the deliberative possibilities al-Sādāt underlined for this interpellated deliberative community, responding to both prenegotiation and reconciliatory needs.

Geared toward this mandate for peace, the KA's political rhetoric has three discernible moves that seek to impact deliberations. The first move, which sets the stage, identifies conditions that can promote peace, defines what al-Sādāt's peace initiative is and is not, names grievances, and calls for reciprocal accountability. Textually, this move is organized around a series of vocalized deliberative questions, advocating for measures that can realize peace. The central and strategically reiterated the question—How can we achieve a permanent peace based on justice? (17)—has multiple functions. Among these functions, this move assumes the viability and feasibility of peace; promotes the desirability of meaningful, collective problem solving; and, therefore, initiates (public) deliberation concerning goals and appropriate processes for realizing peace. The second move, which provides an organizational pattern that addresses interdependent problem-solution and question-answer texts, also relies on iterations of the central question.[16] Together, these texts detail questions (i.e., the negatively evaluated aspects of the situation) that (when resolved) attain a just and durable peace. These problem-solution and question-answer texts focus on interdependent issues like political recognition, safety and security guarantees, occupied territories, and the questions of Jerusalem and Palestine; these issues are textually presented as expedient questions. Discursively, these questions provide a means to address shared problems to be resolved during conflict resolution deliberations. Proposed solutions (or answers to the questions) are presented as workable and legitimate. The third move condenses the first two moves and articulates a framework for an agreement, underlining peace-agreement terms in preparation for the Geneva Convention. Put differently, it begins to develop a diplomatic working paper, focusing on issues that can serve as agenda items; hence the reference to prenegotiation as well as deliberation. Each iteration of the central question comprises an acknowledgement (of a grievance), accommodation, and call for reciprocity; together they point to a distinct discourse of accountability and conflict resolution deliberations.

Conditions Promoting Peace

al-Sādāt poses the first question (i.e., achieving a permanent peace based on justice) soon after he iterates the goal of his visit to Jerusalem as building a new life and establishing peace and identifies peace pursuers who share grave losses to war and the brunt of restoring peace to their respective societies and the international community (17). To respond to the question and initiate the deliberation process, al-Sādāt couples his own commitment and goals with a clarification of the conditions for peace, naming those addressed (i.e., the Israeli people and the entire world) yet again (KA 17). These facts/conditions include asserting the equality of peace pursuers, which results in ascertaining al-Sādāt's credibility as a negotiator, and contextualizing peace processes in relation to both international mandates for peace and principles/practices that optimize peacemaking.

An equal standing of peace pursuers is an indispensable condition for fair negotiations. To ascertain his credibility, al-Sādāt must clarify the logic and goal of his 1977 initiative. He defines his goal (i.e., a durable and just peace) positively many times. However, the political circumstances and al-Sādāt's "solo trip to Jerusalem" mandate a crucial clarification of what his proposed peacemaking agenda is *not*. Accordingly, al-Sādāt affirms that his is neither a third disengagement nor a separate, partial peace; both would undermine his standing to both his domestic and international audience:

> First, I have not come here for a separate agreement between Egypt and Israel. This is not part of the policy of Egypt. The problem is not that of Egypt and Israel.
>
> An interim peace between Egypt and Israel, or between any Arab confrontation state and Israel, will not bring permanent peace based on justice in the entire region.
>
> Rather, even if peace between all the confrontation states and Israel were achieved in the absence of a just solution of the Palestinian problem, never will there be that durable and just peace upon which the entire world insists.
>
> Second, I have not come to you to seek a partial peace namely to terminate the state of belligerency at this stage and put off the entire problem to a subsequent stage. This is not the radical solution that would steer us to permanent peace.
>
> Equally, I have not come to you for a third disengagement agreement in Sinai or in Golan or the West Bank.
>
> For this would mean that we are merely delaying the ignition of the fuse. (17)

al-Sādāt recognizes that lasting, true peace is inconsistent with settling for another disengagement or separate, partial peace. To date, however, this is the most grievous criticism of al-Sādāt's solo trip to Jerusalem. al-Sādāt's (positive and negative) definitions of his peace initiative respond to a non-vocalized, albeit decisive, question of definition/classification: What is this initiative?[17]

His answer to this question relates to yet another dimension of the equality of stakeholders, namely impediments to procedural reciprocity and reciprocal rights, conditions crucial to the workability of the solution. al-Sādāt explains, "no one can build his happiness at the expense of the misery of others," while also asserting that the Arab nation's "drive for permanent peace based on justice, does not proceed from a position of weakness. On the contrary, it has the power and stability for a sincere will for peace" (17). In these statements, he underlines that the pursuit of happiness must be both mutually accepted and empowering to all stakeholders, key characteristics of meaningful peace. Moreover, he contextualizes his proposed initiative in relation to the UN as an institutional reference in all international relations and an immutable power of the international community's will as quoted earlier in the chapter.[18] This reference to the UN helps him underscore the legality and consistency of his proposed solution with UN resolutions.

al-Sādāt's explication of these facts/conditions partially anticipates and prepares the scene for his multidimensional response to the central question, eventually leads to his proposed peace framework, and reflects his attentiveness to issues of expediency, legality, workability, solvency, and optimization of long-term consequences. Expediency, cause (whether it is structural or attitudinal), legality, necessity, cure (in terms of solvency and workability), significance (i.e., severity and magnitude), consequences (material, social, political, etc.), and optimization are recurring stock issues (M. Carter; Jasinski, "Stock Topics"; Pullman). All support the move toward deliberation and are crucial to a positive assessment of his framework: they help al-Sādāt ascertain that his proposal veers away from futile Band-Aid interventions and is worth considering as "the radical solution leading us to durable peace," which seeks the involvement of all stakeholders.

Deliberative Questions

al-Sādāt addresses three questions central to Egyptian/Arab-Israeli peacemaking. At the time, these were about political recognition; the right to land, sovereignty, and security; and Jerusalem and Palestine. What's noteworthy about al-Sādāt's rhetorical choices in the second half of the KA is that they comprise a functional uptake of political accountability, which can be traced using stasis; public, political declarations; and intertextuality. Respectively, they address and assess issues raised in controversies about past acts—like how to attain peace—(Fahnestock and Escor qtd. in Jasinski, "Stasis," 528; Pullman) and declarations made by leaders to lessen tension, for example, which are vital in diplomatic/negotiation discourse.

The KA exists in neither a rhetorical nor ideological vacuum. Accordingly, as it addresses these interdependent questions, it recognizes, evokes, and responds to multiple texts. Some are official international documents, whereas others comprise the voices of varied contributors to the discourse of war and peace. For example, UN resolutions provide important institutional references to potential (re)solutions. Texts indeed often engage or "appropriate previous material establishing a complex system of relationships of opposition, agreement, partial agreement, and reformulation" (Tull 169). These interrelations or intertextuality are rhetorically potent whether manifest as explicit, traceable references or as subtle echoes that contribute to the intelligibility of a statement. As I shed light on the deliberative question addressed, I underline some of these "intrinsic interrelationships of texts" (166), which validate the expediency, solvability, and feasibility of the solutions proposed.

The Question of Political Recognition

The recognition of Israel was a crucial part of the Egyptian-Israeli and Arab-Israeli peacemaking process. In the same section where al-Sādāt indicates rhetorical listening, he addresses the question of recognition and assumes accountability (i.e., expressing the work of symbolic recognition as detailed earlier). In addition to recognizing grievances and assuming accountability, al-Sādāt makes a consequential public declaration, asserting, "I tell *you*, and I declare to the *whole world*, that we accept to live with you in a permanent peace based on justice" (KA 18). This public declaration is significant for a variety of reasons: in addition to allaying Israeli's fears, al-Sādāt's public recognition "in a political sense . . . [is] the acknowledgement of a nation-state's legitimacy of a particular ruler or governing structure" (Malek and Burgess). At a time when Arab leaders denied recognition, the head of the Egyptian state addresses the Israeli political elite in their parliament. al-Sādāt's public declaration was made meaningful because he took the voluntary, high-risk, confidence-building measure of making this declaration in the Knesset, which was witnessed by the Israeli political elite and public and the international community as signaled by *you*, and the *whole world*, at a time when Egypt (and all Arab states) had no formal diplomatic relations with Israel. Though he was criticized for his trip, he knew that "leaders who wish to reconcile with adversaries cannot depend on words alone; they must undertake a coherent and comprehensive strategy that demonstrates credible commitment" (Krepon and Drezin 156). As such, visiting Jerusalem and the Knesset was reinforced by and reinforced his political recognition of the State of Israel; reinforcement is crucial for all public declarations.

Besides recognition, his statement underlines a peacemaking category-bound act ("live with you in durable and just peace") and interpellates addressees and witnesses, thus underlining the relational implication of political recognition. Political recognition "indicate[s] a relationship between parties, be they individuals, groups, or nations, that is important for effective cooperation and/or negotiation" (Malek and Burgess). As such, political recognition and its relational consequences are part of his political, peacemaking endeavors. Because he clearly responds to questions concerning recognition grievances and their consequences, his public recognition affirms accountability and results in what Krepon and Drezin term "declaratory diplomacy," which refers to national leaders' use of "public declarations as part of a broader effort to . . . build trust, lessen tension, and facilitate successful negotiation" (153).

He also complements his declaration with a statement of its necessity, advisability, and expedience for both states (and other frontline states) considering the history of confrontation and the international milieu. His recognition is neither evanescent nor inconsequential for, as he states, both nations lose from belligerence (KA 17). Thus, his declaration is strategically contextualized in relation to the scene across the border. Additionally, he contextualizes his declaration in relation to the international milieu when he explains that "Israel has become a fait accompli, recognized by the world, and that the two superpowers have undertaken the responsibility for its security and the defense of its existence" (18). al-Sādāt's recognition, therefore, relates also to the political relations and political positions of the two superpowers at the time.

If political recognition is the first accommodation move, it functions also indirectly as the first call for reciprocity. al-Sādāt was in a bind: he needed to make peace from a position of strength, not weakness, while accommodating the peacemaking needs/demands of different stakeholders. Calls for reciprocity are crucial to maintaining a balanced articulation of all stakeholders' needs and grievances as well as affirming the legitimacy and equality of their rights. This is where the power of rhetorically efficacious declaration weighs in. "National leaders can use declaratory initiatives to convey to both domestic and foreign audiences an image of self-confidence rather than weakness" (Krepon and Drezin 161). Accordingly, al-Sādāt complements every accommodation move with an explicit or tacit call for reciprocity.

The first significant shift from accommodation to reciprocity follows al-Sādāt's political recognition when he addresses "psychological warfare"; intimidation and threats of annihilation were two of its conspicuous features:

> It was a wall of fear of the force that could sweep the entire Arab nation from one end to another. It was a wall of propaganda that we were a nation reduced to immobility. Some of you have gone as far as to say that even for 50 years to come, the Arabs would not regain their strength. It was a wall that always *threatened with the long arm that could reach and strike anywhere.* It was a wall that *warned us of extermination and annihilation if we tried to use our legitimate rights to liberate the occupied territories.* (KA 18; emphasis added)

The reference to "psychological warfare" serves as both a statement of grievance and a call for reciprocal accountability. al-Sādāt's rhetorical listening to and textualization of the Arabs' grievances sheds light on a crucial dimension of the problem, establishes equal footing, and calls for accountability. Listening to the grievances of the other and voicing the grievances of the self—an indirect call for reciprocal listening—are crucial for mobilizing and acting on conflict resolution goals.[19] An effective prelude to peace negotiations mandates a shift in the representation and footing of Arabs, a shift that hinges on rhetorical listening and recognition. Traces of rhetorical listening lead to the last sentence of the excerpt and seek to counter Israel's dominant representation of the Arabs at the time. This is why there is an indirect reference to the impact of the 1973 war: one of its consequences was that Arabs' military power could no longer be dismissed. The representation, therefore, repositions them (i.e., changes their political orientation so that all stakeholders are on equal footing). The last sentence in the excerpt supports this interpretation as it shifts the focus from the anterior context (reported speech situation) to the posterior context (reporting speech situation), hence short-circuiting a discourse of accusation.[20] In effect, the reference to "psychological warfare" states Arab grievances and indirectly calls for reciprocal recognition of military power.

Recognition of Israeli and Arab grievances entails both accommodation and calls for reciprocity. Similarly, the second set of questions manifests the same pattern of naming a grievance as a problem, proposing a solution, and developing accommodation-reciprocity. Thus, it maintains deliberative momentum and addresses the interrelated issues of land, security and safety, freedom of navigation, and sovereignty.

The Questions of the Right to Land, Sovereignty, and Security

In the second set of questions, al-Sādāt addresses justice and land occupation, explaining that true and lasting peace "is based on justice and not on the occupation of the land of others" (KA 18). al-Sādāt's deliberative rhetoric pinpoints the grave consequences caused by the 1967 war (also known as the Six-Day War), which in effect changed the geopolitical map of the Middle East as noted earlier. Unlike the deliberative question, in which he begins by recognizing the grievances of the other, he initiates this question by expounding claims to territories occupied during the 1967 war and underlining the lessons of shared history of military confrontation:

> With all frankness and in the spirit that has prompted me to come to you today, I tell you [that you] have to give up once and for all the dreams of conquest and give up the belief that force is the best method for dealing with the Arabs.
>
> You should clearly understand the lesson of confrontation between you and us. *Expansion does not pay.* To speak frankly, *our land does not yield itself to bargaining, it is not even open to argument.* To us, *the nation's soil is equal to the holy valley where God Almighty spoke to Moses.* Peace be upon him. (KA 18; emphasis added)

al-Sādāt's call for withdrawal from occupied territories is premised on two principles: expansion is counterproductive and land for Arabs is a sacred entity that is an object neither for debate nor bargaining. His claim for land retrieval and return of sovereignty are consistent with SCR 242: a UN document issued on November 22, 1967, comprising four articles. The first article addresses the issue of land rights, and the resolution generally underlines principles guiding "the inadmissibility of the acquisition of territory by war" (para. 2). This resolution was issued in response to the grave situation caused by the 1967 war. For this reason, SCR 242 affirms measures—when applied—that fulfill UN Charter requirements concerning territorial integrity and sovereignty.

> The Security Council:
>
> *Emphasizing* the inadmissibility of the acquisition of territory by war and the need to work for a just and lasting peace in which every State in the area can live in security,

> . . .
>
> 1. *Affirms* that the fulfillment of Charter principles requires the establishment of a just and lasting peace in the Middle East which should include the application of both the following principles:
>
> (i) Withdrawal of Israel armed forces from territories occupied in the recent conflict;
>
> (ii) Termination of all claims of states of belligerency and respect for and acknowledgment of the sovereignty, territorial integrity and political independence of every State in the area and their right to live in peace within secure and recognized boundaries free from threats or acts of force. (United Nations, "Resolution 242"; emphasis in original)

This section issued calls for termination of belligerency, withdrawal from the territories occupied, political independence of frontline states, and their states' right to live in peace.

Contextualizing his claims for the return of land and regaining sovereignty, al-Sādāt clearly invokes the first and second clauses of the first article of SCR 242. Despite being issued a decade earlier and confirmed by SCR 338 on October 22, 1973, which "aimed at establishing a just and durable peace in the Middle East," nothing had materialized. al-Sādāt's address seems to resuscitate the resolution two days away from its tenth anniversary. This contextualization is corroborated by highlighting the potential of this unique moment, which is juxtaposed with a history of mainly failed diplomatic interventions. al-Sādāt rightly asserts that this occasion is an unprecedented opportunity "if we are really serious in our endeavour for peace" (KA 18). To heighten the mandate, he evokes epideictic's typical blame, asserting that those who fritter away this opportunity will earn "the curse of humanity and of history" (18).

al-Sādāt matches his assertions concerning land rights with a question that reorients everybody's attention to reciprocity as a principle in the deliberative process. He basically reiterates a question posed earlier, "What is peace for Israel?" However, the answer this time focuses on security and safety. al-Sādāt's answer echoes a conversation concerning guarantees consistent with the SCR 242:

> It means that *Israel lives in the region with her Arab neighbors in security and safety*. Is that logical? *I say yes*. It means that *Israel lives within its borders, secure against any aggression*. Is that logical? And *I say yes*. It

means *that Israel obtains all kinds of guarantees that will ensure these two factors*. To this demand, *I say yes*.

Beyond that we declare that we accept all the international guarantees you envisage and accept. We declare that we accept all the guarantees you want from the two super powers or from either of them or from the Big Five or from some of them. Once again, I declare clearly and unequivocally that we agree to any guarantees you accept, because in return we shall receive the same guarantees. (KA 18; emphasis added)

al-Sādāt's answer asserts his openness to guarantees ensuring Israel's security and safety. The first part of his excerpt invokes SCR 242's first article in its reference to the right of all states in the region to live in peace. The second part of the excerpt points to SCR 242's second article, which comprises two clauses: the first clause guarantees the right to international waterways and demilitarized zones: "The Security council, . . . *Affirms* further the necessity (a) for guaranteeing freedom of navigation through international waterways in the area . . . (c) for guaranteeing the territorial inviolability and political independence of every State in the area through measures including the establishment of demilitarized zones" (United Nations, "Resolution 242").

Interestingly, al-Sādāt's public declarations seem to exceed what SCR 242 calls for. It is important to note that between 1967 and 1977, when the KA was delivered, SCR 338 and 339 were issued demanding a ceasefire after the 1973 war; both affirm the authority and binding nature of all SCRs and explicitly refer to SCR 242. However, in invoking a document produced ten years earlier, al-Sādāt voluntarily binds himself to "any guarantees": he transcends those named in SCR 242. To further affirm his stance of openness, accommodation, and accountability, he accepts without reservation Israel's choice of the entity to whom agreeing parties will be bound and accountable. al-Sādāt again uses a self-binding declaration, which foregrounds his stance of accommodation on both substantive (what the guarantees will be about) and procedural (choice of power overseeing the guarantees) matters. More important, towards the end of the declarative summary, which condenses the whole question-answer pattern, the condition of reciprocity is underlined when al-Sādāt notes that the same guarantees are given to the other party. The positive declaration, therefore, highlights the condition of reciprocity, which is common: Krepon and Drezin, for example, explain that "declaratory initiatives can facilitate both bargaining and reciprocity" (161).

As he evokes SCR 242, al-Sādāt reproduces the voices of the other—as italicized in the first half of the excerpt above—calling for living safely and securely. But, he moves beyond demonstrating listening and acknowledgment as signaled by the three "yes" iterations (e.g., "To such logic I say, yes") and adds a self-binding declaration, which is reiterated twice. This discursive pattern highlights the positive declarations, which are "particularly welcome at the beginning phase of negotiation"; to domestic and foreign audiences they signal a stance of openness and strength (Krepon and Drezin 161), and when effective they can generate agreements concerning a framework or agenda and facilitate deliberations of procedural considerations (Berridge 33).

The Questions of Jerusalem and Palestine

The third question (and accommodation-reciprocity move) overlaps with the second. al-Sādāt relates the questions of Jerusalem and Palestine, land rights, sovereignty, and the security and the safety of Israel. To advance earlier discussion concerning the attainment of peace for Israel, al-Sādāt centers on the Jerusalem question, which is contextualized in relation to (1) the history of military confrontation, occupation, and contested land rights; (2) Jerusalem's undisputed significance to all believers of Christianity, Judaism, and Islam, asserting that Jerusalem "should be a free and open city for all believers" (18); and (3) a history of tolerance and respect of religious freedoms. All are evident in the following excerpt:

> There are facts that should be faced with courage and clarity. There are Arab territories[,] which Israel has occupied and still occupies by force. We insist on complete withdrawal from these territories, including Arab Jerusalem.
>
> I have come to Jerusalem, the city of peace, which will always remain as a living embodiment of coexistence among believers of the three religions. It is inadmissible that any one should conceive the special status of the city of Jerusalem within the frame of annexation or expansion. It should be a free and open city for all believers.
>
> Above all, this city should not be severed from those who have made it their abode for centuries. (18)

al-Sādāt's response to the Jerusalem question also underscores the historical rights of Arabs, which are antithetical to "the frame of annexation or expansion." al-Sādāt explains that "The holy shrines [religious sites] of Islam and Christianity are not only places for worship, but a living testimony to our uninterrupted presence here. Politically, spiritually and intellectually" (18). In addition to affirming the political, spiritual, and intellectual rights of Muslims and Christians, al-Sādāt underlines a long history of coexistence, tolerance, and respect for religious freedoms, which is evident in al-Sādāt's reference to Ṣalāḥ al-Dīn and 'Umār ibn al-Khaṭṭāb; these references are both precedents and condensations of peacemaking models. Both leaders were parties to well-known public ṣulḥ or peace pacts, which become precedents. For example, 'Umār ibn al-Khaṭṭāb's peace pact (*al-'ahdah al-'umarīyah*) is often cited as an exemplary treaty for protecting religious freedoms, as mentioned earlier. These two models are antithetical to expansionist logic. Condensing the logic of peace and the logic of expansion, al-Sādāt entreats: "Instead of reviving the precedent of the Crusades, we should revive the Spirit of Omar Emil Khtab [ibn al-Khaṭṭāb] and Saladin, namely the spirit of tolerance and respect for rights" (18).

More important, al-Sādāt reiterates the connection between the question of peace and the resolution of the Jerusalem question, thus responding to solvency as a decisive criterion in the evaluation of his answer. al-Sādāt clarifies that "Complete withdrawal from the Arab territories occupied after 1967 is a logical and undisputed fact. Nobody should plead for that. Any talk about a permanent peace based on justice and any move to ensure our coexistence in peace and security in this part of the world would become meaningless while you occupy Arab territories by force of arms" (KA 18). al-Sādāt's claims for land rights move from a general reference to all territories occupied in 1967 to the question of Jerusalem and finally come full circle to a general reference to all occupied territories, evoking clearly the aforementioned first article of SCR 242.

This third accommodation-reciprocity move addresses the question of Palestine in terms of both statehood and people and advances the problem of recognition of *land rights* and *peoples*. Accordingly, al-Sādāt shifts attention to and recognizes Palestine and Palestinians: "As for the Palestine cause—nobody can deny that this is the crux of the entire problem. Nobody in the world could accept today slogans propagated here in Israel, ignoring the existence of [the] Palestinian people and questioning [even] their whereabouts" (18). In calling for reciprocal recognition of the rights of Palestinians and the establishment of Palestine, al-Sādāt evokes numerous voices of international bodies, superpowers, and publics.

In deliberation, there are always voices of contestation. In conciliatory discourses as a particular case of deliberation, contestation is typical and generative: vocalized contestation can catalyze the surfacing of grievances and/or injustices. Consequently, al-Sādāt underlines voices he is deliberating with: "When some extremists ask the Palestinians to give up this sublime objective ['establishment once again of a state on their land'], this in fact means asking them to renounce their identity and every hope for the future" (18). Some voices, therefore, seek to repeal the inalienable rights of Palestinians. These voices, however, are juxtaposed with those of Israelis who "called for recognition of the Palestinian people's rights to achieve and safeguard peace" (18). al-Sādāt's narrativized reproduction of locution (signaled by "call on" or *yūṭālīb*; "called for" or *ṭālabt*) establishes a web of relations; some voices converge in their harmonious calls for peace, whereas others diverge. These voices transcend the region and include international ones: al-Sādāt argues *with* and *in support of* voices embodied by the international community and the United States as potential sponsors of peace initiatives in the region. Their representation becomes an ethically charged call for attentiveness and responsive listening, which would facilitate the current deliberative moment:

> It [the legitimate rights of Palestinians] is an acknowledged fact, perceived by the world community, both in the East and in the West, with support and recognition in international documents and official statements. It is of no use to anybody to turn deaf ears to its resounding voice, which is being heard day and night, or to overlook its historical reality.
>
> Even the United States of America, your first ally, which is absolutely committed to safeguard Israel's security and existence and which offered and still offers Israel every moral, material and military support—I say, even the United States has opted to face up to reality and admit that the Palestinian people are entitled to legitimate rights and that the Palestine problem is the cause and essence of the conflict and that so long as it continues to be unresolved, the conflict will continue to aggravate, reaching new dimensions. (KA 18)

Here again we have subtle traces of rhetorical listening, echoing deliberating voices as documented in binding international documents besides calls for rhetorical listening to the rights granted/denied to grievable subjects. Interestingly, the representation of these discordant voices enables a reflective stance. al-Sādāt assumes (and models) a partly self-reflective and partly invitational tone:

> Here I tell you, ladies and gentlemen, that it is no use to refrain from recognizing the Palestinian people and their right to statehood as their right of return. We, the Arabs, have faced this experience before with you. And with the reality of the Israeli existence, the struggle which took us from war to war, from victims to more victims, until you and we have today reached the edge of a horrible abyss and a terrifying disaster unless,

> together, we seize this opportunity today [for] a durable peace based on justice. (KA 18)

Encoding a reflective voice, the statement critiques and underscores lessons to be learned from previous military confrontations and diplomatic failures. As he assumes accountability, al-Sādāt foregrounds the consequences of (negatively evaluated) solutions that failed to solve these interrelated problems, resulting in wars, and calls for reciprocity later: "You have to face reality bravely, as I have done" (18). Assuming reciprocal accountability and a reflective stance are decisive endeavors for the transformation of former belligerent parties who together seize the chance to realize peace.

al-Sādāt seizes this potential momentum as he addresses a (mobilized) deliberative community and condenses his previously addressed imperatives for peace, likely impediments, and declarations:

> Peace cannot last if attempts are made to impose fantasy concepts on which the world has turned its back and announced its unanimous call for the respect of rights and facts.
>
> There is no need to enter a vicious circle as to Palestinian rights. It is useless to create obstacles, otherwise the march of peace will be impeded or peace will be blown up. As I have told you there is no happiness [based on] the detriment of others.
>
> Direct confrontation and straightforwardness are the shortcuts and the most successful way to reach a clear objective. Direct confrontation concerning the Palestinian problem and tackling it in one single language [the only meaningful solution] with a view to achieving a durable and just peace lie in the establishment of that peace [establishment of their State]. With all the guarantees you demand, there should be no fear of a newly born State that would need the assistance of all the countries of the world. (KA 18)[21]

Engaging its primary and secondary audiences, this condensed statement calls on peace pursuers to courageously counter discourses of intractability, confront problems, and reflectively balance stances of possibility and recognition of obstacles. Then, they can together optimize the unprecedented momentum for peacemaking by confronting the realities of war, responding to grievances, and embracing accountability.

al-Sādāt and negotiators generally know that a peacemaking momentum needs to be maintained; otherwise "negotiations may . . . falter even if . . . parties . . . are serious about making them a success" (Berridge 54). The condensation of peace imperatives sustains the momentum by foregrounding stances of accountability and reflection, which enable the writing of a mutually accepted agreement and co-constructed alternative peaceful reality. This powerful condensation brings the accommodation-reciprocity moves to an end and initiates another phase of deliberation, namely the articulation of a framework or a working paper, which is shared as a prelude to around-the-table negotiation toward a peace agreement.

Articulating a Framework for a Peace Agreement

In the last deliberative section of the KA, al-Sādāt complements his analysis and answers to questions raised with a peace agreement framework. As Berridge (31) explicates, "Encouraging the belief that negotiations are at any rate worth a try means floating a 'formula' or 'framework' for a settlement." al-Sādāt knew this well and his framework strives for "conceiv[ing] . . . a peace agreement" in Geneva and comprises goal-directed measures that meet the peacemaking needs of all stakeholders. Such an articulation is crucial to impressing on addressees (members of the rhetorically constituted community of peace pursuers) that peacemaking—as a solution to recurring and grave military confrontation—is expedient, viable, workable, and indispensable to moving beyond stalled diplomacy and unrealized resolutions. Accordingly, al-Sādāt's framework invokes SCRs 338, 339, and 242, which call for peacemaking measures like terminating belligerency, initiating negotiation, withdrawing from occupied territories, and recognizing rights, including territorial integrity and sovereignty. Like his other problem-solving endeavors, al-Sādāt addresses guarantees, obligations, and rights and then addresses stances, category-bound acts, and deliberate(d) moves consistent with peace.

al-Sādāt's framework also attends to the mandates of prenegotiation. Though typically the "exit costs" of prenegotiation are low (Zartman 121), a number of variables increase the cost of failure/exit: al-Sādāt's unilateral initiative and highly visible "solo" trip to the Knesset heighten its risk and mandate a prudent balancing of grievances/peacemaking guarantees and an underlining of the terms of a meaningful peace formula. All complicate the articulation of a framework. These variables explain why al-Sādāt constantly evokes UN documents (e.g., SCRs 242, 338, 339), brings to the fore formulas known at the time (e.g., recognition for peace, land for peace), and finally names five measures that would help attain a meaningful peace agreement to the different parties:

> [First,] Ending the occupation of the Arab territories occupied in 1967.
>
> [Second,] Achievement of the fundamental rights of the Palestinian

> people and their right to self-determination, including their right to establish their own state.
>
> [Third,] The right of all states in the area to live in peace within their boundaries, their secure boundaries, which will be secured and guaranteed through procedures to be agreed upon, which will provide appropriate security to international boundaries in addition to appropriate international guarantees.
>
> [Fourth,] Commitment of all states in the region to administer the relations among them in accordance with the objectives and principles of the United Nations Charter. Particularly the principles concerning the nonuse of force and [resolving conflict] among them by peaceful means.
>
> [Fifth,] Ending the state of belligerency in the region. (KA 18)

This framework articulates conditions that would end warfare activities (first and fifth articles), enable peacemaking by recognizing rights of peoples and states (second and third articles), and develop/transform political life in the region to promote peace (fourth article).

Some of these articles are more specific than others because "when parties to a conflict start to explore the possibility of a negotiated settlement they do not, of course, do this in a political vacuum" (Berridge 31) nor work to achieve a singular goal. Therefore, the varied specificity levels serve differing goals. First, a proposed framework must be at once responsive to the context of the negotiated agreement and open to negotiations about guarantees desirable to the other party. For example, an agreement framework must be responsive to people's grievances to "ride out any charge that they are proposing to 'sell out' to the enemy" (31). At the same time, prudent agreements must address mutual responsibilities, as evidenced in articles three, four, and five, while signaling openness to accommodating guarantees and promoting the peacemaking needs and interests of other stakeholders. This openness is clearly signaled throughout the KA and in the formula's third article.

Second, frameworks must invoke the authority of international legal obligations, which are typically well known at least by politicians and diplomats: al-Sādāt clearly evokes and speaks to articles 1i and 1ii of SCR 242 that address withdrawal and the "respect and acknowledgment of the sovereignty, territorial integrity and political independence of every state in the area." SCR articles are mirrored in the first, third, and fifth articles of al-Sādāt's framework (KA 18). Additionally, article four of the framework clearly invokes article 33 (clause 1) of the UN Charter, which asserts that "the parties to any dispute, the continuance of which is likely to endanger the maintenance of international peace and security, shall, first of all, seek a solution by negotiation, enquiry, mediation, conciliation, arbitration, judicial settlement, resort to regional agencies or arrangements, or other peaceful means of their own choice" (United Nations, chapter 6). Third, al-Sādāt's second article engages the General Assembly's 2535 B (XXIV) recognition of the rights of Palestinians. William Mallison and Sally V. Mallison explain that "in 1969 the General Assembly shifted its perspective to acknowledge the Palestinians as a people having rights under the United Nations Charter. The first preambular paragraph of General Assembly resolution 2535 B (XXIV) of 10 December 1969 . . . recognizes "that the problem of the Palestine Arab refugees has arisen from the denial of their inalienable rights under the Charter of the United Nations and the Universal Declaration of Human Rights." UN interventions and resolutions establish a context that transcends that of the polarized groups and expands the membership of this discursively constructed deliberative community. At best, the desires and binding resolutions of the international community—as encoded in the UN Charter, General Assembly, and Security Council resolutions—are well known to all stakeholders: they are intervening voices of authority that cannot be dismissed without risk.[22] Therefore, evoking the authority of the UN and the international community in a highly publicized and contested peace initiative can be consequential: besides providing clarification, it constitutes a community of peace pursuers who not only deliberate means and ends but whose membership hinges on abiding by the binding nature of international law.

al-Sādāt's KA ends in a crescendo in which category-bound acts are infused with an epideictic discourse that calls on both the political elite and the Israeli public to reflect deeply on what is ahead of this deliberative body, noting that "peace is not a mere endorsement of written lines. Rather, it is a rewriting of history" (18). Cogently, the speech ends on a note that abounds with possibility, unlocking the power of a togetherness committed to peace: "It is not my [al-Sādāt's] battle alone. Nor is it the battle of the leadership in Israel alone. It is the battle of all and every citizen in all our territories whose right is to live in peace. It is the commitment of conscience and responsibility in the hearts of millions" (18). This commitment has moved people to transformative action and continues to have an inspirational value.

FORTY YEARS LATER

As I reflect on al-Sādāt's KA, I think it is worth noting that the address calls for scholarship that attends to international and transnational crossings and peacemaking. al-Sādāt's Knesset address lives vicariously in relation to a bundle of other significant political texts: some precede it, while others come later. Of particular importance in this regard are the (un)official reception of the speech, which has not been rhetorically studied to date, and its fruition/constrained potential in the Camp David Peace Accords. In addition, many of the issues addressed are still unresolved. The reception of the KA, its unrealized potentials, and the peace accords are worth rhetorical exploration, especially since in the past few years al-Sādāt's KA has come to the fore.

A few years ago, a crucial piece of information was released about the "coauthor" of the speech. Boutros Ghali—a well-known diplomat, the sixth secretary general of the United Nations, an academic, and the minister of foreign affairs—was at least partly responsible for the writing of the KA. This information suggests numerous research questions for rhetoricians about the role of coauthorship and ghostwriting in relation to political crisis rhetoric, presidential/diplomatic rhetoric, our idealization of the rhetor as an individual, and rhetorical production and work as mainly that of an individual (see, e.g., Brandt's "'Who's the President?'" for a discussion of these issues). This information also underscores the nature of peacemaking, which mandates the involvement of a whole community. If this is the case, who is served by the image of the lone rhetor?

More important, there has long been talk about "cold peace" or "fragile peace," referring to the Camp David Peace Accords. These descriptions, too, are worth exploring. Are they critical of the initiation? Are they critical of sustenance work (i.e., work that sustains the peace momentum) done ineffectively or left undone? In Egypt, after the January 25 Revolution, there were parliamentary and presidential elections. Numerous candidates spoke about the Camp David Accords: some affirmed their respect for all international treaties (including Camp David) while others brought up the need to revise some of Camp David's articles. Rhetoric scholars invested in the study of peacemaking must develop analytical models to study not just the initiation phase, as I did here. We must complement this model with ones that address sustenance work and the reemergence of grievances, especially in contexts of protracted multiparty conflict and conflict resolution. And we must develop ways to respond to calls for revisiting peace treaties not as threats but as occasions to renew and actualize professed commitment to peacemaking.

5

TO GATHER AT COURT

Ṣulḥ as Rhetorical Method

The reconciliation of the selves is a *hardly* attained truth.
But, as an end it cannot be abandoned.

—*Muḥammad Māḍī Abū al-'Azā'im*

The Great Court of Ṣulḥ (GCS) is a deceptively simple, seemingly straightforward, and at times very entertaining, if not funny, dialogue written by Muḥammad Māḍī Abū al-'Azā'im (1869–1937), a well-known theologian and professor of *sharī'ah* (Islamic law). Writing on issues ranging from Qur'ānic interpretation, Sufi poetry and doctrine, and current political and (inter)national issues, he was prolific. GCS was written in the context of international efforts to end World War I and the convening of nations to attempt to end the state of war and find a formula for peace. Eventually, these efforts led to the Treaty of Versailles signed in 1919. At home, Egypt was in a state of turmoil for various economic and political reasons, namely against British occupation and for national sovereignty. Within this context, conflict and conflict resolution loomed large and were addressed by Abū al-'Azā'im in many of his works. Because the dialogue addresses *ṣulḥ* and offers what I consider a rhetorical conciliatory method, it is the focus of this chapter.

GCS's intriguing nature lies in the fact that it is a dialogue whose subject matter is ṣulḥ applied to conflict between parts of the self. More interesting, in addressing ṣulḥ, the dialogue provides an enacted method for reconciliation. This enactment takes the form of a dramatic presentation of conflict and conflict resolution between aspects of the self that gather in a court setting. The dispute is dramatized to capture the dilemmas of the self, which, when projected outward, result in conflict, and their butterfly effects extend to community members, compatriots, and fellow humans. This situation generates a desire for peace. The dramatization of conflict and peace invite deep introspection into the shadow part of the self. Living in an era of colonialism, exploitation, mass killings, and world wars, Abū al-ʻAzā'im meditates on the shadow self—what we choose to repress only to have it haunt our desires, decision, and actions—and all aspects of the self. He also invites us to join this meditation. This call for introspection promises a great reward: "It is in facing the capacity of humanity for evil that we can unleash within ourselves energy to do good" (Villa-Vicencio, "Now That," 45). As we join Abū al-ʻAzā'im and heed his call, we tap into the potential of the text, which provides a method for reconciliation. At best, the method helps guide the pursuit of regaining or attaining a reconciled self.

GCS can be considered a meditation on conflict and peacemaking that models and manifests the conditions of togetherness at a moment when this togetherness is precarious. The contentious conflict invites a discussion of the nature of and differences between the selves and catalyzes a space where arguments, mediation, claims of grievance, exhortation, and conciliatory appeals become necessary. The space where these discussions happen is a courtroom, but the discourse is not just that of litigation.

As a performative exposition of ṣulḥ, GCS has a conspicuous didactic goal: the dialogue teaches us about the nature of ṣulḥ, its doctrinal dimension, and its processes. Such a didactic enactment of ṣulḥ manifests, partly as a discourse of adjudication, partly as a discourse of mediation, and, more important, as an epistemic dialogue, which exceeds just modeling a conflict resolution modality. The dialogue also develops an understanding of the nature of the self; its pursuit of peace and happiness; the conundrum of the pursuit of justice in the context of a multidirectional circulation of the good-evil characterization of claimants and defendants; conflicting understanding of what is good and virtuous; and varied understandings of the relational nature of power and its consequences, all while evoking Islamic philosophy, mystic knowledge, and a tradition of dramatized journeys of self-development in the pursuit of atonement and at-one-ment.

One of the strengths of GCS is that the conflict, litigation scene, and epistemic dialogue are simple, short, and likely to be easily legible across time and space. Though GCS offers a multidimensional reconciliatory model, the dialogue is relatively short (126 pages), is often fast paced, and falls into six scenes with titles that indicate both its reconciliatory goal and its legal setting. The scenes are titled "A Tour within the Self" (13–16), "The First Session" (17–31), "The Second Session" (33–110), "The Euphoria of the Unification of the Selves" (111–17), "The Verdict Session" (117–21), and "The Verdict" (123–26). The scenes of the dialogue tell a story of reconciliation between factions of the self, and its allegorical figures include Justice, Reason, Fairness, Temperance, Courage, Generosity, and Continence as claimants; and Cowardice, Lust, and Folly as defendants. All are virtues and forces of the self that—at the beginning—are contending with one another. Against the realities of contention, the yearning for peace arises and the selves awaken. This is a long process that is neither linear nor easy, but it is supported by dialogue with partners—former adversaries—and facilitated by resources for introspection and transformation-like balance (*wasaṭ*), purification of the selves (*tazkīyah*), and the pursuit of excellence (*kamāl*).

Though the themes of conflict and conciliation are legible across time and space, the dialogue carries the imprint of its time and place and is informed by a relational worldview. It is indeed hard to miss ways in which the dialogue is a culturally inflected meditation on conflict resolution, the nature of the self, and the relational nature of power. This cultural inflection is partly due to its articulation of ṣulḥ, which is historically and culturally informed by Arab-Islamic practices as explicated in the previous chapters. More important, the dialogue draws on a cultural reservoir of sayings and Qur'ānic verses. Because the use of Qur'ānic verses and Ḥadīth was addressed in chapter 1, it is not addressed in this chapter. However, it is important to note that this reservoir informs and grounds the GCS's discourse of peace in relation to its cultural and doctrinal roots. The cultural inflection is also manifest as the dialogue evokes, models, and educates us about interdependent modalities of ṣulḥ, its attendant practices, and its enabling disposition, all while embodying a conception of what I'll refer to as the relational, reconciled self, which will be explored in this chapter. However, the dialogue is also situated in a very specific national and international context, which implies that the relational, reconciled self refers to both the individual and the (international) community.

GCS'S COMPLEX POLITICAL MILIEU

After World War I, Imām Abū al-'Azā'im wrote GCS in a complex political milieu. Nationally and internationally, the political scene was one of turmoil. So what were the dimensions of this national and international situation? On the national stage, Egypt was occupied by Britain (1882–1952). The second decade of the twentieth century was full of upheaval. In particular, 1918 and 1919—the year of GCS's publication—were full of societal, political, and economic turmoil (Goldberg; Shuqruf). Most prominently, numerous articulations of decades-long grievances eventually led to the 1919 revolution.

The November 1918 armistice eventually led to the Paris Peace Conference and the signing of the Treaty of Versailles. Prior to these events, President Woodrow Wilson delivered an important address on January 8, 1918—the speech commonly known as President Woodrow Wilson's Fourteen Points—in which he addressed the potential for peace and what needed to be done to end World War I and move forward. Wilson announced his program for peace, declaring that it was, "the programme of the world's peace, therefore, is our programme and that programme, the only possible programme included fourteen points." Though all fourteen points deserve attention and a comparison with the actual Treaty of Versailles is worth rhetorical consideration, I focus only on point twelve because it was crucial and of special relevance to Egypt and to the 1919 revolution.

Referencing the Ottoman Empire, Wilson pointed to the right to self-determination for all nations that were at the time under the Ottoman rule and clearly stated, "The other nationalities [i.e., Arabs] which are now under Turkish rule should be assured an undoubted security of life and an absolutely unmolested opportunity of autonomous development."[1] Egypt then was partially autonomous in the sense that it was a tributary state of the Ottoman Empire. At that time, it had also been occupied by the British since 1882 and had been a British protectorate since 1914. Egyptian nationalists, led then by Sa'ad Zaghlūl, former minister of education and founder of Ḥizb al-Wafd (the Delegation Party), mobilized for independence. On November 13 (i.e., just two days after the armistice), Zaghlūl and others visited Sir Reginald Wingate, the British High Commissioner at the time, and asked that they be allowed to travel to London to officially present the case for Egypt's independence and unity with Sudan in preparation for the Paris Peace Conference, which was planned to take place in January 1919.

Even though they were considered political agitators and denied the right to travel to London or Paris, Wafdīys (members of al-Wafd) persisted, even when British attempts to contain and foil the movement toward independence escalated: their efforts reached a crescendo when al-Wafd collected thousands of power-of-attorney forms supporting the Egyptian petition for independence and affirming Zaghlūl's rightful representation of the Egyptians. Zaghlūl and other national leaders had to be removed from the scene. On March 9, Egyptian national political leaders were arrested, then exiled to Malta; Zaghlūl was one of these leaders exiled to Malta and then to the

Seychelles. Though these actions were geared toward silencing the political leaders and ending Egypt's pursuit for independence, Egyptians from different walks of life who saw in Zaghlūl a leader—he was named *za'īm al-ummah*, which means the "nation's leader"—carried out a nation-wide revolution, which eventually led to Britain's recognition of Egypt's independence three years later in 1922.

However, the turmoil did not end there. There was also concern about economic injustice and food production and supply. The economic situation, corruption, depletion of resources, and impact of feeding the war machine eventually led to what is known as the Peasants' Revolt of 1919.[2] Because Britain was involved in World War I, Egyptians were conscripted into the Labour Corps—Egyptian low-earning laborers who worked for the British army. The labor conditions were so bad that the conscription of peasants is rightly described as "a new form of corvée" (Elgood qtd. in Killingray 485).[3] Forced labor, destitution, and high mortality rates among conscripts characterized their common plight. The urban working-class peasants toiling the land bore the "yoke of capitalist agrarian economy" (Goldberg 262). Some analysts describe the Peasants' Revolt as a "reaction to the profits reaped by Britain and denied Egyptians" (262). This economy depended on the cotton crop market and witnessed it being "bought up at artificially low prices and sold on the open market at extremely high prices" (262). But the exploitation, corruption, and devastating impacts of the war economy extended to other crops, including cereals, beans, and other staples. There was also a shortage of straw, which was redirected mainly to the army, and this shortage meant there was limited food for peasants and their livestock (268). Eventually, because of the deteriorating conditions, the peasants revolted. The causes of their revolt can be summed in the exploitation that fed the war abroad and that starved the poor on their occupied soil.[4]

Internationally, the world in 1919 was a scene of devastation—a "vast cabal of crime" (Ovid and Sandys).[5] The scene involved massive loss of human life (approximately ten million) and the depletion of economic resources. Though the economic loss experienced by belligerent European states is obvious, it had numerous ripple effects that extended to colonized countries that were used to feed the war machine. After World War I ended on November 11, 1918, treaties—the most important and frequently referenced being the Treaty of Versailles—and institutions, like the International Court and the League of Nations, were established to end the state of belligerence. The professed goals were justice and peace, which history indicates were not attained, especially considering the eruption of World War II.

Much is written about the Treaty of Versailles, which concluded the war using a settlement and established the League of Nations. A number of key players were involved. On one side were Britain, France, the United States, Italy, and Japan who, despite their varied goals, wanted to punish and control the power of Germany (and its allies). The settlement between warring parties resulted in a number of treaties: with Germany, there was the Treaty of Versailles. There were also lesser-known ones with other countries like the Treaty of St. Germain with Austria, Treaty of Neuilly with Bulgaria, Treaty of Trianon with Hungary, and Treaty of Sévres with Turkey. The settlements had devastating consequences and have been critiqued; here I discuss only those critiques that focused on the damaging consequences of the recourse to only punitive justice to enhance—or rather enforce—moral responsibility.

The professed goal of the Treaty of Versailles was peace. However, the articles of the treaty did not just punish but also sought to disarm and humiliate the Germans.[6] Though historians debate the treaty, some argue that, considering the circumstances of World War I, it was the best attainable settlement at the time. Others explain that it was "morally flawed" (Lu 5). Generally, punishment seeks to address multiple goals: abating the destructive force of injustice (Lu), suppressing a perpetrator's false superiority and aggression rationalization (Daye, Lu, Worthington), "vindication of the victim's relative worth" (Lu 14), restoring the moral universe (Stovel), and "establish[ing] goodness" (Hampton qtd. in Lu 14). Enacting a retributive model of justice as a form of "moral accounting," as Catherine Lu explains, "the treaty [of Versailles] assigned blame for the war to Germany (Pt. VIII, Art. 231), called for trials to punish transgressions against the laws of war by defeated powers (Pt. VII), and set up a commission to determine the extent of reparations (Pt. VIII)" (7). However, these goals were not fully realized. Some scholars note that "the ineffectual and selective assignment of responsibility for wrongdoing undermined the treaty's claim to justice" (Lu 13).[7] Many contemporary non-German public intellectuals were critical of the treaty, including Jane Addams (Gorman and Mihalkanin 2) and Abū al-'Azā'im. And "within a couple of years, the justness of the peace settlement [including the Versailles Treaty] seemed flawed to almost everyone" (Lu 10). Not only were the treaties unjust in numerous ways, they resulted—in effect—in impunity and did not end the state of belligerence.

Despite the professed goals of the treaties and the critiques, neither justice nor peace were attained, especially considering the eruption of World War II. GCS was written in response to and as a critique of the forces convening in Paris in 1918 to "establish" peace (Shuqruf 47–48). The war settlements had devastating consequences. Like others, Abū al-'Azā'im was critical of it. Scholars have noted the damaging consequences of the recourse to only punitive justice to enhance moral responsibility, a discussion GCS engages (J.M. Abū al-'Azā'im) and in subtle ways links to the international scene. Further, Abū al-'Azā'im had intimate knowledge and understanding of the plight of colonialism, especially in a time of war, as well as the multidimensional manifestation of this plight at home and internationally. Not only was he aware of this plight, but he also dedicated many of his articles to reflections on colonialism, increasing people's awareness of and warning against colonialism and supporting people's pursuit of liberation (Shuqruf). This was neither the first nor the last time Abū al-'Azā'im was critical of the politics of the day. Because of his political writing against the British occupation and its injustices, Abū al-'Azā'im was imprisoned several times, was fired from his position as a professor at the Gordon Memorial College (currently the University of Khartoum) in Sudan, and was put under house arrest (Shuqruf).

AN INTERVENTIONIST MEDITATION ON CONFLICT RESOLUTION

In response to the multidimensional context of 1919, Imām Abū al-'Azā'im wrote an interventionist meditation on conflict resolution, articulating his vision for the creation of—at one and the same time—a reconciled, peaceful self (*nafsun muṭma'innah*), and (inter)national community (J.M. Abū al-'Azā'im 3); the Imām believed that internal conciliation was the logical precursor to and condition for conflict resolution between peoples and nations, a position articulated in the forward written by his grandson, Dr. Jamāl Mādī Abū al-'Azā'im, a prominent Egyptian psychologist. For Imām Abū al-'Azā'im, internal conciliation meant reconciling competing forces in the self (*al-quwwah al-dāfi'ah wa-al-quwwah al-luwamah*) (J.M. Abū al-'Azā'im 3). His take on reconciliation is evident in GCS's subtitle, which frames it as "A Dialogue between the Demands (*maṭālib*) of the Soul (*rūḥ*) and the Desires (*raghā'ib*) of the Body to Purify Selves and Reform Society."[8]

The self's aspiration to end internal turmoil and conflict is similar to the need for healing and reconciliation on the national and international scenes. Because GCS recognizes the convergence of the self and the national and international yearning for peace, it addresses conflict, domination (domination-submission dynamics), and the limits of punitive justice. It invests in the pursuit of justice, which addresses and balances the needs of all stakeholders, who aspire for both individual and collective good. This pursuit transcends the goals of punitive justice. As Lu explains, "The multiple aspirations of moral regeneration—deterrence of future wrongdoing, moral education of society, rehabilitation of offenders, restoration of victims, transformation of moral norms, and reconciliation with the past—require much more than a retributive model of justice that functions through punishment mainly to defeat wrongdoing rather than establish goodness" (15).

As it meditates on the "aspirations of moral regeneration," GCS goes deeper to transcend the specifics of any one case of conflict and inverts the process, shifting the focus from the other (a characteristic move of blame discourse) to the self (a characteristic move toward accountability). Though this meditation takes the self as its locus, it exceeds the intrapersonal and addresses interpersonal, communal, and (inter)national conflict and peacemaking. In this way, GCS provides a critique against the logic that enables conflict on all levels and provides a vision for peace. As the GCS reflects on the self's yearning for and pursuit of healing and moral regeneration, it demonstrates how the self realizes a state of excellence, a peaceful state that benefits the individual and the collective.

Though GCS maintains its focus on intrapersonal peacemaking as a *requisite* and *condition* for peace on all levels, there are conspicuous references to numerous collectives and to international and national conflicts. To address intrapersonal, interpersonal, and (inter)national conflict, GCS draws on expanded definitions of peace and restorative justice. Rather than just conceptualizing peace as a response to conflict, which is the immediate focus of the dialogue, it also expresses an understanding of peace as "a concept which motivates the imagination, connotes more than the cessation of war. It implies human beings working together to resolve conflicts, respect standards of justice, satisfy basic needs, and honor human rights" (Harris 7). This expanded definition of peace is consistent with a restorative understanding of justice, which as defined earlier, "involve[s], to the extent possible, *those who have a stake* in a specific offense and [seeks] to collectively identify and address harms, needs, and obligations, in order to heal and put things as right as possible" (Zehr 37; emphasis added).

As it engages conciliation on all these levels and draws on an expanded definition of peace, GCS provides a gradual enactment of restorative justice, a dialogic, humanistic model of justice—after juxtaposing it with punitive justice; orchestrates a court scene that brings stakeholders together to reckon with their grievances as well as with denied or dismissed needs; and shows us stakeholders' quest to realize the needs of *all* involved parties.

THE DRAMA OF CONFLICT AND CONFLICT RESOLUTION

The title of the dialogue captures a transspatial and transtemporal site of conflict: the self. As the story unfolds, Abū al-'Azā'im's bidimensional argument for peacemaking and the rationale for his interventionist meditation become clearer. In the Muqaddimah, he uses a healing metaphor to explicate his conception of and obligation to pursue peace. Likening his relation to the community (of Muslims) to that of a part to the whole body, he sees no way but to be accountable to its "health." Generally speaking, for Sufi teachers, the goal of intervention is to address crucial societal problems and to do their part in warding off great dangers. The healing metaphor underlines this mandate for intervention. Accordingly, the dialogue in GCS offers a model for reconciling forces of the self. This model leans into and affirms strengths and confronts and learns from our shadow sides, or repressed aspects of the self, embracing the different needs and goals of the self. As this model strives to counter the negative impact of either/or logic, it introduces a balanced, relational paradigm that seeks to realize all aspects of the self, and fine-tunes endeavors so they are more aligned with the well-being of all. The dialogue, as such, extends to others a Sufi's main focus on the purification of the self and alignment with *ma'īyah* (literally "being with Allāh"), or the surrender of the self to Allāh and attaining God-consciousness, which is consistent with the realization of the rights of others (*ḥuqūq al-'ibād*).

In response to the conflictive (inter)national context, a context which can be read as one of deterioration[9] or as an invitation to learn about the reconciled self, Abū al-'Azā'im writes the dialogue to avert this great danger and to model the work toward the realization of a reconciled self in both the sense of being reconciled with God and being reconciled with fellow human beings; only the latter is focused on in this chapter. Abū al-'Azā'im demonstrates *how* and *why* reconciliation with fellow humans is a worthy goal. This conciliatory work is a precursor to and condition for conflict resolution between nations as it helps cease conflict and establishes an amicable (*muta'ālif*) and cooperative (*muta'āwin*) international society (J.M. Abū al-'Azā'im 3). This multidimensional model for reconciliation unfolds gradually. Its presentation coheres and is simplified by using presence and juxtaposition. Both enable reflection and eventually allow for the layering of the processes that lead to the reconciled self.

Ṣulḥ is typically seen as an external process. The shift to an intrapersonal take on ṣulḥ invites introspection and defamiliarizes the concept and process while drawing on what is legible. The personified and bodied aspects of the self make each present (Perelman and Olbrechts-Tyteca 116–20) for further reflection and reassessment. *Presence* refers to rhetorical choices that make a concept or an object come to life or become a prominent part of one's attention field. Put differently, *presence* refers to interpretive and argumentative acts; the former can be considered an intervention in or an assessment of the relation between an object/concept and ground, whereas the second seeks to guide/influence response to the selected "object-ground" relationship (Tucker). As GCS shifts our gaze inwards, it asks us to attend to the self and its forces and makes the self present, visible, and less abstract. Quoting Stephen Spender, Perelman and Olbrechts-Tyteca explain how presence enables seeing, assessment, and judgment: "Nearly all human beings have an extremely intermittent grasp on reality. Only a few things, which illustrate their own interests and ideas, are real to them; other things, which are in fact equally real, appear to them as abstractions. . . . Your friends are allies and therefore real human beings. . . . Your opponents are just tiresome, unreasonable, unnecessary theses, whose lives are so many false statements, which you would like to strike out with a lead bullet" (117–18). Our conception of forces of the self, desire for courage or pleasure for example, maps well on the ally/foe context. Similarly, our conception of forces of the self is informed by what we value, what seems real, and what we are interested in. All help us assess the desirability and our responsibility to the grievances of these varied forces. Very rarely are these conceptions known, reflected on, or reassessed, though they continue to impact our thoughts, feelings, decisions, and actions.

As a rhetorical text, GCS presents the ensuing conflict: some forces of the self see themselves as more real and beneficial, whereas their *other* is invisible, abstract, and a foe (i.e., their presence is suppressed). The dialogue, by giving the floor to the different aspects of the self, freezes the moment and represents the violence/conflict created by the "suppressed presence" (118). Every aspect of the self is present, and its voice is heard. As such, GCS "make[s] present, by verbal magic alone, what is actually absent" (117). This presence is crucial to a fuller understanding of the self's forces, the process of reconciling these forces, and Abū al-'Azā'im's argument for (inter)national peace. Accordingly, this representation facilitates recognition of the nature of the self as well as the deep, tacit logic (i.e., drives, desires, values) that informs its actions and its articulation of its rights and grievances. This representation and presence has far-reaching consequences. GCS shifts—mainly because of attentiveness to the presence of all stakeholders—from an adversarial conversation to a dialogic encounter.

In addition to presence, juxtaposition brings to sharp relief these different modes of relating and communicating. Warlike interaction is juxtaposed with interaction that strives for reflection and mediation. In very broad strokes, this juxtaposition divides GCS into two main sections. The first represents states of conflict, claims of grievance, and an individualistic worldview, which manifests in power relations characterized by dominance and either/or logic. All these features mandate a legal intervention, which is realized in the form of adjudication and calls for punitive justice. Then, halfway through the dialogue, there is a gradual change. The second part of the dialogue is mainly characterized by a gradual investment in restorative conflict resolution: the rhetoric shifts from that of an adjudicator's cross-examination to an epistemic dialogue and mediation discourse. In turn, this shift realizes a relational worldview where power is shared and used to facilitate transformation. It is in this context that the selves awaken and explore what I will refer to as technologies of becoming: the dialogue highlights wasaṭiyah, tazkīyah, and kamāl as arts consistent with introspection and investment in the realization of a reconciled self. These arts help stakeholders attain reconciliation.

Attaining reconciliation is the central point of the dialogue, and it is condensed halfway through in a comparatively short statement by Hudá (Guidance)—an impactful though not a main character, at least in the number and length of Hudá's turns. Hudá elucidates the goal of the legal intervention:

> Our elusive goal is to counter war with peace so that a human being can live safe from the evils of another. And the strife against microbes, and animals, curing illnesses, and healing grief suffice. The human being was created to work toward their eminent future to which they turn. How could not they, when Allāh created the world with all its low and exalted, conspicuous and invisible forms for the sake of human being and so that Human Being can experience (*yabtalīhi*)?[10] And the human being was created to recognize Allāh (*li-'ibādatihi*). And God prepared for them the great kingdom,[11] bequeathed what is in the sky and earth to their service. . . . In your audience, Esteemed Judges, I propose a conflict resolution plan for this case using undoubtedly clear methods that avoid recourse to tough measures while upholding the values of mercy and compassion. The proposed plan entails al-Ra'īs (the Chief Judge) inviting all litigants, including plaintiffs and defendants to court. They can work together to reach an understanding regarding all their concerns until *ṣulḥ* resolves their conflict, and they are all reconciled. Because each aspect of the self yearns for what it deems good, considers others as contenders, and yearns for what the others shun, they all pine and suffer. Let's clarify to each one of these selves how its good lies in its eternal bliss, which is enabled by striving toward the good of all. Then each self can reach an exalted state, for the soul has needs only attained in the company of the body and

> senses, and the body and senses have needs only attained by the help of the self. Indeed, the outward structure and deeds of the body resemble the inward structure and aspirations of a society. The hand serves the whole body. And if dismembered, it perishes forever. And so would every organ of a human being. (52–53)

The first part of the excerpt lists the goal of countering war with peace, whereas the last part condenses some of the tenets that inform the ṣulḥ process enacted in the dialogue's different scenes. Despite its simplicity, Hudá's statement comes after and responds cogently to a long process of litigants' articulations of grievances and conflicting needs. Hudá's articulation of this central insight is the result of the convergences of two main discourses, namely adjudication, which shifts to a form of mediation in the second half of the dialogue, and epistemic dialogue. Naming reconciliation as central to the collective good and regenerative transformation necessary to recover from and resolve conflict hinges on the successful fusion of the shift from adjudication to mediation and epistemic dialogue, which uncovers the aforementioned three technologies of becoming. However, these technologies hinge, in turn, on introspection, which can be impeded when stakeholders gather to quarrel.

As GCS's simple and allegorical story unfolds, the self is heuristically represented as both a human being (*insān*) and parts of the self. Their conflict and reconciliation events start when the forces of the self express their conflict, explaining how they struggle to meet their physical and spiritual needs, which are pitted against one another and against other aspects of the self's needs. The emplotment of this conflict is clear as early as the opening scene titled "Psychological Travel or Tour". In the dramatic presentation of aspects of the self, their conflictive relations, adoption of an either/or orientation, and ensuing separation are foregrounded. The first scene involves al-Khayāl (Imagination), al-Wahm (Illusion), al-'Aql (Mind), al-Rāwī (Narrator), al-'Adl (the Justice or the Judge), al-Kātib (the Legal Scribe), and al-A'wān (Judge's Assistants). We first hear the initial grievances of the al-Khayāl (Imagination, or the mirror of what is perceived by the senses), who complains about its abilities being undermined and lost in the pursuit of what can be considered temporary, deceptive gains. Similarly, the grievances of al-Wahm (Illusion, or the mirror of meanings) and al-'Aql (Mind) are uncovered. al-Khayāl and al-Wahm commiserate; both are pained by injustices, evils, and false or unattainable desires (*al-munkar wa-al-muḥāl*). As they converse, we observe the evolution of grievance articulation, the establishment of a legal setting, and the initiation of a legal procedure.

The grievances of al-Khayāl and al-Wahm have propositional, affective, and relational dimensions. The propositional and affective dimensions of the conflict are manifest in the very first lines of the scene: al-Khayāl articulates frustration and despondency (i.e., the affective dimension) because of losing the way (*shar'*). al-Khayāl (GCS 13) explains this state by identifying and critiquing choices made (i.e., the propositional dimension) that enslave al-Khayāl and reduce its capacity to fulfill desires (*ahwā'*).[12] In addition, al-Khayāl's grievance statement represents a relation that results in conflict and pain. The relation between al-'Aql (Mind) and al-Nās (People) is depicted and named as one of conflict, which results in separation (i.e., the relational dimension); al-'Aql explains its critique of the ways of people, underlining choices al-Nās (People) makes that result in severing relations between family members, betraying those who should be entrusted, and eroding the moral code of the community (GCS 15).

This articulation of initial grievances—with their propositional, affective, and relational dimensions—leads to writing a complaint (GCS 16). Acting as plaintiffs, al-Khayāl and al-Wahm cede to the suggestion of Al-'aql to seek the intervention of Allāh and legal authorities (GCS 15).[13] al-Rāwī (the Narrator) directs them to take up the suggestion of al-'Aql and begins dictating—acting on their behalf—the complaint, a short condensed document in which the plaintiffs, defendants, and the nature of conflict are identified, initiating—if not building—a legal case. The main plaintiff is Insān (Human Being), who is characterized in the complaint as a being in a state that transcends the limits of human nature and animalistic impulses.[14] In this capacity, Insān files the case to al-'Adl, and thus ushers in the court scenes.[15]

TO GATHER AT COURT: ADJUDICATION, MEDIATION, AND EPISTEMIC DIALOGUE

At court, we have two main scenes. In both, we see the selves gather at court and bring their case to a judge with the hope for conflict resolution. The first is a typical court scene where the selves are cross-examined, the judge plays the role of an adjudicator, and we expect the story of conflict/conflict resolution to come to an end with a verdict. However, the second part of "The Second Session" presents a different discursive model of interaction. The scene shifts from adjudication to a form of mediation, and the forces of the self come to know themselves and others differently and are persuaded to attain a meaningful conflict resolution rather than just settling for punishment.

Conflict can become a tragic illumination, for "disputes illuminate social processes" (Gluckman 636). Together, the aforementioned scenes shed light on numerous discursive and sociopolitical processes that explain the causes of conflict and the path to resolution. The shift from conflict to ṣulḥ hinges on a different understanding of (a) the forces of the self, (b) their functions/aims as well as alternative ways to express these functions, and (c) their relationship to one another. This understanding evolves organically and gradually, is rhetorically mediated, and ensues from a conspicuous shift in the use of discourse. In what follows, the rhetorical impact of forms of discourse like adjudication, mediation, and dialogue are focused on to explicate how this alternative understanding emerges and leads to reconciliation.

Adjudication

"The First Session" is characterized by many of the discursive moves of adjudication. As a third party, al-Ra'īs (literally the Chief Judge who is al-'Adl or Justice) focuses on realizing their "institutional goal—that of settling or disposing of the dispute" (Maley 95). To this end, al-Ra'īs sifts through the litigants' grievances and "decides on legal issues, rights, and penalties" (94). The discursive work of adjudicators entails assuming a reflective disposition and discursive practice including managing others' discursive practices, and it is "norm-governed" (95): they typically "assume neutrality and impartiality" and work toward "keeping order, regulating and facilitating a range of social activities," including examining witnesses; they "are expected or enjoined to adhere to rules of speaking—who speaks to whom, when, about what and how much" (95). In GCS, al-Ra'īs as adjudicator is at the center of the scene, manages the floor, and calls on litigants to state their grievances. al-Ra'īs listens to the grievances of, for example, al-Nafs al-Sab'īyah (Panther Self), al-Nafs al-Shahwānīyah (Appetitive Self), al- Ẓulm (Injustice), and al-Fikr (the Intellect) and conducts an investigation to clarify the issues disputed. al-Ra'īs also asks them to name their defendants. al-Ra'īs controls the process and manages the circulation of floor. When litigants digress, they are guided to focus on relevant (GCS 23) and admissible information in absentia (19).[16] However, toward the end of "The First Session," the litigants become disorderly and clamorous, which causes al-Ra'īs to end the session, detain defendants, and adjourn. "The Second Session" seems to begin on a different note. The roles are slightly but conspicuously modified. al-Ra'īs's role seems to be decentered, and the judge assumes a role more like that of a mediator.

Mediation

al-Ra'īs's role seems to shift to that of a mediator. Like an adjudicator, a mediator engages in sociolegal, discursive activities geared toward justice. Unlike an adjudicator, their role is less structured, for a mediator does not control but instead guides process, substance, or outcome. The discursive shift to mediation is conspicuous at the very beginning of the scene when Rawīyah (Prudence) requests the floor, declaring that al-Ra'īs's intervention was sought after an arduous process. Rawīyah clarifies that the goal is not the extinction of al-Nafs al-Sab'īyah or al-Nafs al-Shahwānīyah, who are recognized as beneficial and crucial to the attainment of the desires of the self. Rawīyah further clarifies that the goal is to purge the excesses of al-Nafs al-Sab'īyah (Panther and Appetitive Selves) so that all involved parties feel fully realized.

Though the decision is ultimately al-Ra'īs's, the request to claim the floor and the articulation of a potential settlement signal the judge's shift to a different role. GCS becomes less formal; al-Ra'īs and the litigants' roles shift as they guide the process and set the agenda. To illustrate, the judge's role shifts to become less "authoritative and decisive"—a characteristic of adjudication (Maley 99).[17] Though al-Ra'īs continues to ask questions and to guide the process, the litigants participate more in the process, claim/negotiate the floor, offer explanations, and name the goals of the process. Like a mediator, al-Ra'īs "facilitates, but does not impose, a settlement between disputing parties. . . . A mediator *empowers* the parties to reach a decision themselves" (Maley 94). Eventually, the verdict, which covers the last two scenes of the dialogue, becomes reiterative, affirming the participatory process of "The Second Session."

The shift toward mediation is gradual, uncovers many different understandings of selves and relations, results in reconciliation, and manifests as an epistemic dialogue. The shift is gradual but rich and complex and abounds with didactic and transformational undertones. More important, the gradual shift from adjudication to mediation implies a state of presence when more stakeholders take the forefront to participate in what becomes an awakening dialogue.

Epistemic Dialogue

The dialogue form is neither incidental nor just a presentational form. Rather, the dialogue is a fundamental part of the message in a variety of ways. Communicative choices invoke and constitute relations. Dialogue connotes a relation of equality, which is different from the relation implied by modalities of communication like debate, argument, controversy, or talking at. In this regard, the form of GCS is consistent with its reconciliatory method. In the early part of the play, the communicative patterns oscillate between conversation and monologue. The characters often engage one another by exchanging short monologues in which uptake signals neither listening nor engagement. Many represent grievances and responses to grievances. Later on, the characters recognize one another, listen to each other's grievances, and try to negotiate a potential solution. Then their communicative practices become dialogic, hence enabling the move toward ṣulḥ. It is important to note that their dialogue catalyzes a space where arguments, mediation, claims of grievance, exhortation, and conciliatory appeals become conduits for better understanding. The dialogue, then, assumes an epistemic function when it allows for the discovery of the nature of and differences between the selves, sharing, and processing of such information. Human Being's imbalanced existence and attempt to reclaim peace minimally entails a better understanding of the problem and learning to problem solve. The dialogue as a form allows interlocutors to reflect on the grievances, and the dramatic litigation setting allows for truth finding and for arguments and counterarguments to emerge.

Epistemic dialogue (Hyland)—characterized by the epistemic activities of argumentation and explanation—is crucial to better understanding discourses that address conditioned, unjust practices and those that enact/model rhetorical, reconciliatory method in GCS. Epistemic dialogue is a *subset of* and *medium for* dyadic interaction, and the beginning of any reconciliation attempt is the coming together of involved parties to the proverbial conversation table to find out the reality, nature, causes, and solutions of a problem faced. Interlocutors at times will only attain a recognition and better understanding of the problem/conflict at hand. In GCS, factions of the self come together, recognize their plight, and sift through what is known and what can be known.

More important, epistemic dialogue enables conceptual understanding of an issue, a level of learning that exceeds the level of problem finding and solving. The difference lies in the fact that the former seeks to "understand the concepts and principles that underlie problem solving," whereas the latter tends to be a discrete, procedural activity more invested in the problem at hand (de Vries, Lund, and Baker 64). Conceptual understanding is flexible, adaptable, and portable. It calls for balancing concept, context, and procedure. As such, it anticipates and invests in a different future because "conceptual understanding is an important prerequisite for interpreting new situations, predicting future states of affairs, and solving types of problems that have not already been practiced" (Tiberghien qtd. in de Vries, Lund, and Baker 64). Because it facilitates conceptual understanding, which in turn can anticipate and inform future action as well as problem solve, epistemic dialogue has both an intrinsic and a nonintrinsic motivation.[18]

The two types of understanding (i.e., the short-term, goal-oriented, problem-solving type and the long-term, conceptual type) are crucial to appreciating how GCS offers a rhetorical method for reconciliation. The conflicting selves who could not listen to one another and were not invested in the potential of dialogue at the beginning come to learn to awaken to each other mainly by understanding four interdependent concepts: the need for the other, the nature of power, the goal of being, and resources for attaining a reconciled self. As we read and observe their case-by-case problem-solving endeavors, we are invited to reflect on the conceptual moves of problem solving, and we observe how they relate to one another differently, attaining both intra- and interpersonal reconciliation.

Ways of Communicating and Relating

GCS juxtaposes communicative styles related to warlike contention and peacemaking endeavors. Relational communication attends to "the interconnection between communication and relationship formation" (Rogers 829). As it underlines this sociality, it helps tease out how communicative choices lead to conflict/conflict resolution and invites us to develop "a relational level focus in order to capture the inherent socialness of relationships" (829). Relational communication, therefore, focuses on the embodied, multidirectional, sociopolitical nature of communication; attends to the different, emerging understandings of any communicative act and event; recognizes the other; acknowledges intended and unintended consequences of communication; and distinguishes between different models of interaction.

Dialectic, *conversation*, and *dialogue* connote talk and imply different relations. Unlike dialectic, which focuses on the intellectual processing of units of thought with the goal of moving toward a better understanding of a concept or an issue, "dialogue is the interaction of concrete particular persons" who might have different perspectives on issues or concepts (Czubaroff 170). Conversation, too, involves a relation, albeit a unidirectional one, in which "individuals interact by engaging in an exchange of ideas" or "negotiation[, which] is trading off, adjusting to each other and . . . 'working something out'" (Kuttner, "Cultivating Dialogue," 316). As such, the existence of two conversing bodies is insufficient for dialogue. The communication between two conversing entities develops into a dialogue when their communicative acts cultivate a way of being (and, accordingly, skills and practices) that can counter "monologic thinking and separateness" (331). A dialogue, therefore, is a bidirectional relation realized in a communicative encounter in which "participants are aware of their radical interdependence, such that their joint action mutually constructs their realities, and their senses of self emerge through and within their unique situation"

(316). By pinpointing the way we relate, relational communication provides us with an analytical prism to study the socialness of relationship and to underline how people "interrelate with others through the process of communication and how different patterns of behavior and meaning characterize and impact their relationship" (Rogers 828). So what relations does GCS attend to, and how is this connected to the development of ṣulḥ as a rhetorical method for conflict resolution?

To understand the relations critiqued and envisioned by GCS, we need to explore yet another concept, namely power.[19] Not only is power a relational phenomenon, but many relations are also identified by their power dynamics. Intriguingly, power relations are manifest in and traceable through forms of interaction (e.g., conversation, talk at, or dialogue) in general and those observable in GCS. Power, therefore, is central to understanding the rhetorical method GCS provides, which attempts to intervene and transform conflictive relations and communicative patterns. Varied relations and different types of power become conspicuous in GCS when the selves articulate their grievances. The first half of the dialogue, which is littered with references to an either/or logic and adversarial relations, exemplifies power-over relations. The second part, however, gradually shifts toward more cooperative relations that counter either/or logic and moves toward building a relation of unity and sharedness, or a power of togetherness.

To illustrate, in "The First Session," which initiates the "legal scene," there is an extended dialogue between al-Ra'īs (the Chief) and al-'Aql ibn al-Qisṭ (literally Mind or Reason Son of Fairness) in which al-'Aql (Mind) articulates a grievance. After praising al-'Adl (the al-Ra'īs or Chief Judge), al-'Aql requests intervention: "I came asking you to support me in my pursuit of vindication (*ji'tu mustanṣiran*)." al-'Aql proclaims that it seeks refuge from the devil of Shayṭān al-Hawá (desire), explaining how desire's overwhelming power has denied al-'Aql's virtues and condemned it to humiliation (*hawān*). Similarly, al-Nafs al-Sab'īyah (Panther Self) states its grievance and discredits al-'Aql on the ground that established scholars have disagreed on the definition, functions, and nature (whether it is manifest entity or an essence) of reason.[20] al-Nafs al-Sab'īyah goes as far as comparing al-'Aql to the devil to whom all bad things are attributed but who is also never seen. al-'Aql is accused of depriving al-Nafs al-Sab'īyah of its animalistic pleasures and desirable excesses. The grievances of al-Nafs al-Sab'īyah and al-'Aql demonstrate the conflictive worldviews of both selves. Within a conflictive world, one's needs are pitted against the other's. To satisfy one's needs, there is no way to achieve this except by controlling and overpowering all others.

Because the recognition of power-over at the level of ideation is not enough, the dialogue also presents the emotional dimension of the grievances. al-'Aql speaks to this clearly, explaining its loss and current state: al-'Aql spells out the erosion of its spiritual life and its loss of the freedom to and pleasures of intellectual and spiritual pursuits. Because of the density and overpowering forces of the animalistic selves, al-'Aql finds itself submissively shackled. In representing the affective consequences of the domination-submission power dynamics, "The First Session" foregrounds many dimensions of conflictive relations. Whoever is deemed other is rendered a devil who overpowers and seeks to subdue, humiliate, or eliminate.[21] Because they cause harm and hurt, they are feared and hated. This attention to the other, however, renders the self invisible and exonerates the self from any responsibility or wrongdoing. The aggregate is a desire to eliminate the other, and the logic of the day seems to be that either one *or* the other exist.

The presentation of this either/or logic and the attendant emotions of fear, anger, and frustration enable a critique of power-over and opposition and explains the centrality of reduced if not negative self-definition to this relational and communicative dysfunction. Litigants define themselves in opposition to one another and create a hierarchy in which a self is better, superior, and more deserving than others, for example.[22] Moreover, articulations of either/or logic and the domination relation underline a negative self-concept: al-'Aql is besieged by desires, and al-Nafs al-Sab'īyah is undermined by al-'Aql: each sees itself vulnerable and under attack in relation to a devilish other.[23] The negative stereotypes of different selves point to self-knowledge and knowledge of others. For example, in knowing itself as overwhelmed by the devilish desire and as besieged, al-'Aql reflects a negative self-concept and negative stereotype of al-Nafs al-Shahwānīyah. Both are consequential. As such, the presence given to the either/or logic, the dynamics of power-over, and the need/desire to subdue or eliminate an other sheds light on the logic that feeds the hierarchical relations between the selves, leading to conflict.

In addition, this presence underlines the logic that justifies resorting to punitive justice to solve problems. Both al-'Aql and al-Nafs al-Sab'īyah protest the denial of their rights, object to the constraints on fully realizing their beings, and take a stand against being reduced to a state of powerlessness. Both recognize their problems as manifestations of being overpowered and rendered powerless. Within this state of conflict, they believe the solution is to strip away power-over, and by doing so the power status of the victim is elevated. This is why al-'Aql's and al-Nafs al-Sab'īyah's statements—in this phase of the dialogue—converge and represent justice as a personal vendetta: justice is presented as a punitive measure or allowance for vigilantism. For example, when al-Nafs al-Sabʿīyah names al-ʿAql as its enemy and articulates its grievance, namely denial of its animal pleasures and constraint of the desirable states of rampant permissibility and celebration of pleasure and vacationing (GCS 20), it pleads for revenge, a measure it contends will bring comfort to people across different class stratifications (*turīḥu kull sulṭān wa fallāḥ*). However, al-Nafs al-Sabʿīyah also requests permission to punch and jab al-ʿAql. Accordingly, al-Nafs al-Sabʿīyah represents justice as eliminating the denial or violation of one's rights not by making things right but by reversing the power-over dynamics. Thus, the claimant—al-Nafs al-Sabʿīyah—can either be allowed to avenge itself or is vindicated by seeing al-Raʾīs exercise the "state's" coercive powers on the defendant. Within this worldview, there is defeat in both the conflict and justice contexts. This conception of justice—consistent with either/or logic, hierarchical relations, and negative self-image—points to an individualistic worldview. Unlike the relational self, which has been touched on in previous chapters, an individualistic worldview "is rooted in a vision of the individual as a separate being, autonomous and unconnected" (Kuttner, "From Adversity," 931). In this worldview, the self's imperative is to elevate their needs and to subordinate those of others (individuals and collective).

The limits of the individualistic worldview are brought to sharp relief with the juxtaposition between what *can/ought* and what *is* and the yearning for the realization of needs. Homing in on the same conflict instantiation, the clash of individualistic worlds becomes clear. al-ʿAql (Reason), as noted earlier, felt reduced because of the excesses of desire. Pleading for help, al-ʿAql explains briefly how it was in an exalted state, enjoying spiritual bliss, until the body, senses, al-Nafs al-Sabʿīyah (Panther Self) and al-Nafs al-Shahwānīyah (Appetitive Self) dragged it to a despicable state of submission to the whims of appetitive desires (GCS 18–19). Similarly, al-Nafs al-Sabʿīyah—very much in character and in a state of excess—assumes the floor for an extended time, represents its grievance, and makes a simple but multidimensional argument against the Highest Self. The argument foregrounds the benefits of al-Nafs al-Sabʿīyah that realize the desires of the body and senses and ward off the troubles of having such desires repressed. al-Nafs al-Sabʿīyah explains how it brings about the joy of embellished dress, delectable refreshments, lascivious encounters with ladies, victorious subduing of enemies, unbridled dominion over property, and virtuousness of people (60). This assertion of benefits mainly focuses on what serves al-Nafs al-Sab'īyah, who sees itself as disconnected and separate, a thing which warrants lack of attention to how these benefits impact and potentially harm others. Similarly, al-Nafs al-Sab'īyah's talk abounds with reference to virtues like justice, courage, generosity, prudence, and self-restraint, which refer to what elevates the needs of al-Nafs al-Sab'īyah (even if this departs from their typical meaning) and disregards how they might impact others. For example, for al-Nafs al-Sab'īyah, justice refers to dominion over others and prudence refers to trickery and sweet talking the affluent out of their riches and virtuousness (60–61).[24]

Both al-Nafs al-Sab'īyah's and al-'Aql suffer, and their suffering evokes sympathy: al-'Aql's short grievance statement underlines the domination-submission storyline, which is a manifestation of an individualistic worldview that results in withholding al-'Aql's right to be and act in ways consistent with spiritual bliss. The other side of the individualistic domination-submission is manifest in al-Nafs al-Sab'īyah's grievance. Though the statement may be dismissed as funny, it helps us see another form of excess. al-'Aql and al-Nafs al-Sab'yah's self-conceptions and goals are very different. al-'Aql's self-conception is almost that of one overcome by the desires of al-Nafs al-Sab'īyah (a negative self-concept), whereas al-Nafs al-Sab'īyah's inflated assertions of its rights at the expense of all others cannot be referred to as just an excessive positive image. Both in a way are dysfunctional self-concepts that are symptomatic of an individualistic worldview even if we respond differently to its consequences: as we read the dialogue we are more sympathetic with al-'Aql. Our asymmetrical response can be explained as relating to the journey of the selves toward their truest potential. al-'Aql's pursuit of its best self is thwarted, whereas al-Nafs al-Sab'īyah's potential is wasted. Both are barred from knowing their true selves.

GCS's emplotment of their plight does not provide us with a simple account of their true selves, but it is rather an account that evolves to match what can be referred to as a gradual awakening. In broad strokes, the selves to this point of the text mainly talk about themselves by referring to what they (used to) *do*, *desire*, or *aspire to*. They tell us about, on the one hand, what they revere but lost while, on the other, they refer to what they detest and fear the other impinges upon—if not thwarts completely. To some extent, their negative self-definitions are prominent and troubling since they feed into a restricted knowledge of the self and one's agency, which leads to submission, the complement to domination, or a crazed lust for power-over. In this context of self-concepts and definitions, needs and aspirations are pitted against one another, and the selves see themselves in an intractable conflict. Each perceives of justice as the punishment and elimination of the other. In their pursuit of justice, we see these selves entangled in warfare, a state indicative of separation and conflict.

This insight into the nature and consequences of power relations, communicative choices, and definitions of the self and justice might be dismissed. However, as readers who join the characters of GCS in this exploration, through this insight we get a glimpse of the writer's critique of power-over and dysfunctional, conflict ridden relations, hence the pursuit of justice that seeks to reverse power-over and heal conflictive relations. This insight, in turn, enables an awakening. This awakening is slow and gradual. The conflict situation, therefore, provides a much-needed juxtaposition and an entry into knowledge of the self (including self-concept), and knowledge of those deemed other. This awakening also underlines the need and yearning to *be* in a state of peace and excellence. As such, GCS highlights two important needs, namely epistemic and constitutive needs. As the dialogue unfolds, GCS addresses the epistemic and constitutive needs and provides an alternative understanding of the self as a relational self that has rights and obligations.

DIALOGUE AS AWAKENING TO THE SELF AND OTHER: TOWARD A RELATIONAL WORLDVIEW

The state of conflict in GCS and the selves' pursuit of conflict resolution reflect an epistemic need to find and articulate a "meaningful frame of reference" that provides an explanation of the self, its relation to others, and "perceptions about how and why the world operates in the way it does" (Burkley and Blanton 290). This epistemic need is coupled with affect. In addition to the recognition and pursuit of a different possibility, there is an articulation of a yearning for change. These needs awaken the desire to know, act, and relate differently. These needs become conspicuous and are taken up in "The Second Session," in which we witness a gradual shift in interaction, especially in the second half of the session, into a dialogic encounter: the characters are open to the views, positions, and needs of the other. This openness initiates reflection on living with oneself and others peacefully.

To this end, GCS brings to the foreground two interrelated, challenging questions: What does it mean to be a human being? How can one live with others peacefully?[25] The dialogue strives to respond to these questions, reflecting Abū al-'Azā'im's interest in better understanding the self in order to attain its reconciliation. In GCS, as the ṣulḥ case unfolds, we witness a variety of selves and their take on their (realized/withheld) needs in action. In their expression of their needs, we witness the way these selves perceive and talk about themselves, underlining a self-conception. At times, this expression evokes the sad response of listening to a grievance, while at others it evokes laughter. Gradually, their expressions lead us to deep reflection on the self. This reflection implies a desire to seek self-betterment and invites a meditation on one's desire for excellence or a state of perfection. This desire is sometimes realized when what *can* or *ought* to be is dramatically juxtaposed to what *is*. Yet, can the state of excellence be defined? Can the desires to attain what is deemed good help move selves toward reconciliation? Can the aspiration for excellence help us understand the selves better and move toward a relational, reconciled self? To respond to these questions, the GCS juxtaposes worldviews, zooms in on the relational worldview, and invites deep reflection.

Unlike the individualistic worldview, which results in conflict and grievances as demonstrated earlier, the second session foregrounds a relational self, which is informed by a relational understanding of the world. To expand on the relational worldview, I compare it to the organic worldview. In contrast to the individualistic worldview which elevates the needs of people who are perceived as "separate, autonomous and unconnected," an organic worldview elevates the needs of the collective, subordinates that of individuals, and emphasizes "community survival or welfare" (Kuttner, "From Adversity," 931, 942). Within the organic worldview, the self is expected to both prioritize the needs of the collective and develop an ethic of devotion, sacrifice, and service. Both the individualist and organic worldviews tacitly assume a tension between the individual and the collective. Their response to this tension diverges—by either elevating the self in opposition to the collective (i.e., individualistic worldview) or by elevating the collective in opposition to the individual (i.e., organic worldview). Alternatively, a relational worldview emphasizes the dynamic and nonpolarized/nonpolarizing relation between people and seeks to balance autonomy and interdependence. The relational worldview is neither the opposite of an individualistic worldview nor an organic worldview. Within a relational worldview, "Individuals are seen as both separate and connected, both individuated and similar. They are viewed as being to some degree autonomous, self-aware, and self-interested but also to some degree connected, sensitive, and responsive to others" (931–32).[26]

The allegorical nature of GCS dramatizes and foregrounds the qualities of self-reflection and responsiveness necessary for a relational worldview when the polarized and conflicting entities come to reckon with the dilemma of not just attaining their goals but also thriving while coexisting with others.[27] To illustrate, at the beginning of "The Second Session," before al-Ra'īs calls on litigants to clarify the situation, Rawīyah (Temperance) assumes the floor and sets the tone for the whole session, indicating a shift toward mediation, restorative justice, and a relational worldview. Rawīyah steps up and declares that the claimants do not seek the elimination of the defendants not only because they recognize that every creation in the universe serves a goal, but also because they recognize that Insān comprises a self, a body, and senses. Rawīyah's statement is the first manifestation of the gradual shift toward a relational conception of the selves. When aspects of the self are purified—not eliminated—they attain a state of physical and spiritual excellence. In this state, they know their selves better, realize their needs, and ward off their excesses. However, when the forces/aspects of the self are in ignorance of or are denied that right to self-purification and excellence, they attain a state of hurtful excess. In this state, they are barred from a state of atonement (i.e., recognizing their excesses) and at-one-ment (i.e., recognizing their unity and interdependence) with their Creator and fellow beings. This is why, al-Quisṭ (Fairness) takes the stand and initiates a long clarification of the nature, relation/interdependence, benefits, and limits of the body, senses, and self. al-Quisṭ, who gives the floor to al-'Ilm (Knowledge) to further explain, provides a counterstatement—to borrow a Burkean term—when a multidimensional representation of the senses, which was previously reduced to appetites, for example, is foregrounded.

With the extended reflective statements of Rawīyah (Temperance), al-Quisṭ (Fairness), and al-'Aql (Reason), there emerges a different vision of the complex nature of the self/selves. The presentation of the nature of the selves is reflective of different worldviews and is related to GCS's meditation on peacemaking. In the separation or fragmentation of aspects of the self, an unbridled, individualistic worldview of warfare is represented. In a state of excess, the selves adopt a conflictive, either/or orientation. Within this view, aspects of the self are either vilified or idolized. In juxtaposition to this worldview, GCS also presents us with a constitutive, relational conceptualization of the self in which a self maintains its integrity but values its interdependence with others. In other words, we come to understand the self as embedded in as well as informed and constituted by a relational worldview.

This relational worldview catalyzes an awakening to a different possibility, a different way to relate to aspects of the self and members of the (international) community. GCS from that point forward manifests conspicuous characteristics of a relational worldview. Partly realized through the discourse of mediation, the relational worldview is mainly actualized through shifts from articulations of either/or statements and punitive justice to an interdependent, transformative existence. This realization results in an awakening; the awakened self recognizes that the assumption of an inherent clash between forces and faculties of the self is just that: an assumption. This realization has a deep impact on the selves' pursuit of justice.

In a relational world, the autonomy and rights as well as the interdependence and responsibilities of the selves are affirmed. Accordingly, in GCS, the selves are not seen as a liability or as deficient. More important, because the impact of a self's health influences the well-being if not livelihood of others, there is a mandate to realize the selves' potential and to respond to their grievances in a way that balances the needs of all stakeholders. Kuttner explains that a relational worldview does not see in a problem an invitation to condemn wrongdoers. Quoting Winslade and Monk, he explains that "through the postmodern lens, a problem is seen not as a personal deficit of the person but as constructed within a pattern of relationships. . . . From this perspective, identity is not fixed, nor is it carried around by the individual largely unchanged from one context to another" ("From Adversity" 932). This perspective highlights flexibility and change, key characteristics of the shift from the excesses of the individualistic worldview to a relational one, or from the "adversarial to a relationally-based integrative mindset," as Kuttner puts it (973). The relational view, generally and as manifest in GCS, is an emergent view that attempts to balance the needs for autonomy while also recognizing the interdependence and responsibilities of the selves to one another.

This shift away from power-over and either/or logic toward a relational, integrative orientation does not hinge only on a redefinition of the self and its relations; there is also important work that actualizes the awakening to the relational self. The second dimension of the shift toward reconciled selves and relations focuses on useful resources for the self to realize its relational nature so it can thrive and enjoy life. This second dimension attends to both the excellences as well as the excesses of the selves, which are better understood in relation to their different goals. When each aspect of the self is understood in relation to both its potential excellence and its potential excess, each is "humanized" and allowed a fuller representation. Both excess and excellence are present at any given time, and in this realm of possibility, the self infinitely dwells in a liminal space of becoming and awakening. In this liminal space, excess as a choice is counterbalanced by wasaṭīyah, tazkīyah, and kamāl, which can be considered technologies of actualizing the moment of dialogic encounter or, simply put, technologies of *awakening* and *becoming* reconciled.

Wasaṭīyah

Wasaṭ, in vernacular Egyptian Arabic, means "a middle between two extremes." However, wasaṭīyah—a noun descriptive of the concept corresponding to wasaṭ—is polysemic. The stance of wasaṭīyah (or embracing the middle way) is doctrinally rooted and is realized (a) in one's individual choice not to fall into the trap of extremes and (b) also in *ummatan wasatan*, or a community characterized by being "just," "justly balanced," or embracing the middle way (Yusuf 384).[28]

The connections between aspects of wasaṭīyah can be seen in Assad's explication of the values undergirding wasaṭīyah and *ummah wasaṭah*:

> Lit., "middlemost community"—i.e., a community that keeps an equitable balance between extremes and is realistic in its appreciation of man's nature and possibilities, rejecting both licentiousness and exaggerated asceticism. In tune with its oft-repeated call to moderation in every aspect of life, the Qur'an exhorts the believers not to place too great an emphasis on the physical and material aspects of their lives, but postulates, at the same time, that man's urges and desires relating to this "life of the flesh" are God-willed and, therefore, legitimate. On further analysis, the expression "a community of the middle way" might be said to summarize, as it were, the Islamic attitude towards the problem of man's existence as such: a denial of the view that there is an inherent conflict between the spirit and the flesh, and a bold affirmation of the natural, God-willed unity in this twofold aspect of human life. (Asad qtd. in Yusuf 384–85)

Asad underlines here wasaṭīyah's shades of meaning, which overlap and are directly related to the conflict between the selves in GCS. These shades of meaning are best understood in relation to two criteria that motivate, inform, and ground the stance of wasaṭīyah. These criteria are "Excellence or Goodness and Between Two Limits" (Ushama 188).

Asad highlights the belief that there is no "inherent conflict between spirit and flesh," and we can also add reason. This tension is brought up several times in the first part of GCS, and within the pervasive either/or logic, al-'Aql and Shayṭān al-Hawá call for the extermination of the other. The stances of the competing forces of the self underpin one of the key forces of injustice that wasaṭīyah seeks to ward off, namely excess (*ghulūw* and *ifrāṭ*) in both action and/or omission (Ushama 189); in denying the right to sensual pleasure or intellectual pursuits, one becomes unjust. Similarly, one is unjust when one exceeds the bounds in the pursuit of justice (e.g., the excessive sentence of exterminating an opponent). In contrast, since wasaṭ assumes the value of all (spirit, flesh, and reason) and counters assumed tension, it calls for moderation in exercising the faculties of each and warns against their excesses. Heeding the advice and the warning counters conflict (like that between Desire and al-'Aql). In the absence of conflict, heeding the advice and warning, wasaṭīyah becomes an aspect of the code of conciliatory conduct that supports a proactive take on reconciliation.[29] Tazkīyah is another aspect.

Tazkīyah

In the Arab-Islamic tradition, tazkīyah (purification) refers to a bidimensional investment whereby a person abstains from bad deeds and strives for good ones, hence the term *jihād*;[30] though the concept of tazkīyah is legible because there is a long history of a cross-cultural investment in the purification of the self, the concept jihād is misrepresented and misunderstood when reduced to an argument for (just) war. The goal of the purification of the self is understood as one of the dimensions of *al-jihād al-akbar* (the greater strife) and is addressed in the Holy Qur'ān, Ḥadīth, and in a short epistle by the well-noted scholar Ibn Taymīyah, who frequently refers to the Holy Qur'ān and Ḥadīth as grounds for his explication of tazkīyah. Muḥammad Māḍī Abū al-'Azā'im—a scholar of theology and sharī'ah—knew of tazkīyah and probably of Ibn Taymīyah's meditation on *tazkīyat al-nafs* (the purification of the self), which warrants a quick reference.

Ibn Taymīyah's (1263–1328 CE) meditation on the purification of the self takes an epistolary form—commonly used for commentaries and explications of central concepts in the Middle Ages. The text, which was written in 735 (Hijrīy Year), is relatively short (sixteen pages long).[31] Tazkīyah refers to a variety of practices but can be explained as both giving away (an excess) of something (e.g., money, desire, fame) and seeking a state of excellence and purification. For example, we give away money—in the form of charity—to detach ourselves from an obsession with money (a state of excess/excessive attachment)—a state in which we cede to money's power-over us—and to recognize the potential of money to bring (others) good. This leads to a state of excellence in relation to money: money is neither denied its power to bring good nor given too much power-over our lives. Accordingly, Ibn Taymīyah's book addresses how the deliberate practice of tazkīyah ultimately aims to realize *huqūq Allāh* and *ḥuqūq al-'ibād* (the rights of Allāh and people, respectively). Both are attained when one wards off excess, guides the self to strive against bad and hurtful deeds, and encourages the pursuit of good ones (Ibn Taymīyah 37–52).[32]

In GCS, tazkīyah is addressed as both a goal and a deliberate practice.

Tazkīyah is mentioned (GCS 33) at the beginning of "The Second Session" when Rawīyah (Temperance) claims the floor, declaring that the claimants do not seek the extermination of the defendants because they are crucial to everyone's well-being. Rather, they desire their tazkīyah, explaining that Insān's (Human Being) complex nature—comprising body, senses, and soul—can attain a state of worldly and spiritual excellence when it embraces tazkīyah. Otherwise, when tazkīyah is forsaken, it debases itself to (a state of) hell manifest in escalating conflict. Therefore, tazkīyah's main goal is to ward off excess, and this goal is best realized by the pursuit of excellence or kamāl.

Kamāl

Elsewhere, Abū al-'Azā'im underlines the potential for excellence and the perfect (hu)man, and in GCS he addresses excellence and the related concept of the perfect (hu)man as a resource to counter internal turmoil and conflict with others.[33] As a Muslim mystic, Abū al-'Azā'im was interested in the soul's yearning for a state of excellence and the needs of the self to thrive in a material world. As a professor of theology and a religious leader, he was interested in explicating and modeling this move toward excellence.

In Islamic mystic thought, the perfect human "exemplifies all virtuous moral qualities, which in turn represent the qualities that exist in God" (Leaman 80).[34] The pursuit of excellence is informed by a belief in Allāh, whose perfected attributes guide all actions. As justice is one of the ideals to be realized by humans, we are expected to assume a mindful, reflective disposition that strives for warding off excesses and injustice to both self and others.[35] This expectation is the reason that, in numerous places, ṣulḥ pursuers in GCS bring up the idea of attaining a state of excellence and the realization of the noble virtues. To illustrate, in a long discussion (59–73) among al-'Aql (Reason), al-'Ilm (Knowledge), al-Ra'īs, and al-Nafs al-Sab'īyah (Panther Self), al-'ilm engages al-Nafs al-Sab'īyah in a long epistemic conversation—up to this point al-Nafs al-Sab'īyah has resisted the logic of wasaṭīyah, interdependence, and reconciliation. al-'Ilm responds to a long statement made by al-Nafs al-Sab'īyah by addressing excellence, among other issues. However, to understand al-'Ilm's statement, we first need to understand to what al-'Ilm is responding.

al-Nafs al-Sab'īyah had spoken earlier about its grievance, underlined its benefits to the body and the senses, and articulated what is perceived as good and beneficial on personal and national levels. al-Nafs al-Sab'īyah stays in character, and overall the language used in this section evokes reflection on al-Nafs al-Sab'īyah's articulation of its own raison d'être and modi operandi, which is one of the main goals of awakening (of both the selves and the reader). al-Nafs al-Sab'īyah first talks about the virtues it realizes, which were addressed earlier. To reiterate this earlier reference, al-Nafs al-Sab'īyah explains that, for example, valor is deceit of the vulnerable; dominion over the weak; coercion of parents, spouses, and offspring into submission; harming animals and equals like any beast; and flattering superiors like a sly fox (GCS 60–61). Then al-Nafs al-Sab'īyah explains the details of its domination-submission game in its different phases and scales. Accordingly, it talks about what it takes real pleasure in doing and states that it especially gets a kick out of tempting those whom it has tricked into divisive arguments and hatred, which eventually weakens all of them, enslaves them to dutiful service, and establishes al-Nafs al-Sab'īyah's dominion. To sustain such domination-submission dynamics, al-Nafs al-Sab'īyah explains how it undermines people's virtues and affirms their vices until their forefathers' legacies become extinct and their exemplars are dismissed to oblivion. al-Nafs al-Sab'īyah continues to boast about its abilities, exclaiming, "How many nations were brought to their knees like so, losing their aspirations after attaining a state of 'excellence'" (62).

In response, al-'Ilm offers an explanation, which can be considered a counterstatement, and reframes al-Nafs al-Sab'īyah's raison d'être and its excellence, explaining that al-Nafs al-Sab'īyah was prudently created for a conspicuous reason for those who choose to be reflective. al-'Ilm further underlines al-Nafs al-Sab'īyah's transformative powers, reframes its relational dynamics, and connects its excesses and abuse of power with hindrance in attaining its state of excellence. For example, al-'Ilm explains that in a balanced state, al-Nafs al-Sab'īyah holds the strength to ward off harm and vice, contain evildoers, and vindicate the vulnerable or victimized (GCS 65). But, in a state of demise, al-Nafs al-Sab'īyah misses appearances for reality and deflects its attention from other relations and pursuits (66–67). In such a state, a self can settle for temporary pleasures (like that of victory over an adversary—even if wrongful—in a state of anger). However, when a self seeks excellence, it aspires to a compassionate stance that restrains vindictive gloating over an adversary (68).

As the engagement continues to unfold, it becomes clear that the concepts of excellence and the perfect human respond to and foreground an understanding of the self as abounding with potential and as transformable. Leaman speaks to this important understanding in Islamic mystic thought when he explains, "The important thing to realize about human beings is that we are open to a wide range of possibilities. We do not have fixed natures, and we can become more or less anything. We can become perfect, or we can become corrupt and evil" (81). The epistemic engagement between al-Nafs al-Sab'īyah and al-'Ilm demonstrates both the different possibilities of relations that exceed that of the domination-submission game and the transformability of any self. As such, to Abū al-'Azā'im, the pursuit of excellence is an imperative because it helps humans attain self-knowledge, realize their potential, get closer to knowing Allāh, and realize peaceful relations with others.

A RECONCILED SELF

Toward these ends, the three technologies (i.e., wasaṭīyah, tazkīyah, and kamāl) together counter excesses, abuse of power, negative self-definition, and moral/relational degeneration. Each impinges on realizing the potential of facets of the self and communities.[36] Though my reflections have referenced each separately, they are addressed together in different places in the dialogue. To illustrate, the three technologies GCS proposes help respond to grievances disturbing the relation between Rawīyah and Tahūr (Impulsiveness). Rawīyah speaks of all three arts, namely wasaṭīyah, tazkīyah, and kamāl. All facilitate the process of becoming reconciled with the self and with those othered because these technologies help realize the potential of the different selves and promote mindful, peaceful relations with others. As such, the dialogic, relational awakening as actualized by wasaṭīyah, tazkīyah, and kamāl charts a path for transformation and regeneration that eventually leads to reconciliation. Together, they form a method and a path, which draws on an Islamic response to the question of conflict and to the yearning for justice, regeneration, and reconciliation.

In its attempt to purify the soul and reform (international) society, the dialogue uses the form of a play to create a "pious entertainment" (Hirschkind). The text relies on a familiar plot, yet it is rich with details, clamorous voices, and insight into reconciliation. The dramatized conflict and conflict resolution take place mostly in a court setting, which makes the situation, interactions, and unfolding events familiar despite the fact that the dialogue models the complex work of introspection. Aspects of the self assume anthropomorphic qualities. They gather, articulate grievance claims, contest the grievances, and toward the end, they move toward a dialogic interaction, which eventually leads to their reconciliation.

The form helps simplify and model a responsive, reflective method for conflict resolution. The enacted reconciliatory method draws on and weaves knowledge, value systems, and social investments together to realize a relational worldview. For this reason, the dialogue takes up and modifies the trope of the journey—a journey within the self—as a transspatial and transtemporal trope for growth. Within the context of this journey, the dialogue affirms Islamic virtues cultivated *in actu* during the process of adjudication/mediation. The journey of awakening is crucial for mystics in general, and since this play is written by a Sufi teacher and leader, the process of facing the self's logic of contention and scarcity becomes a paramount duty/necessity for a meditation on interpersonal and intrapersonal conciliation. However, the dialogue, in affirming virtues that are cultivated for the benefit of both the individual and the community, allegorically foregrounds two contrasting models of public sociality (the relation of conflict vs. the relation of conciliation), demonstrating their short- and long-term consequences. More important, from the dialogue we can extrapolate a rhetorical method for conciliation comprising a functional interaction of three discourses: (1) a bidirectional, reciprocal discourse of expressing and listening to grievances; (2) an introspective, reflective discourse; and (3) a visionary discourse, articulating a vision for peace. As such, the dialogue provides a versatile, rhetorically mediated method for a functional, collaborative move from grievance claims to the establishment of a restorative peace.

The Great Court of Ṣulḥ is indeed deceptively simple. Written in a context of deterioration of (inter)national life after the Treaty of Versailles and the establishment of the League of Nations, it presents an interventive argument: internal conciliation between warring factions of the self is a model for, precursor to, and condition for the resolution of world conflicts and the establishment of a cooperative international society. This argument manifests as literary rhetoric, which differs from and complements the domains of activity and types of ṣulḥ rhetoric addressed in previous chapters. Yet it manifests the same goal of ṣulḥ, namely to bring about reconciliation and peace. Though intrapersonal ṣulḥ is the least visible and the most taxing, it is indispensable to realizing personal transformation and as a prelude to other forms of reconciliation. When realized, intrapersonal ṣulḥ is a gift, a new beginning, and act of grace.

CONCLUSION

The Gift of Possibility

This book points to a seldom-told story. This is a story of the gift of realizing an alternative possibility. Every time we witness conflict, we are given the two-sided gift of possibility: on one side we have plight, and on the other we have possibility. Plight offers us a necessary—only because we deem it so—juxtaposition, insight into, and a yearning for what *can* and *ought* to be. A possibility for peace, one foreclosed by violence, emerges. This book focuses on the gift of possibility and the rhetorical work that realizes this gift in terms of *ṣulḥ* practices. Indeed, the practices and rituals of ṣulḥ prove to be enduring, generative, and malleable, and they abound with possibilities for conflict resolution in different settings.

To underscore such possibilities, this book focuses in on three unique features of ṣulḥ initiation using commitment in addition to apology-forgiveness discourse, its mobilization of commissive witnesses, and its reconstitution of a deliberative community. This interpellated community comprises peace pursuers and beneficiaries who reach a mutually accepted peace framework, negotiating peacemaking needs and responsibilities. People, as peace pursuers and beneficiaries, grapple with the possibility of peacemaking. Peace pursuers' rhetorical activities are examined using varied case studies. Each sheds light on decisive features of the rhetoric of ṣulḥ and underlines discursive conditions that catalyze and sustain ṣulḥ's peacemaking potential. Together, they demonstrate how ṣulḥ is malleable enough to counter inter/intrapersonal and national and international conflict. Ṣulḥ also travels easily across medieval times up to the present and across social, legal, and political domains. Ṣulḥ's malleability and transformative potential is manifest in cases of public, international ṣulḥ, like al-Sādāt's 1977 peace initiative; the *in actu* sociopolitical contract and Constitution of Medina; and the literary uptake of ṣulḥ practice in epistemic dialogue. The book celebrates this potential and testifies to the complex, arduous, rhetorical work entailed: ṣulḥ's seemingly nonguaranteed output and delayed reward.

Ṣulḥ discourses—like other restorative models—typically contend and often collide with numerous failed ṣulḥ cases, which causes people to reduce ṣulḥ to a narrative of submission, the coming back of the unjust, a misplaced tradition in a world that is run—or should be run—by institutions, or the loss of a tradition that has become an anomaly in a world besieged by conflict. Therefore, *Shades of Ṣulḥ* accounts for, recognizes, and also invites further reflection on the limitations of ṣulḥ and other restorative justice practices and the forces with which they contend.

THE VEIL OF (IM)POSSIBILITY

Though this is the first book-length rhetorical analysis of the Arab-Islamic culturally inflected ṣulḥ practice, there is so much work needed to further the exploration of the rhetorics of ṣulḥ, and there are many more documents to mine. Such a recovery project must contend with the complexities of ṣulḥ as it reaches forward to realize the "faith in the ultimate justice of things"—to use DuBois's phrase—as well as cases of ṣulḥ failure. Very often, the pursuit is impeded or thwarted discursively, a phenomenon that warrants rhetorical attention.

Often critiqued, misunderstood, or altogether dismissed, ṣulḥ—and other restorative justice models—and ṣulḥ studies must contend not only with the realities of violence but, more importantly, with the accumulated history of reductive representations or malpractice of ṣulḥ; all become arguments—at best—cautioning against peacemaking rhetoric. This accumulated history or collective misconception exceeds ṣulḥ; it works in similar ways to undermine restorative justice, generally, despite increasing attention to its potential. To begin probing these misconceptions, we can consider those pertaining to the concept and nature of peacemaking and peacemaking rhetoric, the domains of conciliatory rhetorical activity, processes entailed, and anticipated results.

We seize the potential of peacemaking to interrupt violence. The initiation of ṣulḥ, the focal point of this project, is often critiqued as overpromising and underdelivering. This critique mistakes the work of initiation for the work of sustenance and renewed commitment. Because of the complexity of this work, I separate these phases of the process, focusing mainly on the initiation of ṣulḥ. However, our collective explorations of ṣulḥ, ṣulḥ rhetorics, and peacemaking rhetorics in general must attend to the processual nature of reconciliation practices, which mandates the development of complementary models for the different phases of reconciliation and their manifestations in varied contexts.

Additionally, we need to attend to the invisible work of ṣulḥ, which can be observed in numerous cites. To illustrate, I point out two types of invisible rhetorical work. The first is that done in private spaces. Ṣulḥ enlists the rhetorical work of mediators and arbiters; their work is typically part of visible tribal/familial/communal sociopolitical networking. Ethnographic case studies provide a good starting point to study this rhetorical work. However, ethnographic studies focus on public/formal ṣulḥ practices and eclipse the invisible contributions of women—family elders and mothers. In many ways, their work including rhetorical work is part of the invisible economy of communities. They, too, contribute to ṣulḥ as a mode of restorative justice, which is typically simpler, expeditious, and cost effective; but because their work, as valuable and productive as it is, remains under the radar like many other work done by women in private spaces, they are invisible even to scholars. Yet they inform collective memory and the passing down of rhetorical conciliatory practices. This work and its potential calls for research on the discursive economy that supports its invisibility as well as research on the rhetorical knowledge and practices that this "private" ṣulḥ entails.

The second invisibility relates to internal reconciliatory work that supports interpersonal reconciliatory rhetorical moves. There is a tendency to project outward the responsibility for conflict and conflict resolution. Our disciplinary investment in interpersonal rhetoric eclipses the self as a crucial locus for rhetorical work; in relation to South Africa's Truth and Reconciliation Commission (TRC) and inflated expectations of what TRCs can accomplish for communal or national healing, Villa-Vicencio ("Now That") writes that healing involves much more work, including the work of personal healing and reconciling with oneself. Despite the crucial role of internal rhetoric to peacemaking, this rhetorical work continues to be outside the territory of rhetoric since internal rhetorics are perceived to be under the dominion of psychology; this perception invites renewed interest in internal rhetorics in general and in relation to mindfulness and peacemaking in particular.

Moreover, peacemaking rhetoric's attempt to realize relational responsibility is often considered an excess, especially when what is deemed valuable is investment in punitive measures only, which realize responsibility in the legal sense. Culturally inflected peacemaking practices are often displaced by attention to the justice practices of the state. Some—when juxtaposed with punitive justice institutions—seem indecisive or unpredictable as they negotiate the variable and context-dependent conciliation needs of stakeholders. Though the discourse of punitive justice and the discourse of ṣulḥ talk against power-over (i.e., domination-submission), they are different. In addition to contending with power abuse and the resultant violation, ṣulḥ discourse contends with power abuse's subtle and morphing manifestations. These include minimal, delayed, or deferred accountability; dysfunctional systems for rights advocacy; logics of expediency and efficiency that settle for punitive justice, leaving behind gaping wounds; and euphemistic discourse that pits rights against one another or prioritizes some over others. All—in effect—foil the move toward the relationally motivated healing of violated individuals and their moral universe. More important, morphing and subtle manifestations of violence are often underrecognized by penal codes and even by members of a community until someone persuasively claims them to be unjust. However, morphing and subtle manifestations of power abuse can be addressed by restorative models of justice when they are recognized as trailblazing the discourse of conflict resolution and affirmation of rights. But, does this actually happen?

Often dismissed as a relic of a tribal past, ṣulḥ rhetorics and practices contend with a plethora of reductive representations and assumptions about ṣulḥ and traditions of peacemaking in the Arab-Islamic world. These reductive representations and assumptions partly map on geographical imaginaries, and these imaginaries encode an understanding of a moral, civilizational, and cultural geography that grapples with the formative dynamic relation among space/place/location, environment, and people when questions of violence, moral accountability, justice, and moral regeneration are concerned. To some extent, historical accounts of violence as an inherent cultural characteristics of the Middle East are manifestations of these enduring geographical imaginaries. Though rightly critiqued by many, these imaginaries endure, morph, and are impactful. (Consider, for example, Huntington's recent iteration of the clash of civilization.) A case in point: urban spaces, where state legal institutions are typically located, are more often linked with an informed, fair, determinate pursuit of justice. These imaginaries have the long-term consequence of deflecting attention away from traditions—often locally practiced—of peacemaking rhetorics. Similarly, though there is a growing body of work on culturally inflected peacemaking practices, their potential continues to be received in academia with a reticent hope that punitive justice is enough or is the only option. Rather than seeing these imaginaries and misconceptions as a pessimistic testimony to human nature, they can be seen as a tragic illumination of the convergences of complex variables and societal changes that led to this skepticism, tacit critique of restorative justice models, and dismissal of the effectiveness of the rhetorical work they entail. Such tragic illumination or critique is generative in our attempt to study what limits the potential of peacemaking rhetorics. However powerful these imaginaries, they are at odds with old and new cases of (inter)national peacemaking practices, including ṣulḥ documents.

Peacemaking rhetoric will continue to be practiced and needed because conciliatory exigence is an enduring rhetorical phenomenon. Disciplinary investment in the study of discursive conditions that enable and sustain peacemaking efforts on micro and macro social domains will continue to be rewarding; study of these conditions sheds light on the complexity and fragility of human interaction and responds to nagging questions about how and to what extent rhetorically potent language interrupts destruction and attains peace. This book contributes to this ongoing discussion by offering a corrective account that underlines such possibilities.

RHETORICAL INTERRUPTION AND POSSIBILITY

It is hard to overestimate the role rhetoric plays in the complex processes of ṣulḥ, which harnesses rhetorical power to begin the work of interruption: uncover, document, and disseminate knowledge about acts of injustice; mobilize intervention; call for accountability; and initiate and sustain peacemaking. This book explores such rhetorical work and addresses mainly two overlapping and underrecognized lines of inquiry. There is a dearth of scholarship on culturally inflected models of peacemaking—ṣulḥ included—and scholarship on Arab/Arab-Islamic rhetorics, which to date continues to be mainly focused on pragmastylistics, stylistic analyses, translation studies, contrastive rhetoric, or work on the translation movements of the Middle Ages.

As the book responds to these gaps, it develops a three-dimensional contribution that transcends the specificity of the cases studied. First, the book suggests that peacemaking rhetoric hinges on balance; the rhetorical work of peacemaking strives to regain or attain balance in more than one sense. Second, the book develops an analytical matrix that can match the complexity of the rhetoric of peacemaking. Finally, *Shades of Ṣulḥ* is one of few book-length studies that focus on culturally rooted peacemaking practices and one of even fewer projects situated in rhetorical studies. Therefore, the book, which is informed by comparative rhetoric, tries to develop a vocabulary that honors the cultural iteration of peacemaking while remaining legible to those who are not familiar with such history and culture.

First, the different chapters present a story of the rhetoric of peacemaking as a rhetoric that seeks to regain balance. The balance manifests as a discourse that does not settle with the critique against war and violence but exceeds it to articulate a vision, a critique toward realizing peace. The critiques *against* war and *for* peace are complementary and balance investment in problems faced, desired goals, and necessary policy measures. This balance also manifests as a discourse that resolves potential tension between varied and often incompatible restorative needs. Moreover, the analyzed cases uncover the discourse of intervention that orchestrates and balances rhetorical work done by peace pursuers. This discourse is manifest in attempts to balance interpersonal and intrapersonal rhetorical engagement with the reality of conflict; self- and other-oriented suasive moves; problem-solving and constitutive goals; verbal suasion, functional silence, rhetorical listening, and ritual practice; symbolic and procedural dimensions of reconciliation; and accommodation measures and calls for reciprocity. This intricate discourse of balance allays the fears of former belligerent parties, helps them embrace the power of togetherness, and guides the process of co-constructing a mutually agreeable conflict resolution. More important, the interdependent critiques *against* and *for* mandate and call for a balanced investment in different modes of *knowing, doing* and *being.*

These critiques call forth subjects who are reconstituted as peace pursuers rather than as enemies, which is a polarizing designation. Their new membership in the community of peace pursuers hinges on consistently choosing and actualizing category-bound acts that realize their commitment to peace. Through the process, ṣulḥ pursuers become rhetors par excellence. Using rhetorically persuasive text and talk, ṣulḥ pursuers listen to grievances, balance often incompatible needs, and reconstitute the belligerent stance of conflicting parties. Their rhetorical work can pour balm on open wounds, enable healing, and promote the pursuit of justice. As such, this study provides insight into peacemaking that transcend ṣulḥ as a peacemaking modality and encourages further reflection on peacemaking rhetorics in general.

Second, the book develops an analytical matrix. To match the intricate and unique exigence and constraints of conciliatory rhetoric, the analytical matrix must be multidisciplinary, data driven, and allow for fine-grained analysis. By drawing on reconciliation and peace studies, diplomacy, international relations, international law, anthropology, sociology, social work, and theology, this study develops an insight into the multilayered, contextually rich, and complex nature of peacemaking rhetorical work. More important, the analysis demonstrates how varied analytical concepts can be brought together to undertake a fine-grained analysis, which can in turn respond to the complexities of peacemaking rhetorics. For example, from rhetorical, sociolinguistic, and critical discourse analyses concepts—like rhetorical narratives, cultural reservoirs of sayings (condensed arguments), representation of locution, intertextuality, internal rhetoric, functional listening, and silence—can complement one another. Together, these concepts help probe and tease out the voices that contend with the dilemmas of peacemaking. Also, analytical terms like *categorization of membership* (sociolinguistics/pragmatics) and *constitutive rhetoric* (rhetoric studies) were used together to explicate how peace pursuers are interpellated. And to underline rhetorical work done to initiate, embrace, and be held accountable for actualizing this membership, the distribution of self- and other-oriented (suasive) moves, which tap into the discourse of moral agency, can be traced. This discourse has numerous manifestations, which can be probed using rhetorical listening and representation of locution/ideas that respond to claims of grievance and for recognition.

The chapters include numerous examples of how analytical lenses can be put together to uncover the richness of peacemaking discourses. The analytical matrix transcends a minimalist definition of rhetoric as persuasion, or as just an instrument, and seeks to counter what Krista Ratcliffe, in a different context, refers to as a divided logos that separates and displaces some rhetorical practices like listening and by extension creates walls of separation between insights attained in different disciplines or disciplinary corners, which can converge to fine-tune analyses of discourse.

Third, as this book focuses on ṣulḥ as a culturally rooted peacemaking practice, it suggests a different route to the study of Arab/Arab-Islamic rhetoric. Often, rhetorical studies of Arabic rhetoric take the route of the Greek tradition by focusing on the translation movement. The book takes a different route, one beyond the Greco-Roman tradition, and therefore contributes to and extends current discussion in comparative rhetoric and histories of rhetoric. The book also suggests areas for further research by looking at and pointing to texts that predate ones explored by the translation movement. Uniquely, the book turns to texts that have not been analyzed rhetorically and sheds light on a plethora of texts that document ṣulḥ practices and agreements or draw on ṣulḥ process and ritual. The book, however, does not touch at all on other discourses that contribute to/impede/call for justice in varied ways. These include, for example, poetry. A vibrant poetic tradition addresses valor, moral responsibility, the mandate to strive for justice, and so forth that remains untapped from a rhetorical perspective. There is also literature on khuṭab (singular: khuṭbah) or religious homilies and how they address war, military intervention, rights at times of war and peace, and the mandate for peace. Though this book situates all of the texts analyzed in relation to ṣulḥ, it has not even begun to scratch the surface of this line of inquiry.

The book suggests numerous studies that can add to, and might indeed complicate, its findings. For example, the book suggests the undeniable importance of internal rhetorics as a way to tap into deliberative work and acts that precede the interpersonal rhetoric of peacemaking deliberations and calls for a renewed interest in internal deliberations. I would also like to invite others to consider developing models and ways to think about the rhetorical work of sustenance, rhetorical work that affirms and extends the life of peacemaking beyond the moment of initiation. We can do this, for example, by comparing al-Sādāt's Knesset address and the Camp David Accords especially since critique of the accords was taken up in the Egyptian presidential election discourses in 2012 and 2014.

Further, this book invites attention to the interrelation of different justice discourses. There is a variety of interrelated, historically rich justice practices and discourses. Some manifest in adjudication, mediation, and arbitration practices, which to the best of my knowledge have not been rhetorically studied. These projects would extend current work in rhetoric scholarship, translation studies, Middle Eastern studies, and rhetorical studies. As they exceed the bounds of the translation movement, they underline the critical need for work on Arab/Arab-Islamic rhetorics and the rhetorics of peacemaking. Scholars of rhetoric can illuminate these spheres of rhetorical activity, and the discipline will continue to grow as we study rhetorical practices and rhetorical agency in places and spaces we have not often frequented. I hope the journey of this book will continue in these explorations.

NOTES

INTRODUCTION: DISCURSIVE SPACES FOR PEACE

1. The intersection of rhetoric—or communication—and culture is addressed by different areas of inquiry. These include contrastive rhetoric, comparative/cultural rhetoric, and intercultural rhetoric. Contrastive rhetoric emerged as a result of and in response to Kaplan (Kaplan's "doodles article"), and the work in the following four decades morphed into intercultural rhetoric (Connor).

2. Since the 1980s there have been waves of reflection on the history and historiography of rhetoric (Brooks; Graff and Leff; Walzer and Beard). These reflections continue. Some of the crucial contributions to this ongoing conversation include *Octalogs* I, II, and III (Murphy et. al.; Enos et. al.; Agnew et. al.) as well as the recently published edited collections, *Theorizing Histories of Rhetoric* (Ballif) and *The Present State of Scholarship in the History of Rhetoric* (Gaillet and Horner). This work sheds light on types of historiography and their differing imperatives (Vitanza), the responsibilities of scholars of the history of rhetoric, and the task of theorizing the histories of rhetoric (Ballif).

3. A dispersed body of work needs to be synthesized and processed. There is also a need for rhetorical studies of different rhetorical practices and traditions. Then we can begin building the typological map of Arabic/Arab-Islamic rhetorics. For more on medieval *khuṭbah* and religiopolitical texts, see Qutbuddin; for the

study of the rhetoric of women, see Khoury; and for work on organizational rhetoric, see Diab. Arabic transliterations follow the Library of Congress guide.

4. George Kennedy's *Classical Rhetoric and Its Christian and Secular Traditions* suggests a typology of rhetoric, which comprises philosophic, sophistic, literary, epistolary, and religious rhetoric.

5. Many traditional communities developed ways to deal with conflict. Post-conflict reconciliation is manifest in a number of practices that go beyond the desire to punish wrongdoers (i.e., punitive justice) to seek the healing and restoration of the lives of all involved parties, hence the term *restorative justice*. These peacemaking practices/traditions include the South African *ubuntu* (Kamwangamalu; Murithi), the Hawaiian *ho'oponopono* (Hosmanek; Wall and Callister), and Native American peacemaking circles (Metoui; Nielsen and Zion). A few articles in rhetoric and composition studies deal with peacemaking traditions or cultural influences on dispute-resolution measures (Chen; Dissanayake; Xiao).

CHAPTER 1. PEACEMAKING TOPOI: CULTURAL ITERATIONS OF RELATIONAL AND MORAL NEEDS

1. While I focus on these topoi, there are other variables to attend to, including the nature and gravity of the conflict/violence; the economic, social, political, historical, and psychological dimensions of the experiences of parties involved; ensuing hurt and its scale; and the impact of all these variables on emerging claims of rights. Each variable needs to be treated as a unique force that affects the conciliation discourse.

2. A history of oppression and trauma can be encoded in individual and/or collective memory. However, this issue is not addressed here in detail.

3. For more on the "memory of publics" and the "publicness of memory," see Phillips.

4. Katherine Mack ("Hearing Women's Silence") touches on tension arising from (dys)functional silence and listening practices as they engage the dilemmas of remembering, telling, and forgetting as she analyzes public memory in Achmat Dangor's *Bitter Fruit* and South Africa's Human Rights Violations Committee.

5. Shaw explains that their silence also reflected a spiritual concern because some were concerned that their words "could also summon forth the violence in a more spiritual sense" (9).

6. Some countries of the global East and the South adopted Western legal models because of colonial contact, among other reasons.

7. Restitution and procedural justice are also consistent with restorative justice, which I address later in the chapter.

8. Crime was considered a violation of victims (or their rights); however, this changed between the tenth and eleventh centuries when William the Conqueror developed a legal system centralizing power. Then his son King Henry I "issued laws

detailing offenses against the 'King's peace'" (Estrada-Hollenbeck 67). For more on the history of legalistic justice, see Estrada-Hollenbeck (66–68), and for more on its limitations, see Stovel and Estrada-Hollenbeck (69–74).

9. For more on ubuntu, see Murhiti's "Practical Peacemaking."

10. Tully offers a multidimensional understanding of recognition as (1) based on the liberal ideals of free and equal; (2) informed by norms of mutuality in which every citizen of a given community—including the global community—reciprocates, is fully recognized, and fully recognizes comembers of the community; and (3) affirming participation rights: subjects of recognition have a say over their right to recognition.

11. Truth Commissions fit the restorative model, and they can offer victims substantive forms of justice in the terms of restitution.

12. Everyone can be lured by the seduction of propaganda. This has been affirmed by Lifton in his study *The Nazi Doctors*: "Under certain conditions, just about anyone can join a collective call to eliminate every last one of the alleged group of carriers of the 'germ of death,' which the Nazis attributed to Jews and other Lebensunwertes Leben ('life unworthy of life'). . . . The moral challenge here was to be sure that one could empathize without sympathizing or excusing. As the definition of Michael Bosch has it: Empathy involves resonating with the other's unconscious affect and experiencing his experiences with him while the empathizer maintains the integrity of his self intact" (qtd. in Shriver 36).

13. For an extensive study of historical apologies, see Weyeneth's "The Power of Apology and the Process of Historical Reconciliation."

14. Aristotle defines *phronesis* (often translated as prudence) as an intellectual virtue (qtd. in Ruderman 414) that helps us deliberate about means. Moreover, "Aristotle . . . encourages *phronesis* to reason about such things as the relative importance of (potentially conflicting) ends, and even about the full implications of an end perhaps only dimly perceived at the start" (415). Therefore, he addresses the pursuit of wisdom in relation to deliberated means and ends.

15. Justice intersects with memory in ways that invite rhetorical exploration. As Daye explains, impunity fosters an environment in which memory is fragmented between an official narrative, which does not hold perpetrators equally accountable for their transgressions, and an unofficial narrative, which identifies perpetrators, holds them accountable for their transgressions, and details grievances. As such, impunity might be one of the causes behind contested histories. This intersection between justice and memory brings about dysfunctional stances and limiting subject positions. Both are inconsistent with the pursuit of peace. But, lack of (or insufficient) justice has serious political consequences as well. A deliberate forgetting of victims' rights undermines the legitimacy of the state, "for protecting and upholding victims of injury is one of the basic raison d'être of the state" (Biggar,

"Making Peace," 8). Moreover, deliberate (and selective) forgetting is consequential, for "grievances without redress tend to fester. . . . [and] infect future generations with an indiscriminate hatred of the perpetrators and their descendants—and also with an endemic mistrust of the state that, having failed in its duty to vindicate victims past, seems ready to tolerate the injury of victims future" (8). For more on contested histories and the pursuit of reconciliation, see Biggar ("Concluding Remarks"), and for rhetorical studies on forgetting and public memory, see Vivian and Phillips.

16. I am using *leadership* here in an expansive sense. As such, leadership is not exclusive to positional leadership.

17. *Ṣaḥīḥ al-Bukhārīy* is a ninth-century recognized collection of *aḥādīth* (or the sayings of the Prophet; plural form of *ḥadīth*); *af 'āl* (or the actions; plural of *fi'l*), which sometimes relate to the context of a Qur'ānic verse; and *taqrir* (or tacit approval) of Prophet Muḥammad. Put differently, *Ṣaḥīḥ al-Bukhārīy* is an anthology that comprises texts compiled to preserve Islamic knowledge and traditions by recording Prophet Muḥammad's sayings, acts, and tacit approval of practices, for example. *Ṣaḥīḥ al-Bukhārīy* is organized topically, and book forty-nine is devoted to ṣulḥ or peacemaking. All accounts are authenticated using the tradition of *isnād*—a method used to ascertain the report of one of the Prophet's sayings, for example, by tracing the chain of its credible narrators.

18. This is consistent with a verse in al-Nisā' ("The Women") or chapter 4 of The Noble Qur'ān, which states that the best of deeds are those directed toward charity, good and righteous deeds, or conciliation between people (al-Nisā' 114).

19. The case also exemplifies the intervention of state authorities and community notables to end the cycle of violence. Though the news report does not explicitly underline this, it is clear that both state law and ṣulḥ were made use of to end violence and heal the community. The story is available at http://m.almasryalyoum.com/news/details/392862.

20. The Noble Qur'ān and the tradition of Ḥadīth are replete with references to the remembrance of God (*dhikr*). Consider for example the following verses: "And men who remember Allāh much and women who remember—Allah has prepared for them forgiveness and a vast reward" (al-Aḥzāb 35) and "Remember Me and I shall remember you. Be grateful unto Me and deny Me not" (al-Baqarah 152). The significance of dhikr is multifaceted but can be condensed as a practice of recollecting God, Divine love and protection, and the way to attain God consciousness and its realization in a righteous, fair, and just life, that is a heavenly state.

21. Mu'āwiya and al-Ḥasan reached a peace settlement that is documented. One of the texts documenting this historical event is *Ṣaḥīḥ al-Bukhārīy*, an authenticated book providing accounts of many historical events and doctrinal teachings as noted earlier. A digital copy of chapter 49 on peacemaking is available through the

University of Southern California, Center for Muslim-Jewish Engagement, at http://www.usc.edu/schools/college/crcc/engagement/resources/texts/muslim/hadith/bukhari/049.sbt.html. It is worth noting that this type of ṣulḥ—to the best of my knowledge—has not been researched to date, yet it was recognized and classified by al-Bukhārīy, a prominent scholar, in his book on peacemaking. In popular parlance, it is considered a manifestation of forgiveness.

CHAPTER 2. THE POWER OF SWEET PERSUASION: CULTURAL INFLECTIONS OF INTERPERSONAL ṢULḤ RHETORICS

1. Nādiah Muṣṭafá is an Egyptian singer, who was born in Cairo in 1963. Her song was in an album with the same title (i.e., *al- Ṣulḥ Khayr*, which is part of a Qura'anic verse [al-Nisā' 128]). The song was written by the well-known lyricist al-Shandāwīlī. For more on Muṣṭafá and Muṣṭafá al-Shandāwīlīy, see Qābīl.

2. One of the reasons I choose to begin this chapter on interpersonal ṣulḥ by a reference to Nādiah Muṣṭafá is to foreground and honor the contribution of women, who often in the private space of home intervene to heal rifts and make peace. Their contribution has yet to attract scholarly attention. As an Egyptian who has lived thirty years in Cairo, I certainly knew about ṣulḥ and women's role in effecting ṣulḥ even when it was not referred to as ṣulḥ (in Egypt, I often heard colleagues and family members say *ḥa-nu''ud sawā wi nitṣāfá*, which can be literally translated as "we will sit together and make peace"; usually this takes place at one of the involved parties' or a friend's house, and typically food and beverages, signs of hospitality, are part of the setting. This conciliatory act is confirmed by Lang, who writes about the pervasiveness of this practice: "Throughout the Galilee, as in many parts of the Middle East, the Arab population has traditionally practiced a ritualized process of conflict resolution known as ṣulḥ" (53). Though the significance of the safe, private, intimate space of the home as a condition for ṣulḥ is not underlined in research on ṣulḥ, women's role in ṣulḥ has been recognized in Pakistan, for women and men are hired by courts to help resolve marital problems (Hussain).

3. Smith studied the practice of ṣulḥ at a macrosocial domain when he looked at how conflict and peace are "perpetuated in the minds of participants according to the symbols and motifs of their culture and history" (53); one of these cultural motifs and symbols is the communal practice of ṣulḥ. Lang examined ṣulḥ "as it is practiced in Galilee villages in tandem with the state justice system" at a microsocial domain, investigating how family, and among families, blood disputes are resolved and how peace and friendliness are restored (52). Sometimes, ṣulḥ involves a formal agreement or a peace treaty (Irani "Islamic Mediation").

4. Smith's and Lang's accounts depict the ṣulḥ process, ritual, and event. It is, however, crucial to note that Smith and Lang studied only the use of ṣulḥ to resolve conflict and violence resulting from blood feuds. This limitation has implications

for some of the details in their accounts. The general principles of ṣulḥ, however, continue to be portable and common to other ṣulḥ practices.

5. As a city dweller, I did not witness ṣulḥ processes to have all these rituals. This difference may be due to regional variation and the kinds of disputes, which in my experience were less grave.

6. Smith does not explain the value of the killer taking bitter coffee at the victim's family's house. The bitter coffee is equivalent to black coffee (i.e., no sugar and no milk). Smith's informants focused on the worst-case scenario, murder, and in this context bitter coffee seems to be a trace of another ritual, which is very relevant. At Arab funerals, there is a consoling ritual in which family, friends, and neighbors visit the family of the deceased and are offered black or bitter coffee, which is symbolic of the solemn situation. It strikes me that the killer goes to the home of the victim and takes coffee, which is an act of showing sympathy; likewise, the fact that the killer is offered coffee by the victim's family is a sign that the killer's visit and condolences are respected and accepted. If not a symbolic indicator of social reconstitution within this context, then the act is certainly establishing a welcoming gesture because the moment a person enters a house, that person is a guest, which earns them the rights of being welcomed and treated honorably.

7. For a comparison of an individualistic and a relational worldview in relation to mediation practices, see Sable and Kornhauser.

8. Suasory goals correspond to predisposition variations. They range, according to Simons (23–24), from shaping or reinforcing to terminating or changing response. To terminate a response, encoders can either resort to diffusion or neutralization. To shape a response, encoders aim at the acquisition of new beliefs or attitudes, while to reinforce a particular response, encoders either work to strengthen a recipient's beliefs or to increase their resistance to change using intensification, activation, and deterrence. Finally, to change a response, encoders aim at conversion of belief, which seems to correspond to some definitions of persuasion.

9. In an expansive take on rhetoric, Burks, and later Nienkamp, revisit the work of rhetoricians who have shed light on the two meanings of dialectic. The primary meaning of dialectic refers to a heuristic exercise that relies mainly on questions and answers and encourages people to discover things for themselves (Burks 112). This exercise tends to focus on external, dialogic, inquisitive interaction. Dialectic can be interpersonal and intrapersonal, for "what is required formally for dialectic is not two actually diverse minds, but rather an actual diversity or duality, an opposition or conflict, and this may occur within the borders of a single mind. When it does, that mind is likely to carry on dialectic thinking" (Adler qtd. in Burks 112). Explicating the two different types of dialectic, Adler then emphasizes duality or diversity of positions rather than the number of involved parties as indicative of (an internal) dialectic leading to or impeding suasion and later action. However, Burks

(12) and Nienkamp note how internal dialectic or "individual deliberation" has been backgrounded. Numerous rhetoricians have paid attention to internal rhetoric (Burks; Nienkamp). Nienkamp explains how rhetoric's attention to public modes of deliberation besides the "Platonic split between speech and thought" resulted in the marginalization of internal deliberation despite its continued reference in works that date as far back as the Homeric *Iliad* (xi).

10. Here I use the word recognition in its expansive sense, which would include both recognizing the rights of the other and being answerable to affirming this right or countering its violation.

11. Krista Ratcliffe (23–25) explains Martin Heidegger's critique of divided logos by simply stating that the tendency in the Western rhetorical tradition is to accent productive skills. Heidegger, in *What Is Called Thinking?* "claims [that] we have inherited in the West, the *logos* that speaks but does not listen" (qtd. in Ratcliffe 23).

12. Ratcliffe explains: "*A rhetoric of dysfunctional silence offers interlocutors three dysfunctional rhetorical stances—denial, defensiveness and guilt/blame*" (88; italics in original). Denial is antithetical to apology and recognition, and this is unequivocal in Ratcliffe's definition of denial as a "failure to recognize obvious implications or consequences of a thought, act, or situation" (88). An apology that enables recognition, responsiveness, and accountability counters dysfunctional silence. A rhetoric of recognition based on an awareness of and the courage to admit and own up to the consequences of "a thought, act, or situation" is the logic behind ṣulḥ affording a wrongdoer the chance to recognize and be held answerable to their acts of violence.

13. Keith Gilyard uses the term positive tension to refer to tension that can be used as generative moments.

14. Money materializes the recognition of one's act of violation (a self-oriented move) and materializes recognition of grievances and hurt incurred (other-oriented move). Giving money, therefore, is part of the rhetoric of listening and accountability, namely acting on one's recognition of violation. At best, ṣulḥ settles for no less than peace and does not settle for just restitution. Hence, in ṣulḥ, the referential meaning of reconciliation equals neither apology nor restitution.

CHAPTER 3. *WE* THE RECONCILED: THE CONVERGENCE OF ṢULḤ AND HUMAN RIGHTS

1. For an introductory set of medieval and contemporary human rights instruments, see Bassiouni. My analysis makes use of the Arabic text of the CM document as published in Bassiouni (27–29). Excerpted English-language translation is from Guillaume's translation of the covenant of Medina (231–233).

2. It is worth noting here that the conceptualization of human rights in the CM varies from the conceptualization of human rights in the UDHR. The

conceptualization of rights and obligations in the CM is relationally and communally defined, and it is premised not on an attempt to just counter a violation of rights. Rather, it is premised on the collective participation of all community members in the realization of obligations to one another and to the city-state, which is consistent with individual rights.

3. There were twelve different Arab tribes; the most prominent two were al-ʻAws and al-Khazraj. The Arabs were pagan and believed in the goddess Manāt. There were ten Jewish tribes, the most prominent of which were Banū Qaynuqāʻ, Banū al-Naḍīr, and Banū Qurayẓah. It is worth noting that there is scholarly debate concerning whether the Jewish tribes were Arabs who converted to Judaism or immigrants who fled Palestine after Roman persecution (for more on this debate, please see Watt ctd. in Yildirim). Though Barakat believes there were no Christians, according to Hamidullah, Christians made up 1 to 4 percent of the total population, whereas the Jewish tribes made up almost 50 percent.

4. The people of Mecca feared the alliance mainly for political and commercial reasons. Yathrib was different from Mecca: it was a fertile land with agricultural trade. Yathrib also had arms trade, an industry quarter, and gold markets (Barakat 25–36). Mecca, whose wealth mainly came from trade, depended on good relations with neighbors like Yathrib. However, Mecca's leaders also wanted dominance. Indeed, Mecca's leaders were threatened by Muḥammad's migration to Yathrib and the anticipated increase in his power, especially since many traders who migrated with Muḥammad took their wealth with them, which shifted the monetary and commercial dynamics. It was this shift that incited Muḥammad's failed assassination.

5. Soon after Muḥammad's emigration, Yathrib was referred to as the Madīnatu al-Nabī (literally the "city of the prophet"), to be later called Medina, as it continues to be referred to.

6. The role played by *shūrá* (dialogue and discussion) in the formulation of the charter is discussed in detail in Bulaç.

7. This was a name given to him by Meccans.

8. I use here the term *rhetorical leadership*, appropriating the commonly used *rhetorical presidency*. The term is used here to invoke rhetoric's potential for (re) defining political and social reality. However, because of Muḥammad's multidimensional role in his community, and because of the rise of Medina as a city-state, *presidency* is not an appropriate term, so I'll use *rhetorical leadership* to refer to the consistent use of the power of discourse to mediate and redefine *in actu* the sociopolitical reality of Medina. For more on the rhetorical presidency and presidential rhetoric, please see Zarefsky's "Presidential Rhetoric and the Power of Definition."

9. The process of fractionation, which was identified by Follett in 1942 and later

named by Fisher in 1971, fits the conflict resolution measure that the CM neatly captures. The CM in its current form clearly isolates contentious issues and the parties involved and seeks to efficaciously address them. Rhetoricians may conceive of fractionation as an interventive discourse that isolates in a systematic way contentious issues. As noted earlier, bloodwite was a source of conflict in Medina; it was isolated from other problems and addressed.

10. For more on this, see Serjeant's explanation of Document C.

11. For more on the rights of refugees and their responsibilities, and documents relating to early Islam, see the special issue of *Refugee Survey Quarterly* dedicated to refugee rights and Islam (Türk, Supramaniam, and Liew).

12. In conflict resolution scholarship, there are four different types of goals: process, content, relational, and interaction goals (Hocker and Wilmot).

13. Because this book focuses on ṣulḥ, this chapter's exploration of rights is limited. Ṣulḥ manifests itself in the form of written, legally binding contracts and unilateral pledges or constitutions affirming the rights of citizens (like political and religious rights) while also asserting citizens' obligations (mainly perfect obligations) to one another and to the community. However, documents in the Arab-Islamic tradition that affirm rights are not the exclusive domain of ṣulḥ agreements, for such documents extend to religious and religiopolitical rhetoric, among other genres. For example, two of the most prominent orations on human rights are Prophet Muḥammad's last speech (10 AH/630 CE), known as *khuṭbat al-wadāʿ* (farewell speech) and Abū Bakr's address to Muslims (11AH/631 CE). In the former, the equality of all Muslims and all peoples as well as the rights of women are affirmed. In the latter, Abū Bakr addresses the political rights of the people (holding their leadership accountable) and the equality of all before the law. He also commits himself to a moral leadership consistent with the tenets of Islam (for more on human rights instruments in early Islam, please see Bassiouni). I define religiopolitical rhetoric here drawing on the work of Tahera Qutbuddin, who includes doctrinally driven, pious counsel under religious discourse and ritual as well as legislative discourses under the category religiopolitical oratory (Qutbuddin).

14. For a detailed account of human, civic, and political rights, as well as the rights of people at war, see Mawdūdīy.

15. The charter strikes a surprising balance between representing the Jewish community as a group and recognizing intragroup differences.

16. It is worth noting here that establishing close relations with other Jewish communities that did not reside in Medina was beyond the CM at the time. An alliance with other religious communities in the region was crucial as a way to counter religious persecution, but at the time expansive unity beyond the territory of Medina was difficult, hence the focus on Medina. For more on this, see Rubin. Arjomond's analysis rereads the CM and makes the claim that the last part of the text

was actually a pact with other Jewish communities and was attached to the original pact with the Jewish groups at a later date which Barakat estimates to be 650.

17. Rights in Islam are not conceptualized as separate from obligations. This view of rights is mainly due to the relational logic of ṣulḥ as an indigenous mode of conciliation as well as a relational worldview. Individual and communal rights overlap, so in this section of the CM, affirmations of religious rights sometimes are manifest textually as statements of obligation, which is also consistent with the contractual language of the charter. This approach can be succinctly explained: "The Medina charter represents an example of fractionation [a strategy of conflict resolution that seeks to separate issues to resolve them] that maintains a distinctly Islamic cultural understanding of conflict. The charter does not address individuals; rather it addresses communities and tribes, calling not for individual reparations or settlements, but for the creation of a new community" (Yildirim, "The Medina," 444).

18. The following verse from the Holy Qur'ān elucidates this use of nafs: "Whosoever kills a soul (without any reason like) manslaughter, or corruption on earth, it is as though he had killed all mankind; and whoever keeps it alive, it is as though he kept alive all mankind" (5:32).

19. This article might be misread as being antithetical to religious freedom. However, in its sociopolitical context, the second half of the article as quoted is read in relation to Abrahamic faith traditions, which implies inclusion of Judaism and Christianity. In addition, in the original Arabic text of the CM, Allāh is just the Arabic word for God.

20. It is important to note here that the moral sanction is listed in the CM before the sociopolitical sanction. In the second part of the CM, we find statements that invoke a moral code and a political imperative. To illustrate, the moral code and political imperative are clear in article 37, where loyalty is referred to as the condition (perfect duty) for the stability of the community. This emphasis on the importance of loyalty is coupled with a positive sanction declaring "Yathrib shall be a sanctuary for the people of this document" (CM 39). Together, the moral code, political imperative, and reward (loyalty and a safe haven), the negative sanction (treachery and its negative consequences), in addition to terms of actualization and agency resources, provide the unified citizenry with a morally grounded, relationally rich, hospitable universe where their recognized rights and aspirations for a safe city-state can be realized.

21. In its historical context, the term *believers* as used in the CM refers to those who embraced Islam. It is used neither to positively evaluate nor to privilege a sect. Rather, it is used instrumentally to unite the emigrants in a communal life based on equal and reciprocal rights and obligations.

CHAPTER 4. FROM THE EGYPTIAN PEOPLE'S ASSEMBLY TO THE ISRAELI KNESSET: AL-SĀDĀT'S KNESSET ADDRESS, ṢULḤ, AND DIPLOMACY

1. Symbolic and procedural reconciliation can be seen as two different and alternative routes. This is what happened in Australia (Altman and Hunter). However, scholars critical of procedural reconciliation in Australia and others believe that symbolic and procedural forms of transformation are complementary.

2. I used the Arabic version of the Knesset address as published in al-Sādāt's *Al-Baḥth 'an al-Dhāt* and used the English translation published in the *New York Times*. I revised excerpts from the KA in brackets to correct translation mistakes and to add important features of the Arabic text.

3. There are many structural and discursive affinities between problem-solution and question-answer structures. Both are recursive structures: a negative evaluation of either the solution or the answer sends interlocutors back to the moment of initiation, that is, stating a problem or posing a question (Hoey 194–95). The basic structure of both models comprises categories like situation, problem/question, answer/solution, and evaluation (Hoey and Winter 130). Besides being organizational strategies, these macrostructures signal an encoder's perspective or frame, which, if negatively evaluated, can necessitate the use of other (recursive) rhetorical models.

4. Bassiouni includes ten prominent Islamic instruments that regulate relations: some affirm positive peace while others respond to the mandates of negative peace, that is, addressing grievances and regulating life in a way that prevents cycles of violence from re-erupting. The ten documents cover a vast territory, take different forms, and are named differently, but all comprise measures establishing and promoting peace. Unfortunately, to date there is no study explicating these instruments from the perspective of genre, discourse, or rhetoric. However, these documents have numerous conspicuous features. Textually, they are sociopolitical contracts. Similarly, they recognize and exchange responsibilities and affirm rights. Discursively, they vary a great deal, reflecting different contextual exigencies and acknowledging different power dynamics; that is documents pertaining to positive peace tend to be hortatory, underlining rights that should be affirmed. For example, Abū Bakr's inaugural sermon details the responsibilities of a political leader and a public (Bassiouni 34); his statement functions like a list of guarantees and commitments whereby he binds himself to serve the people well and honorably, abiding by the regulations of Islam. As to negative peace, 'Umar's agreement with the people of Jerusalem (37), also referred to as *Ṣulḥ al-Quds* (the peace pact of Jerusalem), exemplifies a different kind of document: using a pact form, 'Umar guarantees the religious freedoms (comprising both belief and practice) of the people of Jerusalem. Their reciprocal responsibility is to pay taxes (*jizyah*) like other places under

Islamic rule did at the time. This treaty exchanges responsibilities but emphasizes guarantees for religious freedom because assimilation to the dominant religion was a common practice by political entities in power. In contrast to this treaty, which can be considered a unilateral guarantee (encoded in one of its popular titles, 'Umar's Commitment or *al-'ahdah al-'umarīyah*), there is another treaty that documents bilateral guarantees. This is Ṣulḥ al-Ḥudaybīyah, or the Ḥudaybīyah treaty, between Prophet Muḥammad and the people of Quraysh. Both parties agreed on a ten-year truce, mutually guaranteeing safety to pilgrims and travelers and freedom of belief and membership, among other guarantees (30).

5. Drawing on Aristotle and John Dewey's reflections on the relation between time and deliberation, Hart and Dillard note that deliberations, peacemaking ones included, are haunted by internecine or immutable desires, fears, and experiences. They explain how deliberation is "haunted by the past, or more appropriately, by people's unique personal histories and preexisting allegiances . . . ; haunted yet again by the future, by calculations of the probable and the improbable. . . . ; haunted by the present. Because the past speaks with so many voices and because the future speaks not at all, deliberative bodies are constantly caught in the turmoil of what to do" (211).

6. al-Sādāt criticized the format of the Geneva Convention as comprising un(der)actualized "battery of public speeches" and as conducive to dysfunctional stances and discourses (al-Sādāt, "Speech to the EPA"). His assessment can be understood in light of the first Geneva Convention held in response to SCR 338, which "consisted chiefly of 'a battery of public speeches' rather than serious secret negotiation" (Berridge 37). The resolution asked for a ceasefire and the initiation of negotiations. Arabs, Israelis with the United States, and the Soviet Union convened in December of 1973 under the auspices of the UN. Four years later, after lengthy preparation for the second convention, there were neither signs of progress nor a peacemaking framework. On the contrary, there were still significant signs, including war threats, of a stalemate.

7. The political rhetoric of crises—whether rhetoric is used to create or respond to a crisis—attracted scholarly attention. For more on this, see Kiew, Kuypers, and Dow.

8. A copy of the hand-written letter is produced in Quandt. Carter also reproduces the letter in his memoir.

9. He doesn't recognize this peace ritual, however, as informed by and evoking a cultural resource.

10. al-Sādāt clearly names this as the second "psychological barrier" (the first being psychological warfare), explaining that "this wall constitutes a psychological barrier between us, a barrier of suspicion, a barrier of rejection, a barrier of fear,

of deception, a barrier of hallucination without any action, deed or decision" (KA 17).

11. Aristotle explains that the theme of epideictic rhetoric is blame and praise. This entails an interest in the noble and virtuous. Similarly, Arnhart centers the epideictic on two dichotomies, namely noble/ignoble and virtue/vice (77). In relation to the yearning for peace, this theme transcends the limits of time and place.

12. Malmkjær (491) explains, "S[peaker] intends that the utterance of U make her/him responsible for doing A [whatever is being proposed]" as well as "S[peaker] intends that the utterance of U will place her/him under an obligation to do A." Commissives might also include declarations, assertions, and espousals (Malmkjær 490).

13. Despite reductive perception of the complexities of ṣulḥ, the crucial role of commissives in ṣulḥ and their relevance in situations of contested histories and double victimization, commissive speech acts have yet to attract the attention of rhetoricians interested in reconciliation and peacemaking.

14. In his article "Ten Imperatives for Peace," John Richardson lists ten proactive strategies "not only [for] conflict prevention, but also [for] conflict stabilization." His second imperative, which addresses "polarizing political rhetoric," clearly underlines the significance and consequence of membership categories in creating (or foiling the potential of) peacemaking encounters: "Polarizing political rhetoric and tactics must be foregone, however tempting their short-term benefits may seem" (15). Here he identifies "polarizing political rhetoric" as one of the roots of conflict. This mandates closer attention to categorization of membership for it is one of the crucial features of polarizing rhetoric, and peacemaking efforts can be facilitated by efficacious recategorization of membership.

15. These Biblical references are not represented in the *New York Times* translation.

16. Structurally, the question-answer is more conspicuous than the problem-solution structure. The question-answer organizational structure signals the deep semantic relations between clusters of information that underscore problems that must be addressed to establish peace. As al-Sādāt responds to the questions, he nests problem-solution structures, which acknowledge the peacemaking demands from the perspective of Arabs and Israelis.

17. Though this might be read as repetitive, it is crucial to his goals, namely to involve all stakeholders and ward off fears of double-crossing his compatriots and Arabs. This is why all stakeholders, as judges, are solicited to seize this kairotic moment, co-construct peace together: the Israeli people and the entire world are asked to listen, reciprocate, and materialize the potential of this historical moment

(KA 17). This collective summoning is consistent with peacemaking in general but especially with the prenegotiation mandate: "The mere agreement to deliberate on important matters can signal that longstanding rivals have chosen to submit themselves to the vagaries of human interaction" (Hart and Dillard 211). al-Sādāt knew this too well, considering the aforementioned history of failed negotiations and initiatives; agreeing to deliberate is an essential prelude to negotiation. This is why he frames this moment as history rewriting, advocating peace as a common goal. Indeed, "as prominent negotiation theorists emphasize, successful negotiations change perceptions of conflict from a zero-sum to a win-win situation" (Krepon and Drezin 159). Simultaneously, al-Sādāt's public declarations, committing to and building confidence in the peace process, balance domestic and foreign needs (Krepon and Drezin). To balance these needs and to affirm that deliberations can lead to a win-win situation, al-Sādāt introduces his answer by uncovering facts/ conditions concerning peace.

18. Despite its failure in productively intervening to solve the Palestinian question, end settlements, and impede seizing lands of others, al-Sādāt chooses to underline the positive potential of the UN and affirms that his answer to the central question and his calls for peace are congruous with the UN resolutions, which are a "cogent expression of the international community's will." This is why they are adopted by weak and strong publics around the world.

19. Earlier in the chapter the role rhetorical listening plays in recognizing Israeli is presented as an efficacious, reconciliatory rhetorical move. Rhetorical listening functions in a similar way in this excerpt, but with a change in directionality. In situations of contested and/or multiple grievances, accommodation/reparative articulations must balance the needs of all stakeholders. Similarly, al-Sādāt's address to the Knesset—as a public declaration—must attend to both domestic and foreign audiences, Arabs and Israelis, self and other. It is important to note that while uncovering conflict-enticing acts, his statement of grievance does not initiate blame discourse for a number of reasons. The projected locutions are neither represented verbatim nor indirectly as "you said/claimed that." Instead, projections of locutions are filtered through the speaker's perspective, who offers condensed forms of speech signaled by nominalized verbs of locution and locution verbs, as in "intimidation" (*takhwīf*), "alleged" (*tarwīj*), "forecast" (*qāla*), and "threatened" (*wa haddada*). This type of minimalist representation is actually more backgrounded and distanced than indirect speech (Short 293–98), hence short-circuiting blame-guilt discourse.

20. Containing accusation discourse helps promote peacemaking, but this is not the only textual feature that underlines how peace is negotiated, for the positioning of grievances and calls for reciprocity are significant. The positioning of the psychological warfare statements as a grievance ascertains this interpretation: they are

sandwiched between two sections. The first is devoted to Israel's recognition as a decision and a political reality. The second is devoted to the psychological barrier (a barrier of suspicion, fear, distrust, animosity, deception, etc.), which implies a list of category-bound acts consistent with Arabs and Israelis as partners. Its location, therefore, (i.e., following the accommodation of Israel's calls for recognition) renders it a call for reciprocity.

21. The *New York Times* mistranslates this part of al-Sādāt's speech. al-Sādāt in the Arabic text states that the durable and just peace depends on establishing a Palestinian State (*an taqūm dulatuhum*).

22. Scholars of international politics explain the reward of abiding by international law that regulates relations between states. For example, Berridge explains that "among other reasons, . . . natural inhibitions to law-breaking exist in the relations between states that do not obtain in the relations between individuals, and because a reputation for failing to keep agreements will make it extremely difficult to promote policy by means of negotiation in the future" (73–74). However, there are conspicuous power asymmetries that increase the impunity of some key international players and undermine the right to just reward and punishment for all those who do not abide by international law or internationally recognized bodies for intervention.

CHAPTER 5. TO GATHER AT COURT: ṢULḤ AS RHETORICAL METHOD

1. Point twelve states that "the Turkish portion of the present Ottoman Empire should be assured a secure sovereignty, but the other nationalities which are now under Turkish rule should be assured an undoubted security of life and an absolutely unmolested opportunity of autonomous development, and the Dardanelles should be permanently opened as a free passage to the ships and commerce of all nations under international guarantees." The speech is available at to http://avalon.law.yale.edu/20th_century/wilson14.asp.

2. For more on the Peasants' Revolt, see Goldberg.

3. There are varied estimates of the conscripted soldiers. According to one, there were 327,000 conscripts (Killingray 485).

4. The revolt ended tragically. Goldberg documents this event, explaining that "when the revolt began, rail and communication lines were cut by peasants, and Cairo was isolated from the countryside for weeks. The revolt was only put down when tens of thousands of British troops were sent into the country and, aided by aircraft, restored by force the control of the central government on an essentially unarmed population" (261).

5. Though in this section, I focus on the aftermath of World War I. Abū al-'Azā'im witnessed many moments of transformation worldwide. In his biography of Abū al-'Azā'im, Shuqruf explains how Abū al-'Azā'im's critique of national

and international plights and woes was informed by a series of events. As he grew up, Egypt was under British occupation, and between the late 1890s and 1919, the country witnessed two major revolutions, namely the revolution of 'Uraby, the 1919 revolution, and numerous crucial events related to the failure of the former and the success of the latter. In addition, there was a 1906 peasants' revolt in Egypt caused by the injustices of "harsh exemplary punishment" enforced by the British occupation's military forces and targeting Egyptian peasants (commonly known as the Denshawai Incident), which galvanized national sentiment against the injustices of occupation. There was also the Mahdi Revolution in Sudan (1899), another in Somalia (1892), the Unionists in Turkey (1907), and the Indian Revolution (1908) against British colonialism. In his biographic account, Shuqruf emphasizes Abū al-'Azā'im's revolutionary work against the injustices of occupation in the Arab world and in other places, his investment in the pursuit of justice, and his recognition of the long-term ramifications of injustice.

6. For more, see Keegan's *The First World War.*

7. Citing Article 227 of the Treaty of Versailles, Lu underlines the mismatch between the treaty's goal to punish and what actually happened. Kaiser Wilhelm II (1859–1941) was the last German emperor and king of Prussia (Mommson). Though there was a lot of debate about how to punish the Kaiser, eventually "the Big Four did override the dissenting American and Japanese reservations attached to the Final Report of the Commission on Responsibility of the Authors of the War, indicting the Kaiser in early April 1919 for the "'violation of international morality'" and the "'violation of the sanctity of treaties'" (Treaty of Versailles qtd. in Kampmark 535). This punishment was in response to the world's recognition of the Kaiser's responsibility, whether as a culprit or an instigator, for bellicose foreign policies and for bringing about the Great War. However, the Kaiser, who went into exile in the Netherlands, "lived out his life in Holland without ever facing prosecution. The vast majority of those German soldiers charged with war crimes escaped a guilty verdict or were allowed to escape from prison" (Robertson ctd. in Lu 13).

8. This declaration of intention situates the play in relation to Islamic literature and art (though the text is categorized by the author as a "dialogue," it is typically cited as a prominent example of Islamic theater) and related to the national and international scenes after World War I, which underscore the interventionist goal of the dialogue. Moreover, the dialogue taps into a cross-cultural investment in what it means to be human and how to manage different aspects of the self. These are important questions to Islamic philosophy as manifest in, for example, al-Kindī's translation of Aristotle's *Book of the Soul.* Though cross-cultural, philosophical reflection is informative, it is beyond the scope of this chapter. For more on Arab-Islamic philosophical responses to these enduring questions, see Baddar ("From Athens"), Fākhūrīy and Jurr, Jolivet, and Leaman.

9. The context of deterioration or degeneracy seems to be a cross-cultural exigence for reconciliation. Doxtader, in "Reconciliation—A Rhetorical Concept/ion" writes about the desire to "[indemnify] the city."

10. All translations of the dialogue are mine. To the best of my knowledge, there is no translation of the dialogue to English. I chose to translate the word *yabtalīh* as experience. It is possible of course to read the sentence as a reference to *ibtilā'* (test). In both cases, however, *experience* (or *test*) only makes sense when we consider its location in relation to a moral view of the world that underscores moral choice and its consequences.

11. This is potentially a reference to heaven, which would match the previous reference to moral choice in *yabtalīh* and duty to recognize Allāh.

12. Al-Khayāl details these choices, listing for example acts like letting oneself fall prey to imagining the aggression or malice (*'adāwāt*) of those who deserve to be loved and honored like parents and children.

13. In the dialogue, Al-'aql seeks the intervention of Allāh and those who are experts in conflict resolution (*walī al-'amr*).

14. Ḥasan Jad Ḥasan, a professor of Arabic literature, in his introduction to GCS, describes Insān or Human Being using the same terms.

15. The reference to this character is worth noting. When justice is introduced with the definite article *al-* in Arabic, the reference is usually to Allāh, using one of his attributes, namely the Most Just or the Utterly Just. In the dialogue, it references the character that will take the role of the judge or adjudicator.

16. Maley explains that adjudicators and mediators are constrained by a number of sociolegal norms, which direct their discursive contributions. Typically, adjudicators and mediators impact, albeit differently, the legal process, the substance or content of discussion, and the outcome, hence the terms *control of process*, *control of substance*, and *control of outcome*, respectively (96).

17. Maley explains that the discursive practices of mediators and adjudicators are better thought of as a complex range of activities. The former tends to rely more on facilitation and the latter more on authoritative intervention. "It is the degree of authoritative intervention and the variety and range of intervention that distinguishes judicial from mediatory discourse" (108).

18. Yang explains this distinction as follows: "There is . . . an important distinction between actions as instrumental means and actions as constitutive means. . . . If an action is moved by an intrinsic motive, the action is constitutive of the end and good in itself, subjectively or objectively. If an action is moved by a nonintrinsic motive, the action is an instrumental means to the end it realizes and is good (subjectively or objectively) because of its relation to some further ends" (118–19).

19. Though theories of power identify different dimensions of power (Jasinski "Power"; Thye), they also underscore common features: power is recognized as

a relational phenomenon (Thye). Communicative events manifest a modality of *power use/exercise*. Power is not in the air. Rather, it is a dimension of the relation between interlocutors—in both the personal and political domains. Because of this realization, "theories of power take as their focus the relationship between two or more actors, and not the characteristics of actors themselves" (Thye). Recognizing power as a relational phenomenon (Burbules; Foucault; Thye), scholarship on power distinguishes between its different types and underlines its multidimensionality. To illustrate, the literature distinguishes between power-over (domination-submission), power *with* (collaboration, unity, solidarity), and power *to* and *through* (facilitative power). Often reconfigured in the moment and the ever-present history of relations between peoples, power is manifest in and is informed by different communicative practices. It is hard to overestimate the discursive nature of power-over and how it results in and sustains suppression of the value of an entity, which eventually results in its oppression.

20. GCS abounds with philosophical references, including ontological ones concerning the distinction between and interdependence of essence and instantiation. This argument between al-'Aql (Reason) and hwá (desires) illustrates the dramatization of philosophical questions and evokes a history of philosophic debates. For more on Islamic philosophy, see Leaman, especially chapters 2 and 5, which are devoted to major controversies and ontological questions, respectively.

21. This is an exaggerated articulation of power-over in which complete control happens by extermination.

22. Smeed and colleagues distinguish among three manifestations of power in organizations: elitism, corporatism, and populism. The elitists are relevant here. Smeed et al. explain that "for elitists . . . there are two groups in society—the rulers and the ruled. . . . Elitists consider the rulers to be naturally superior to the ruled" (29).

23. Self-concept and self-concept needs are very complex. A negative self-concept (e.g., I am bad at math) is very often naturalized and seen as part of the nature of things (e.g., women tend to be bad at math), a phenomenon psychologists name system justification theory, which explains and justifies how things "are" even if this works against the good of an individual or a community. Because there is a need to find a "meaningful frame of reference," as Burkley and Blanton explain (290), "this need for system justification is sufficiently strong that at times it will override the individual's need for positive self and group evaluations" (291). I do not distinguish between different types of negative self-concept; for a detailed explanation of chronic and functional self-concepts, please see Burkley and Blanton.

24. The reference is to deceiving women in particular.

25. The first question echoes Robert Bush and Joseph Folger's foundational philosophical question that helps us transform adversarial relations into amicable

ones (Bush and Folger qtd. in Kuttner, "From Adversity" 931). The pursuit of being *insān* (human) in the Arab-Islamic tradition is explored by Imtiyaz while investigating how Islam and Buddhism responded to dilemmas faced by humans by charting a way, namely *Wasaṭīyah* in Islam and The Middle Way in Buddhism.

26. For more on the differences among organic, individualistic, and relational worldviews, see Kuttner ("From Adversity") and Bush and Folger.

27. However, this state of recognition of the other depends on an emergent understanding, which is the reason for what seems to be extended discussions of the nature of the self as well as the value and the assumed lack of value of some of the selves in the dialogue. There are lengthy discussions about the nature of different aspects of the self and the different branches of knowledge that shed light on different aspects of the self. These discussions seem to complicate conflict resolution, but actually they work to provide the grounds for a different understanding of the conflict and conflict resolution between the contentious factions of the self.

28. The expression ummah wasaṭah comes from *The Qur'ān* (al-Baqarah: 143). The translations of the term used here are Yusuf's.

29. I reference wasaṭīyah here as a response to assumed conflict between different facets of the self. Yusuf (385–87) and Ushama explain, while drawing on Quranic verses, Ḥadīth, and well-known exegetes (Ushama 186–95) the different facets of realizing the virtue of wasaṭīyah. For example, the call for moderation and a middle way also applies to intra- and interreligious relations, where Muslims are enjoined to deal with members of (different) religious groups with *birr*, or respectfully and amicably. In addition, moderation implies resisting the urge for power-over. Instead, Muslims are called to "adhere to fairness and equity" (Yusuf 386) in all their dealings, be this in relation to business, social, or familial relations. Furthermore, the reference to ummah wasaṭah—a Quranic reference—evokes rightly for a Western reader the golden mean, but the golden mean here references both a preferable or desirable stance as well as an obligation that realizes both *ḥuqūq* Allāh and *ḥuqūq al-'ibād* ("the rights of Allāh" and "the rights of people"). Like Mawdūdiīy, Daryabadi (both are well-known Qur'ānic exegetes) explains that "*Ummatan wasatan* are people who have hit the golden mean: not inclined to either extreme; well poised in every virtue: A nation conforming, or conformable, to the just mean; just; equitable" (Daryabadi qtd. in Ushama 187).

30. Jihād means "strife." The bigger jihād is strife against one's own excesses or dysfunctional thought, feelings, and actions.

31. According to Muḥammad al-Qathanīy's new edition of the epistolary text, it was written in 735 (Ḥijrīy Year), and the new edition accounts for 150 lines missing from previous editions. For more, please see al-Qathanīy's edition of the text (37–77).

32. Ibn Taymīyah epistle addresses different types of diseases of the selves that

relate to a person's relation to other people and to Allāh, an approach that makes cross-cultural interest in the purification of the self grounded in Arab-Islamic culture. For example, he refers to *shirk* (idolatry), which violates the principle of *tawḥīd* (monotheism). In this expanded approach, he lists a variety of practices that guide the pursuit of tazkīyah. These include repentance (48), *tawḥīd* (49), *ikhlāṣ* or "sincere, pure intentions" (49–50), generosity, *jihād al-nafs*, or "strife against unbridled desires of the self" (54), patience with the self in one's pursuit of tazkīyah (54), and responsiveness to grievances (62).

33. Shuqruf, one of Abū al-'Azā'im's biographers, refers to numerous publications on the issue of *al-insān al-kāmil*, or "the perfect human." Noteworthy, the Arabic word *insān* is gender neutral. However, often scholars addressing the concept of *insān al-kāmil*, which is a key concept in mysticism, translate it as "the perfect man." To avoid assuming a gender bias in the language used by mystics, (hu) man will be consistently used. The yearning for this state of excellence is indeed cross-cultural and, as Shuqruf rightly notes, it is conspicuous in ancient Egyptian wisdom literature, Buddhist thought, and ancient Greek and Roman writings (e.g., *orator perfectus*). Many scholars of Islamic philosophy—in the early and contemporary history of Islamic philosophy—sought to address this state of excellence in relation to Islam's doctrine. For more, see Shuqruf (135–39).

34. The role of the perfect (hu)man is more complex. However, different dimensions of the potential of the perfect human exceed the focus of this chapter on reconciliation. For example, in Islamic mystic thought, the perfect (hu)man models and catalyzes excellence for others: "His task is to help others to span the gap that exists between this world and the next, the world of reality; and as one might expect, the perfect man is often identified with the prophet, who has precisely this role" (Leaman 80).

35. Because, Abū al-'Azā'im was a mystic, the state of excellence as described here is just a phase in a multiphased mystic journey, which enables a human to know Allāh, not just about Allāh.

36. Excess here would include both laxity in the pursuit of justice and excessiveness in terms of undermining or usurping rights. These manifestations of excess are observable in personal, national, and international domains.

WORKS CITED

'Abd al-Salām, Ja'far. *Mu'āhadat al-Salām al-Miṣrīyah al-Isrā'īlīyah: Dirāsah Ta'ṣīlīyah wa-Taḥlīlīyah 'alá Ḍaw' Aḥkām al-Qānūn al-Duwalī* [Egypt-Israel Peace Accords: A Foundational and Analytical Study based on International Law]. al-Qāhirah: Dār Nahḍat Miṣr, 1980. Print.

Abdul-Raof, Hussein. *Arabic Rhetoric*. Hoboken: Taylor & Francis, 2006. Print.

Abū al-'Azā'im, Muḥammad Māḍī. *Maḥkamāt al-Ṣulḥ al-Kubrá* [*The Great Court of Ṣulḥ*]. Cairo: Dār al-Sha'b, n.d. Print.

Abū al-'Azā'im, Muḥammad Māḍī. "Muqaddimah" [Introduction]. *Maḥkamāt al-Ṣulḥ al-Kubrá* [*The Great Court of Ṣulḥ*]. Cairo: Dār al-Sha'b, n.d. 9–11. Print.

Abū al-'Azā'im, Jamāl Māḍī. "Tamhīd." [Foreword]. *Maḥkamāt al-Ṣulḥ al-Kubrá* [*The Great Court of Ṣulḥ*]. By Muḥammad Māḍī Abū al-'Azā'im. Cairo: Dār al-Sha'b, n.d. 3–4. Print.

Abu-Nimer, Mohammed. "A Framework for Nonviolence and Peacebuilding in Islam." *Journal of Law and Religion* 15.1/2 (2000): 217–65. Print.

Abu-Nimer, Mohammed. *Nonviolence and Peace Building in Islam: Theory and Practice*. Gainesville: UP of Florida, 2003. Print.

Agnew, Lois, Laurie Gries, and Zosha Stuckey. Introduction. "Octalog III: The Politics of Historiography in 2010." *Rhetoric Review* 30.2 (2011): 109–10. Print.

Agnew, Lois, et al. "Octalog III: The Politics of Historiography in 2010." *Rhetoric Review* 30.2 (2011): 109–34. Print.

Al-Bukhārīy, Muḥammad. "Book XLIX: Ṣulḥ Peacemaking." Trans. M. M. Khan *Ṣaḥīḥ al-Bukhārīy*. Lahore, Pakistan: Kazi Publications, 1983. Print.

Al-Sādāt, Muḥammad Anwar. *Al-Baḥth 'an al-Dhāt* [*In Search of Identity*]. Cairo: al-Maktab al-Miṣrīy al-Ḥadīth, 1978. Print.

Al-Sādāt, Muḥammad Anwar. *In Search of Identity: An Autobiography.* New York: Harper & Row, 1978. Print.

Al-Sādāt, Muḥammad Anwar. "Interview with President Sadat on Canadian Television." Anwar Sadat Chair for Peace and Development, Department of Government and Politics. *Anwar Sadat Archives.* Presidential Remarks to the Press. Web. 2 Oct. 2006. http://sadat.umd.edu/archives/remarks/AAEV%20Canadian%20TV11.16.77pdf.PDF.

Al-Sādāt, Muḥammad Anwar. "Speech to the Egyptian People's Assembly" (Arabic). *Al-Ahram Newspaper* 9 Nov 1977. al-Ahram Archive. 2002. Print.

Al-Sādāt, Muḥammad Anwar. "Speech to the Inaugural Session of the Egyptian People's Assembly." Anwar Sadat Chair for Peace and Development. *Anwar Sadat Archives.* Presidential Speeches. Web. 2 Oct. 2006. http://sadat.umd.edu/archives/speeches/AAES%20Speech%20to%20Assembly%2011.26.77pdf.

Al-Sādāt, Muḥammad Anwar. "Speech to the Knesset" (Arabic). *Al-Baḥth 'an al-Dhāt* [*In Search of Identity*]. 1979. Cairo: al-Maktab al-Miṣrīy al-Ḥadīth.

Al-Sādāt, Muḥammad Anwar. "Transcripts of Sadat and Begin Addresses." *New York Times.* New York Times Article Archive 1851–1980. 21 Nov 1977. *ProQuest.* Web. 2 Mar. 2015.

Altman, Jon, and Boyd Hunter. "Monitoring 'Practical' Reconciliation: Evidence from the Reconciliation Decade, 1991–2001." Australian National University, Center for Aboriginal Economic Policy Research (Paper No. 254). Camberra, Boyol, 2003. Web. 20 Feb. 2009.

Aristotle. *On Rhetoric: A Theory of Civic Discourse.* Trans. George Kennedy. New York: Oxford UP, 1992. Print.

Arjomand, Said Amir. "The Constitution of Medina: A Sociolegal Interpretation of Muhammad's Acts of Foundation of the Umma." *International Journal of Middle East Studies* 41.04 (2009): 555–75. Print.

Arnhart, Larry. *Aristotle on Political Reasoning: A Comment on the "Rhetoric."* DeKalb: Northern Illinois UP, 1981. Print.

Assefa, Hizkias. *The Meaning of Reconciliation. European Platform for Conflict Prevention and Transformation.* 1999. Web. 30 September, 2006. http://www.gppac.net/documents/pbp/part1/2_reconc.htm.

Assefa, Hizkias. "Reconciliation." *Peacebuilding: A Field Guide.* Ed. Luc Reychler and Thania Paffenholz. Boulder, CO: Lynne Reiner, 2001. 336–342. Print.

Atwater, Deborah F. *African American Women's Rhetoric: The Search for Dignity, Personhood, and Honor.* Lanham, MD: Lexington Books, 2009. Print.

Austin, John. *How to Do Things with Words.* Oxford: Oxford UP, 1962. Print.

Ayoub, Victor. "Conflict Resolution and Social Reorganization in a Lebanese Village." *Human Organization* 24.1 (1965): 11–17. Print.

Baca, Damián, and Victor Villanueva. *Rhetorics of the Americas: 3114 BCE to 2012 CE.* New York: Palgrave Macmillan, 2009. Print.

Baddar, Maha. "The Arabs Did Not 'Just' Translate Aristotle: Al-Farabi's Logico-Rhetorical Theory." *The Responsibilities of Rhetoric.* Ed. M. Smith and B. Warnick. Long Grove, Ill: Waveland P, 2010. 230–42. Print.

Baddar, Maha. "From Athens (Via Alexandria) to Baghdad: Hybridity as Epistemology in the Work of Al-Kindi, Al-Farabi, and in the Rhetorical Legacy of the Medieval Arabic Translation Movement." ProQuest. 2010. Web. 30 March 2013.

Ballif, Michelle, ed. *Theorizing Histories of Rhetoric.* Carbondale: Southern Illinois UP, 2013. Print.

Barakat, Ahmed. *Muhammed and the Jews: A Re-examination.* New Delhi: Vikas Publishing House, 1979. Print.

Bar-Joseph, Uri. "Last Chance to Avoid War: Sadat's Peace Initiative of February 1973 and Its Failure. *Journal of Contemporary History* 41.3 (2006): 545–56. Print.

Barnes, Catherine, ed. *Owning the Process: Public Participation in Peacemaking. Accord: An International Review of Peace Initiatives* 13 (2002). 1–99. Print.

Bassiouney, Reem. *Arabic Sociolinguistics: Topics in Diglossia, Gender, Identity, and Politics.* Washington, DC: Georgetown UP, 2009. Print.

Bassiouni, Cherif, ed. "Al-Wathā'iq al-Islāmīyah [Islamic Instruments (Arabic)]." *Al-Wathā'iq al-Dawlīyah al-Ma'nīyah bi-Ḥuqūq al-Insān [International Instruments on Human Rights*]. Ed. Cherif Bassiouni. Vol. 2. Cairo: Dār al-Shurūq, 2006. 23–44. Print.

Beer, Francis. *Meanings of War and Peace.* College Station: Texas A&M UP, 2001. Print.

Begin, Menachem. "*Prime Minister Begin's Speech to the Egyptian Public.*" Anwar Sadat Chair for Peace and Development. *Anwar Sadat Archives.* Presidential Speeches. Web. 2 Oct. 2006. http://sadat.umd.edu/archives/speeches%5CAADJ%20Begin%20Speech%20to%20Knesset%2011.20.77.pdf.

Beitler, James Edward. *Remaking Transitional Justice in the United States: The Rhetorical Authorization of the Greensboro Truth and Reconciliation Commission.* New York: Springer, 2013. Print.

Ben-Ami, Shlomo. *Scars of War, Wounds of Peace: The Israeli-Arab Tragedy.* Oxford: Oxford UP, 2006. Print.

Berridge, Geoff R. *Diplomacy: Theory and Practice.* 3rd ed. New York: Palgrave Macmillan, 2005. Print.

Berridge, Geoff R., and Alan James. "Diplomatic Solution." *A Dictionary of Diplomacy.* 2nd ed. Basingstoke: Palgrave Macmillan, 2003. Print

Biggar, Nigel. "Concluding Remarks." *Burying the Past: Making Peace and Doing Justice after Civil Conflict.* Ed. Nigel Biggar. Washington, DC: Georgetown UP, 2001. 270–85. Print.

Biggar, Nigel. "Making Peace or Doing Justice: Must We Choose?" *Burying the Past: Making Peace and Doing Justice after Civil Conflict.* Ed. Nigel Biggar. Washington, DC: Georgetown UP, 2001. 6–22. Print.

Bitzer, Lloyd F. "The Rhetorical Situation." *Philosophy & Rhetoric* 25 (1992): 1–14. Print.

Black, Deborah L. *Logic and Aristotle's Rhetoric and Poetics in Medieval Arabic Philosophy.* Leiden, Netherlands: E.J. Brill, 1990. Print.

Booth, Wayne. "Introduction: The Rhetoric of War and Reconciliation." *Roads to Reconciliation: Conflict and Dialogue in the Twenty-First Century.* Ed. A.B. Brown and K.M. Poremski. Armonk, NY: M.E. Sharpe, 2005. 3–13. Print.

Booth, Wayne. *The Rhetoric of Rhetoric: The Quest for Effective Communication.* Malden, MA: Blackwell, 2004. Print.

Borrowman, Shane. "The Islamization of Rhetoric: Ibn Rushd and the Reintroduction of Aristotle into Medieval Europe." *Rhetoric Review* 27.4 (2008): 341–60. Print.

Brahm, Eric. "Sovereignty." September 2004. Beyond Intractability. Ed. Guy Burgess and Heidi Burgess. Conflict Research Consortium. 15 April 2009. http://www.beyondintractability.org/essay/sovereignty/.

Brandt, Deborah. "'Who's the President?' Ghostwriting and Shifting Values in Literacy." *College English* 69.6 (July 2007): 549–71. Print.

Brooks, Kevin. "Reviewing and Redescribing the Politics of Historiography: Octalog I, 1988." *Rhetoric Review* 16.1 (1997): 6–21. Print.

Brown, Penelope, and Stephen C. Levinson. *Politeness: Some Universals in Language Usages.* Cambridge, UK: Cambridge UP, 1987. Print.

Bruck, Peter A. "Strategies for Peace, Strategies for News Research." *Journal of Communication* 39.1 (1989): 108–29. Print.

Buber, Martin. *I and Thou.* Trans. Ronald George Smith. Edinburgh: T. & T. Clark, 1937. Print.

Bulaç, Ali. "The Medina Document." *Liberal Islam: A Sourcebook.* Ed. Charles Kurzman. New York: Oxford UP, 1998. 169–78. Print.

Burbules, Nicholas C. "A Theory of Power in Education." *Educational Theory* 36.3 (1986): 95–114. Print.

Burke, Kenneth. *A Rhetoric of Motives.* U of California P, 1969. Print.

Burkley, Melissa, and Hart Blanton. "The Positive (and Negative) Consequences of Endorsing Negative Self-Stereotypes." *Self and Identity* 8.2–3 (2009): 286–99. Print.

Burks, Don M. "Persuasion, Self Persuasion and Rhetorical Discourse." *Philosophy and Rhetoric 3* (1970): 109–19. Print.

Bush, Robert A. Baruch, and Joseph P. Folger. *The Promise of Mediation: The Transformative Approach to Conflict.* San Francisco: Jossey-Bass, 2005. Print.

Butterworth, Charles E. "Translation and Philosophy: The Case of Averroës' Commentaries." *International Journal of Middle East Studies* 26.1 (1994): 19–35. Print.

Butler, Judith. *Frames of War: When Is Life Grievable?* London: New York, 2009. Print.

Carter, Jimmy. *Keeping Faith: Memoirs of a President.* New York: Bantam Books, 1982. Print.

Carter, Michael. "Stasis and Kairos: Principles of Social Construction in Classical Rhetoric." *Rhetoric Review* 7.1 (1988): 97–112. Print.

Carter, Sue. "Using the Needle as a Sword: Needlework as Epideictic Rhetoric in the Woman's Christian Temperance Union." *Rhetorical Agendas: Political, Ethical, Spiritual.* Ed. Patricia Bizzell. Mahwah, NJ: Erlbaum, 2006. 325–34. Print.

Charland, Maurice. "Constitutive Rhetoric: The Case of the Peuple Quebecois." *Landmark Essays on Rhetorical Criticism.* Ed. Thomas B. Benson. Davis, California: Hermagoras P, 1993. 213–25.

Chen, Guo-Ming, ed. *Chinese Conflict Management and Resolution in Intercultural Context.* Spec. issue of *Intercultural Communication Studies* 9.1 (2000): 1–175. Print.

Coben, James, and Penelope Harley. "Intentional Conversations about Restorative Justice, Mediation and the Practice of Law." *Hamline Journal of Public Law and Policy* 25 (2004): 235–45. Web. 30 Jan. 2014.

Conley, Thomas M. *Rhetoric in the European Tradition.* New York: Longman, 1990. Print.

Connor, Ulla. "Intercultural Rhetoric Research: Beyond Texts." *Journal of English for Academic Purposes* 3.4 (2004): 291–304. Print.

Corbett, Edward J. *Classical Rhetoric for the Modern Student.* New York: Oxford UP, 1971. Print.

Crosswhite, James. *Deep Rhetoric: Philosophy, Reason, Violence, Justice, Wisdom.* Chicago: U of Chicago P, 2013. Print.

Cull, Nicholas J. "Public Diplomacy: Seven Lessons for Its Future from Its Past." *Engagement: Public Diplomacy in a Globalized World.* Foreign and Commonwealth Office.

Web. 2 Jan. 2009. http://uscpublicdiplomacy.org/sites/uscpublicdiplomacy.org/files/useruploads/u26739/Engagement_FCO.pdf.

Cull, Nicholas J. "'Public Diplomacy' Before Gullion: The Evolution of a Phrase." USC Center on Public Diplomacy. Web. 25 Oct. 2009. http://uscpublicdiplomacy.org/blog/060418_public_diplomacy_before_gullion_the_evolution_of_a_phrase.

Czubaroff, Jeanine. "Dialogical Rhetoric: An Application of Martin Buber's Philosophy of Dialogue." *Quarterly Journal of Speech* 86.2 (2000): 168–89. Print.

Daye, Russell. *Political Forgiveness: Lessons from South Africa*. Cossining: Orbis, 2004. Print.

De Vries, Erica, Kristine Lund, and Michael Baker. "Computer-Mediated Epistemic Dialogue: Explanation and Argumentation as Vehicles for Understanding Scientific Notions." *The Journal of the Learning Sciences* 11.1 (2002): 63–103. Print.

Derrida, Jacques. "On Forgiveness." *On Cosmopolitanism and Forgiveness: Thinking in Action*. Trans. Mark Dooley and Michael Hughes. New York: Routledge, 2001. 27–60. Print.

Diab, Rasha. "Peacemaking and the Chancery in Medieval Cairo: Revisiting Medieval Arabic Rhetoric." *Rhetoric across Borders*. Ed. Anne Demo. Long Grove, Ill: Waveland P, 2015. 121–33. Print.

Dingo, Rebecca. "Linking Transnational Logics: Feminist Rhetorical Analysis of Public Policy Networks." *College English* 70.5 (2008): 490–505. Print.

Dissanayake, Wimal. "Peace and Communication: A Buddhist Point of View." *Media Development* 30.2 (1983): 7–9. Print.

Dobel, J. Patrick. "Political Prudence and the Ethics of Leadership." *Public Administration Review* 58.1 (1998): 74–81. Print.

Dow, Bonnie J. "The Function of Epideictic and Deliberative Strategies in Presidential Crisis Rhetoric." *Western Journal of Speech Communication* 53.3 (1989): 294–310. Print.

Doxtader, Erik. "The Faith and Struggle of Beginning (with) Words: On the Turn between Reconciliation and Recognition." *Philosophy and Rhetoric* 40.1 (2007): 119–46. Print.

Doxtader, Erik. "On the Turn between Reconciliation and Recognition." *Philosophy and Rhetoric* 40.1 (2007): 119–46. Print.

Doxtader, Erik. "A Question of Confession's Discovery." *Rhetoric Society Quarterly* 41.3 (2011): 267–81. Print.

Doxtader, Erik. "Reconciliation—A Rhetorical Conception." *Quarterly Journal of Speech* 89.4 (2003): 267–92. Print.

Doxtader, Erik. "The Rhetorical Question of Human Rights—A Preface." *Quarterly Journal of Speech* 96.4 (2010): 353–79. Print.

Doxtader, Erik. *With Faith in the Works of Words: The Beginnings of Reconciliation in South Africa*. East Lansing: Michigan State UP, 2009. Print.

Doxtader, Erik. "Works of Faith, Faith of Works: A Reflection on the Truth and Justification of Forgiveness." *Quest: An African Journal of Philosophy*. XVI.1–2 (2002): 50–61. Print.

Drieskens, Barbara. "A Cairene Way of Reconciling." *Islamic Law and Society* 13.1 (2006): 99–122. Print.

Du Bois, W.E.B. "The Sorrow Songs." *Souls of Black Folk*. Chicago: A.C. McClurg & Co., 1904. Print.

Engels, Jeremy, ed. "Forum on the Violence of Rhetoric." Spec. issue of *Quarterly Journal of Speech* 99.2 (2013): 180–232. Print.

Engels, Jeremy. "Introduction to the Forum on the Violence of Rhetoric." *Quarterly Journal of Speech* 99.2 (2013): 180–81. Print.

Ellsworth, Elizabeth Ann. "The US Holocaust Museum as a Scene of Pedagogical Address." *Symploke* 10.1 (2002): 13–31.

Elshtain, Jean Bethke. "Politics and Forgiveness." *Boston University Studies in Philosophy and Religion.* 20 (1999): 32–47. Print.

Enos, Richard, et al. "Octalog II: The (Continuing) Politics of Historiography." *Rhetoric Review* 16.1 (1997): 22–44. Print.

Esposito, John L. *Islam: The Straight Path.* New York: Oxford UP, 1988. Print.

Estrada-Hollenbeck, Mica. "The Attainment of Justice through Restoration, Not Litigation: The Subjective Road to Reconciliation." *Reconciliation, Justice, and Coexistence: Theory and Practice.* Ed. Mohammad Abu-Nimer. Lanham, MD: Lexington Books, 2001. 65–85. Print.

Ezzaher, Lahcen E. "Alfarabi's *Book of Rhetoric*: An Arabic-English Translation of Alfarabi's Commentary on Aristotle's *Rhetoric*." *Rhetorica: A Journal of the History of Rhetoric* 26.4 (2008): 347–91. Print.

Ezzaher, Lahcen E. *Three Arabic Treatises on Aristotle's Rhetoric: The Commentaries of al-Farabi, Avicenna, and Averroes*. Carbondale: Southern Illinois UP, 2015. Print.

Fahmy, Ismail. *Negotiating for Peace in the Middle East: An Arab View.* Baltimore: Johns Hopkins UP, 1983. Print.

Fākhūrī, Ḥannā, and Khalīl Jurr. *Tārīkh al-Falsafah al-'Arabīyah* [The History of Arabic Philosophy]. Beirut: Dār al-Ma'ārif, 1963. Print.

Felstiner, William L F. "Influences of Social Organization on Dispute Processing." *Law and Society Review* 9.1 (1974): 63–94. Print.

Fetherston, A. Betts. "Peacekeeping, Conflict Resolution and Peacebuilding: A Reconsideration of Theoretical Frameworks." *International Peacekeeping* 7.1 (2000): 190–218. Print.

Fitzmaurice, Redmond. "Other Religions and Reconciliation: Reconciliation in Islam." Ed. Michael Hurley. *Reconciliation in Religion and Society.* Belfast, Ireland: Institute of Irish Studies, 1994. Print.

Foss, Sonja K., and Cindy L. Griffin. "Beyond Persuasion: A Proposal for an Invitational Rhetoric." *Communications Monographs* 62.1 (1995): 2–18. Print.

Foucault, Michel. *Power/Knowledge.* Ed. Colin Gordon. New York: Pantheon, 1980. Print.

Foucault, Michel, and Jay Miskowiec. "Of Other Spaces." *Diacritics* 16.1 (1986): 22–27. Print.

Funk, Nathan C., and Abdul Aziz Said. *Islam and Peacemaking in the Middle East.* Boulder: Lynne Rienner, 2009. Print.

Gaillet, Lynée Lewis, and Winifred Bryan Horner, eds. *The Present State of Scholarship in the History of Rhetoric: A Twenty-First Century Guide.* Columbia: University of Missouri P, 2010. Print.

Galaway, Burt, and Joe Hudson. *Perspectives on Crime Victims.* Saint Louis: C.V. Mosby, 1981. Print.

Galtung, Johan. "Cultural Violence." *Journal of Peace Research* 27.3 (1990): 291–305. Print.

Gearhart, Sally Miller. "The Womanization of Rhetoric." *Women's Studies International Quarterly* 2.2 (1979): 195–201. Print.

Gilyard, Keith. "Literacy, Identity, Imagination, Flight." *College Composition and Communication* 52.2 (2000): 260–72. Print.

Glenn, Cheryl. "Remapping Rhetorical Territory." *Rhetoric Review* 13.2 (1995): 287–303. Print.

Glenn, Cheryl. *Unspoken: A Rhetoric of Silence*. Carbondale: Southern Illinois UP, 2004. Print.

Gluckman, Max. "Limitations on the Case-Method in the Study of Tribal Law." *Law and Society Review* 7 (1973): 613–41. Print.

Goffman, Erving. "On Face-Work." *Psychiatry* 18.3 (1955): 213–31. Print.

Goldberg, Ellis. "Peasants in Revolt-Egypt 1919." *International Journal of Middle East Studies* 24.2 (1992): 261–80. Print.

Gopin, Marc. "Forgiveness as an Element of Conflict Resolution in Religious Cultures: Walking the Tightrope of Reconciliation and Justice." *Reconciliation, Justice, and Coexistence: Theory and Practice*. Ed. Mohammad Abu-Nimer. Lanham, MD: Lexington Books, 2001. 87–99. Print.

Gorman, Robert F., and Edward S. Mihalkanin. *Historical Dictionary of Human Rights and Humanitarian Organizations*. Lanham, MD: Scarecrow, 2007. Print

Gorsevski, Ellen W. "Nonviolent Theory on Communication: The Implications for Theorizing a Nonviolent Rhetoric." *Peace and Change* 24.4 (1999): 445–75. Print.

Gorsevski, Ellen W. *Peaceful Persuasion: The Geopolitics of Nonviolent Rhetoric*. Albany: State University of New York P, 2004. Print.

Gorsevski, Ellen W. "The Physical Side of Linguistic Violence." *Linguistic Violence*. Spec. issue of *Peace Review: A Journal of Social Justice* 10.4 (1998): 513–16. Print.

Graff, Richard, and Michael Leff. "Revisionist Historiography and Rhetorical Tradition(s)." *The Viability of the Rhetorical Tradition*. Ed. Richard Graff, Arthur E. Walzer, and Janet M. Atwill. Albany: State University of New York P, 2005. 11–30. Print

Green, Keith. (1995). "Deixis: A Revaluation of Concepts and Categoies." *New Essays in Deixis: Discourse, Narrative, Literature*. Ed. Keith Green. Amesterdam: Rodopi, 1995. 11–25. Print.

Gregg, Benjamin. *Human Rights as Social Construction*. Cambridge UP, 2012. Print.

Gronbeck, Bruce E. "Underestimating Generic Expectations: Clinton's Apologies of August 17, 1998." *American Communication Journal* 2.2 (1999). Web. 20 Feb. 2009.

Guillaume, Alfred. *The Life of Muhammad. A Translation of Ishaq's Sirah Rasul Allah*. Karachi: Oxford UP, 1955. Print.

Habermas, Jürgen. "Towards a Theory of Communicative Competence." *Inquiry: An Interdisciplinary Journal of Philosophy* 13.1–4 (1970): 360–75. Print.

Halldén, Philip. "What Is Arab Islamic Rhetoric? Rethinking the History of Muslim Oratory Art and Homiletics." *International Journal of Middle East Studies* 37.1 (2005): 19–38. Print.

Hallett, Brien. "Overcoming Linguistic Violence." *Linguistic Violence*. Spec. issue of *Peace Review: A Journal of Social Justice* 10.4 (1998): 511–12. Print.

Halliday, Michael Alexander, and Christian Matthiessen. *An Introduction to Functional Grammar*. 3rd ed. London: Arnold, 2004. Print.

Hamidullah, Muhammad. *The First Written Constitution of the World: An Important Document of the Holy Prophet*. Lahore: Ashraf Printing P, 1994. Print.

Hardimon, Michael O. "The Project of Reconciliation: Hegel's Social Philosophy." Philosophy and Public Affairs 21.2 (1992): 165–95. Print.

Haron, Mohammad, Zeinoul Abedien Cajee, and Suleman Essop Dangor. "Initiating Transformation, Visualizing a Future: The Case for Constructing a Charter for Muslims in South Africa." *Journal of Muslim Minority Affairs* 31.4 (2011): 615–30. Print.

Harris, Ian. *Peace Education*. Jefferson, NC: McFarland, 1988. Print.

Hart, Roderick P., and Courtney L. Dillard. "Deliberative Genre." *Encyclopedia of Rhetoric*. Ed. T.O. Sloane. New York: Oxford UP, 2001. 209–17. Print.

Ḥasan, Jadd Ḥasan. "Taqdīm [Introduction]." *Maḥkamāt al-Ṣulḥ al-Kubrá* [*The Great Court of Ṣulḥ*]. By Muḥammad Māḍī Abū al-'Azā'im. Cairo: Dār al-Sha'b, n.d. 5–7. Print.

Hatch, John B. "Beyond Apologia: Racial Reconciliation and Apologies for Slavery." *Western Journal of Communication* 70.3 (2006): 186–211. Print.

Hatch, John B. *Race and Reconciliation: Redressing Wounds of Injustice*. Lanham: Lexington, 2008. Print.

Hauser, Gerard A. "The Moral Vernacular of Human Rights Discourse." Philosophy and Rhetoric 4.4 (2008): 440–66. Print.

Hauser, Gerard A. *Prisoners of Conscience: Moral Vernaculars of Political Agency*. Columbia: U of South Carolina P, 2014. Print.

Herman, Judith Lewis. *Trauma and Recovery*. New York: Basic Books, 1997. Print.

Hesford, Wendy, and Eileen Schell. "Introduction: Configurations of Transnationality: Locating Feminist Rhetorics." *College English* 70.5 (2008). 461–70. Print.

Hirschkind, Charles. "Civic Virtue and Religious Reason: An Islamic Counterpublic." *Cultural Anthropology* 16.1 (2001): 3–34. Print.

Hocker, Joyce, and William Wilmot. *Interpersonal Conflict*. 2nd ed. Dubuque, IA: William Brown Publishers, 1985. Print.

Hoey, Michael. "Overlapping Patterns of Discourse Organization and Their Implications for Clause Relational Analysis of Problem-Solution Texts." *Studying Writing: Linguistic Approaches*. Vol. 1. Ed. C.R. Cooper and S. Greenbaum. London: Sage, 1986. 187–214. Print.

Hoey, Michael, and Eugene Winter. "Clause Relations and the Writer's Communicative Task." *Functional Approaches to Writing: Research Perspectives*. Ed. B. Couture. London: Francis Pinter, 1986. 120–41. Print.

Hoigilt, Jacob. *Islamist Rhetoric: Language and Culture in Contemporary Egypt*. Hoboken: Taylor & Francis, 2010. Print.

Hosmanek, Andrew J. "Cutting the Cord: Ho'oponopono and Hawaiian Restorative Justice in the Criminal Law Context." *Pepperdine Dispute Resolution Law Journal* 5 (2005): 359–75. Web. 20 Dec. 2013.

Hudson, Valerie M., ed. *Culture and Foreign Policy*. Boulder, CO: Lynne Rienner, 1997. Print.

Hum, Sue, and Arab Lyon. "Recent Advances in Comparative Rhetoric." *The Sage Handbook of Rhetorical Studies*. Ed. Andrea Lunsford, Kirt Wilson, and Rosa Eberly. Thousand Oaks, CA: Sage, 2008. 153–65. Print.

Hurley, Michael. "Introduction." *Reconciliation in Religion and Society*. Ed. Michael Hurley. Belfast, Ireland: Institute of Irish Studies, 1994. 1–5. Print.

Hussain, Jamila. *Islam: Its Law and Society*. 3rd ed. Annandale, N.S.W: Federation P, 2011. Print.

Hyland, Drew A. "Why Plato Wrote Dialogues." *Philosophy and Rhetoric* 1.1 (1968): 38–50. Print.

Ibn Taymīyah, Taqī al-Dīn. *Tazkīyat al-Nafs* [*The Purification of the Self*]. Ed. Muḥammad al-Qaḥṭānīy. Riyadh: al-Muslim, 1994. Print.

Irani, George E. "Acknowledgement, Forgiveness and Reconciliation in Conflict Resolution: Perspectives from Lebanon." *Chronos* 5 (2002): 195–220. Print.

Irani, George E. "Islamic Mediation Techniques for Middle East Conflicts." *Middle East Review of International Affairs* 3.2 (1999): 1–17. Print.

Irani, George E., and Nathan Funk. "Rituals of Reconciliation: Arab-Islamic Perspectives." Notre Dame, IN: Joan B. Kroc Institute for International Peace Studies, University of Notre Dame, 2000. Print.

Jackson, Ronald L., and Elaine B. Richardson, ed. *Understanding African American Rhetoric: Classical Origins to Contemporary Innovations*. New York: Routledge, 2003. Print.

Jasinski, James. "Power." *Sourcebook on Rhetoric: Key Concepts in Contemporary Rhetorical Studies*. Ed. James Jasinski. Thousand Oaks: Sage, 2001. 444–55. Print.

Jasinski, James. "Stasis." *Sourcebook on Rhetoric: Key Concepts in Contemporary Rhetorical Studies*. Ed. James Jasinski. Thousand Oaks, CA: Sage, 2001. 528–31. Print.

Jasinski, James. "Stock Topics/Issues in Policy Debates." *Sourcebook on Rhetoric: Key Concepts in Contemporary Rhetorical Studies*. Ed. James Jasinski. Thousand Oaks, CA: Sage, 2001. 531–36. Print.

Jiryis, Sabri. "The Arab World at the Crossroads: An Analysis of the Arab Opposition to the Sadat Initiative." *Journal of Palestine Studies* 7.2 (1978): 26–61. Print.

Jolivet, Jean. "Alkindi." *A Companion to Philosophy in the Middle Ages*. Ed. J. Gracia, T. Noone, and M.A. Malden. Oxford, UK: Blackwell, 2003. EBSCOhost. Web. 19 Jan. 2014. eBook.

Jung, Carl G. *AION: Researches into the Phenomenology of the Self.* Trans. R.F.C. Hull. Part II of *The Collected Works of C.G. Jung*. 2nd ed. Bollingen Series XX. Princeton, NJ: Princeton UP, 1968. Print.

Kamel, Mohamed Ibrahim. *The Camp David Accords: A Testimony*. Boston, MA: KPI, 1986. Print.

Kampmark, Binoy. "Sacred Sovereigns and Punishable War Crimes: The Ambivalence of the Wilson Administration towards a Trial of Kaiser Wilhelm II." *Australian Journal of Politics and History* 53.4 (2007): 519–37. Print.

Kamwangamalu, Nkonko M. "Ubuntu in South Africa: A Sociolinguistic Perspective to a Pan African Concept." *Critical Arts* 13.2 (1999): 24–41. Print.

Kaplan, Robert B. "Cultural Thought Patterns in Intercultural Education." *Language Learning* 16.1–2 (1966): 1–20. Print.

Keegan, John. *The First World War*. New York: Knopf, 1999. Print.

Kelley, Andrew. "On Listening." *Linguistic Violence*. Spec. issue of *Peace Review: A Journal of Social Justice*. 10.4 (1998): 529–32. Print.

Kelman, Herbert C. "The Psychological Impact of the Sadat Visit on Israeli Society." *Peace and Conflict: Journal of Peace Psychology* 11.2 (2005): 111–36. Print.

Kemal, Salim. *The Philosophic Poetics of Alfarabi, Avicenna and Averroës: The Aristotelian Reception*. London: Routledge, 2003. Print.

Kennedy, George A. *Classical Rhetoric and Its Christian and Secular Tradition from Ancient to Modern Times*. Chapel Hill: U of North Carolina P, 1999. Print.

Kennedy, George A. *Comparative Rhetoric: An Historical and Cross-Cultural Introduction*. New York: Oxford UP, 1998. Print.

Khan, Ali. "The Medina Constitution." Social Science Research Network. 2006. 1–7. http://papers.ssrn.com/sol3/papers.cfm?abstract-id=945458.

Khoury, Nicole. "(Re)Positioning Lebanese Feminist Discourse A Rhetorical Study of 'Al-Raida' (Pioneer) Journal, 1976–1985." ProQuest, 2012. Web. 30 March 2015.

Kiewe, Amos. Introduction. *The Modern Presidency and Crisis Rhetoric*. Ed. Amos Kiewe. Westport, CT: Praeger, 1994. xv–xxxvii. Print.

Killingray, David. "Labour Exploitation for Military Campaigns in British Colonial Africa 1870–1945." *Journal of Contemporary History* (1989): 483–501. Print.

Kirkwood, William. "Narrative and the Rhetoric of Possibility." *Communication Monographs* 59.1 (1992): 30–47. Print.

Krepon, Michael, and Jenny S. Drezin. "Declaratory Diplomacy and Confidence Building?" *Declaratory Diplomacy: Rhetorical Initiatives and Confidence Building.* Ed. Michael Krepon and Jenny S. Drezin. Washington, DC: Stimson Center, 1999. 153–77. Web. Jan. 2009.

Kriesberg, Louis. "Changing Forms of Coexistence." *Reconciliation, Justice, and Coexistence: Theory and Practice.* Ed. M. Abu-Nimer. Lanham, MD: Lexington Books, 2001. 47–64. Print.

Kriesberg, Louis. "The Conflict Resolution Field." *Peacemaking in International Conflict: Methods and Techniques.* Ed. I. W. Zartman. Rev. ed. Washington, DC: United States Institute of Peace, 2007. 25–60. Print.

Kriesberg, Louis. "Reconciliation: Aspects, Growth, and Sequences." *International Journal of Peace Studies* 12.1 (2007): 1–21. Print.

Kruse, Noreen Wales. "The Scope of Apologetic Discourse: Establishing Generic Parameters." *Southern Journal of Communication* 46.3 (1981): 278–91. Print.

Kuttner, Ran. "Cultivating Dialogue: From Fragmentation to Relationality in Conflict Interaction." *Negotiation Journal* 28.3 (2012): 315–35. Print.

Kuttner, Ran. "From Adversity to Relationality: A Buddhist-Oriented Relational View of Integrative Negotiation and Mediation." *Ohio State Journal on Dispute Resolution* 25.4 (2010): 931–74. Print.

Kuypers, Jim A. "From Chaos, Community: The Crisis Leadership of Virginia Tech President Charles W. Steger." *American Communication Journal* 9.1 (2007). Web. Jan, 2009.

La Caze, Marguerite. "The Asymmetry between Apology and Forgiveness." *Contemporary Political Theory* 5.4 (2006): 447–68. Print.

Lakoff, George, and Mark Johnson. *Metaphors We Live By.* Chicago: U of Chicago P, 1980. Print.

Lambourne, Wendy. "Justice and Reconciliation: Postconflict Peacebuilding in Cambodia and Rwanda." *Reconciliation, Justice, and Coexistence: Theory and Practice.* Ed. Mohammad Abu-Nimer. Lanham, MD: Lexington Books, 2001. 311–37. Print.

Lameer, Joep. *Al-Fārābī and Aristotelian Syllogistics: Greek Theory and Islamic Practice.* Leiden, Netherlands: E.J. Brill, 1994. Print.

Lang, Sharon. "Sulha Peacemaking and the Politics of Persuasion." *Journal of Palestine Studies* 31.3 (2002): 52–66. Print.

Lawrence, Bruce B., and Karim, Aisha. "General Introduction: Theorizing Violence in the Twenty-first Century." *On Violence: A Reader.* Ed. Bruce B. Lawrence and Aisha Karim. Durham, NC: Duke UP, 2007. 1–15. Print.

Leaman, Oliver. *Islamic Philosophy.* Hoboken, NJ: Polity, 2013. Print.

Lederach, John Paul. *Building Peace: Sustainable Reconciliation in Divided Societies.* Washington, DC: United States Institute of Peace P, 1997. Print.

Lévinas, Emmanuel. "Philosophy, Justice and Love." *Entre Nous: On Thinking-of-the-Other.* Trans. Michael B. Smith and Barbara Harshaw. New York: Columbia UP, 1998. 103–22. Print.

Leudar, Ivan, Victoria Marsland, and Jiri Nekvapil. "On Membership Categorization: 'Us,'

'Them' and 'Doing Violence' in Political Discourse." *Discourse & Society* 15.2–3 (2004): 243–66. Print.

Lewis, Arnold. "The Peace Ritual and Israeli Images of Social Order." *Journal of Conflict Resolution* 23.4 (1979): 685–703. Print.

Long, William J., and Peter Brecke. *War and Reconciliation: Reason and Emotion in Conflict Resolution*. Boston: MIT P, 2003. Print.

Lipson, Carol, and Roberta A. Binkley, eds. *Ancient Non-Greek Rhetorics*. Anderson, SC: Parlor, 2009. Print.

Lipson, Carol, and Roberta A. Binkley, eds. *Rhetoric before and beyond the Greeks*. New York: State University of New York P, 2004. Print.

Littlefield, Robert S. "The Rhetoric of Balance: An Analysis of Selected Speeches by Anwar El-Sadat." Paper presented at the joint meeting of the Central States Speech Association and Southern Speech Communication Association, 1987. ERIC.

Lu, Catherine. "Justice and Moral Regeneration: Lessons from the Treaty of Versailles." *International Studies Review* 4.3 (2002): 3–25. Print.

Lucaites, John Louis, and Celeste Michelle Condit. "Re-constructing Narrative Theory: A Functional Perspective." *Journal of Communication* 35.4 (1985): 90–108. Print.

Lyon, Arabella. *Deliberative Acts: Democracy, Rhetoric, and Rights*. University Park: Pennsylvania State UP, 2013. Print.

Lyon, Arabella, and Lester C. Olson. *Human Rights Rhetoric: Traditions of Testifying and Witnessing*. Spec. issue of *Rhetoric Society Quarterly* 41.3 (2011): 203–12. Print.

Lyons, Scott Richard. *X-Marks: Native Signatures of Assent*. Minneapolis: University of Minnesota P, 2010. Print.

Mack, Katherine. *From Apartheid to Democracy: Deliberating Truth and Reconciliation in South Africa*. University Park: Pennsylvania State UP, 2014. Print.

Mack, Katherine. "Hearing Women's Silence in Transitional South Africa: Achmat Dangor's Bitter Fruit." *Silence and Listening as Rhetorical Arts* 2011: 195–213. Print.

Maiese, Michelle. "Rights." Ed. Guy Burgess and Heidi Burgess. August 2003. Conflict Research Consortium. Web. 24 May 2011. http://www.beyondintractability.org/essay/rights/.

Malek, Cate, and Heidi Burgess. "Recognition." *Beyond Intractability*. Conflict Information Consortium, University of Ed. Guy Burgess and Heidi Burgess. Boulder, CO. Web. 12 Feb., 2007.

Maley, Yon. "From Adjudication to Mediation: Third Party Discourse in Conflict Resolution." *Journal of Pragmatics* 23.1 (1995): 93–110. Print.

Mallison, William Thomas, and Sally V. Mallison. *An International Law Analysis of the Major United Nations Resolutions Concerning the Palestine Question*. United Nations, 1979. UN Doc. S/SG/SER.F/4. Web. 20 Dec. 2008.

Malmkjær, Kirsten. "Speech Acts." *The Linguistic Encyclopedia*. 2nd ed. Ed. K. Malmkjær. London: Routledge, 2004. 486–95. Print.

Mao, LuMing. "Doing Comparative Rhetoric Responsibly." *Rhetoric Society Quarterly* 41.1 (2011): 64–69. Print.

Mao, LuMing. "Reflective Encounters: Illustrating Comparative Rhetoric." *Style* 37.4 (2003): 401–25. Print.

Mao, LuMing, ed. "Studying Chinese Rhetoric in the Twenty-First Century." *College English* 72.4 (2010): 329–429. Print.

Mao, LuMing, and Morris Young. *Representations: Doing Asian American Rhetoric*. Logan: Utah State UP, 2009. Print.

Maoz, Zeev, and Dan S. Felsenthal. "Self-Binding Commitments, the Inducement of Trust, Social Choice, and the Theory of International Cooperation." *International Studies Quarterly* 3.2 (1987): 177–200. Print.

Mawdūdīy, Sayyid Abū al-A'lá. *Human Rights in Islam*. Lahore, Pakistan: Islamic Publication, 1977. Print.

McCann, Bryan J. "Entering the Darkness: Rhetorics of Transformation and Gendered Violence in Patty Jenkins's Monster." *Women's Studies in Communication* 37.1 (2014): 1–21. Print.

McCann, Bryan J. "On Whose Ground? Racialized Violence and the Prerogative of 'Self-Defense' in the Trayvon Martin Case." *Western Journal of Communication* 78 (2014): 1–20. Print.

McPhail, Mark Lawrence. *The Rhetoric of Racism Revisited: Reparations or Separation?* Lanham, MD: Rowman & Littlefield, 2002. Print.

Merry, Sally E. "Mediation in Nonindustrial Societies." *Mediation Research: The Process and Effectiveness of Third-Party Intervention*. Ed. K. Kressel and D. Pruitt. San Francisco: Jossey-Bass. 1989. 68–91. Print.

Metoui, Jessica. "Returning to the Circle: The Reemergence of Traditional Dispute Resolution in Native American Communities." *Journal of Dispute Resolution*. 2007.2 (2007): 517–39. Web. 20 Feb. 2014.

Miller, Thomas P. "Reinventing Rhetorical Traditions." *Learning from the Histories of Rhetoric: Essays in Honor of Winifred Bryan Horner*. Ed. Winifred Bryan and Theresa Enos. Carbondale: Southern Illinois UP, 1993. 26–41. Print.

Minow, Martha. *Between Vengeance and Forgiveness: Facing History after Genocide and Mass Violence*. Boston: Beacon P, 1998. Print

Mommsen, Wolfgang J. "Kaiser Wilhelm II and German Politics." *Journal of Contemporary History* 25.2 (1990): 289–316. Print.

Montville, Joseph V. "Justice and the Burdens of History." *Reconciliation, Justice, and Coexistence: Theory and Practice*. Ed. Mohammad Abu-Nimer. Lanham, MD: Lexington Books, 2001. 129–43. Print.

Murithi, Timothy. "Practical Peacemaking Wisdom from Africa: Reflections on Ubuntu." *Journal of Pan African Studies* 1.4 (2006): 25–34. Print.

Murphy, James. *Medieval Eloquence: Studies in the Theory and Practice of Medieval Rhetoric*. Berkeley: California UP, 1978. Print.

Murphy, James, et al. "Octalog I: The Politics of Historiography." *Rhetoric Review* 7.1 (1988): 5–49. Print.

Murray, Jeffrey W. "Bakhtinian Answerability and Levinasian Responsibility: Forging a Fuller Dialogical Communicative Ethics." Southern Communication Journal 65.2 (2000): 133–50. Print.

Nielsen, Marianne O., and James W. Zion. *Navajo Nation Peacemaking: Living Traditional Justice*. Tucson: University of Arizona P, 2005. Print.

Nienkamp, Jean. *Internal Rhetorics: Toward a History and Theory of Self-Persuasion*. Carbondale: Southern Illinois UP, 2001. Print.

Nilan, Pam. "Membership Categorization Devices under Construction: Social Identity Boundary Maintenance in Everyday Discourse." *Australian Review of Applied Linguistics* 18.1 (1995): 69–94. Print.

Oliver, Robert Tarbell. *Communication and Culture in Ancient India and China*. Syracuse, NY: Syracuse UP, 1971. Print.

Oliver, Robert Tarbell. *Culture and Communication: The Problem of Penetrating National and Cultural Boundaries*. Springfield, IL: Charles C. Thomas, 1962. Print.

Ovid, and George Sandys. *Ovid's Metamorphosis*. Cambridge: Chadwyck-Healey, 1992. Print.

Perelman, Chaim, and Lucie Olbrechts-Tyteca. *The New Rhetoric: A Treatise on Argumentation*. Trans. J.W.P. Weaver. Notre Dame, IN: U of Notre Dame P, 1969. Print.

Peters, Ifeanyi. *Conflict Management, Prevention and Resolution*. Nigeria Network of Non-Governmental Organisations (NNNGO), Ibadan, Nigeria. Web. 24 December, 2006.

Phillips, Kendall R., ed. *Framing Public Memory*. Tuscaloosa: U of Alabama P, 2004. Print.

Philpott, Daniel. "Sovereignty: An Introduction and Brief History." *Journal of International Affairs*. 48.2 (1995): 353–68. Print.

Porter, James E. "Intertextuality and the Discourse Community." *Rhetoric Review* 5.1 (1986): 34–47. Print.

Poulakos, John. "Rhetoric, the Sophists, and the Possible." *Communication Monographs* 51.3 (1984): 215–26. Print.

Pough, Gwendolyn D. *Check It While I Wreck It: Black Womanhood, Hip Hop Culture, and the Public Sphere*. Boston: Northeastern UP, 2004. Print.

Powell, Malea. "Rhetorics of Survivance: How American Indians Use Writing." *College Composition and Communication* 53.1 (2002): 396–434. Print.

Pullman, George L. "Deliberative Rhetoric and Forensic Stasis: Reconsidering the Scope and Function of an Ancient Rhetorical Heuristic in the Aftermath of the Thomas/Hill Controversy." *Rhetoric Society Quarterly* 25.1–4 (1995): 223–30. Print.

Qābīl, Muḥammad. *Mawsū'at al-ghinā' al-Miṣrī fī al-qarn al-'ishrīn* [*The Encyclopedia of Singing in the Twentieth Century*]. Cairo: al-Hīy'ah al-Maṣrīyah al-'Āmmah lil-Kitāb, 1999. Print.

Quandt, William B. *Camp David: Peacemaking and Politics*. Washington, DC: Brookings Institution P, 1986. Print.

Qutbuddin, Tahera. "*Khutba*: The Evolution of Early Arabic Oration." *Classical Arabic Humanities in Their Own Terms: Festschrift for Wolfhart Heinrichs*. Ed. Beatrice Gruendler and Michael Cooperson. Leiden: Brill, 2008. 176–273. Print.

Rafeeq, Mona. "Rethinking Islamic Law Arbitration Tribunals: Are They Compatible with Traditional American Notions of Justice." *Wisconsin International Law Journal* 28 (2010): 108–39. Print.

Rafman, Sandra. "Restoration of a Moral Universe: Children's Perspectives on Forgiveness and Justice." *Women's Reflections on the Complexities of Forgiveness*. Ed. Wanda Malcom, Nancy DeCourville, and Kathryn Belicki. New York: Routledge, 2008. 215–34. Print

Rand, Erin J. "Thinking Violence and Rhetoric." *Rhetoric and Public Affairs* 12.3 (2009): 461–77. Print.

Ratcliffe, Krista. *Rhetorical Listening: Identification, Gender, Whiteness*. Carbondale: Southern Illinois UP, 2005. Print.

Richardson, Elaine B., and Ronald L. Jackson, ed. *African American Rhetoric(s): Interdisciplinary Perspectives*. Carbondale: Southern Illinois UP, 2004. Print.

Richardson, John. "Ten Imperatives for Peace." *The Futurist* (2006): 14–17. Print.

Rogers, L. Edna. "Relational Communication Theory." *Encyclopedia of Communication*

Theory. Ed. Stephen W. Littlejohn and Karen Foss. Thousand Oaks, CA: Sage Reference, 2009. 828–33. Print.

Rivenburgh, Nancy K. "Seeking Discursive Spaces for Peace in Media-Sport Narratives." *Conflict and Communication Online* 8.2 (2009): 2–11. Print.

Royster, Jacqueline Jones. "Disciplinary Landscaping, Or Contemporary Challenges in the History of Rhetoric." *Philosophy and Rhetoric* 36.2 (2003): 148–67. Print.

Royster, Jacqueline Jones. *Traces of a Stream: Literacy and Social Change among African American Women*. Pittsburgh: University of Pittsburgh P, 2000. Print.

Rubin, Uri. "The 'Constitution of Medina': Some Notes." *Studia Islamica* 62 (1985): 5–23. Print.

Ruderman, Richard S. "Aristotle and the Recovery of Political Judgment." *American Political Science Review* 91.2 (1997): 409–20. Print.

Sable, Sandy C., and Eric Kornhauser. "Some Reflections on a Relational World View." *ADR Bulletin* 2.7 (1999): 63–65. Web. 2 July, 2012. http://epublications.bond.edu.au/adr/vol2/iss7/2/.

Sacks, Harvey. "The Baby Cried. The Mommy Picked It Up. Chapter 3: Lecture 1(R)." *Lectures on Conversation*. Oxford: Basil Blackwell, 1992. 243–51. Print.

Sacks, Harvey. "Invitations; Inexhaustable Topics; Category-Bound Activities (Part I; Lecture 8)." *Lectures on Conversation*. Ed. Gail Jefferson. Vol. 1. Oxford: Basil Blackwell, 1992. 175–81. Print.

Said, Abdul Aziz. "Precept and Practice of Human Rights in Islam." *Universal Human Rights* 1.1 (1979): 63–79. Print.

Sassen, Saskia. "Local Actors in Global Politics." *Current Sociology* 52.4 (2004): 649–70. Print.

Sassen, Saskia. "The Repositioning of Citizenship: Emergent Subjects and Spaces for Politics." *Berkeley Journal of Sociology* 46 (2002): 4–26. Print.

Schooley, Kimberly. Y. "Cultural Sovereignty, Islam and Human Rights—Toward a Communitarian Revision Comment." *Cumberland Law Review* 25 (1994–1995): 651–714. Print.

Searle, John R. *Speech Acts: An Essay in the Philosophy of Language*. Cambridge, UK: Cambridge UP, 1969.

Serjeant, Robert Bertram. "The Sunnah Jamiah, Pacts with the Yathrib Jews, and the Tahrim of Yathrib: Analysis and Translation of the Documents Comprised in the So-called 'Constitution of Medina.'" *Bulletin of the School of Oriental and African Studies* 41.1 (1978): 1–42. Print.

Shaub, Mark. "Rhetorical Studies in America: The Place of Averroës and the Medieval Arab Commentators." *Alif: Journal of Comparative Poetics* 16 (1996): 233–254. Print

Shaw, Rosalind. *Rethinking Truth and Reconciliation Commissions: Lessons from Sierra Leone*. Washington, DC: United States Institute of Peace P, 2005. Print.

Sheard, Cynthia Miecznikowski. "The Public Value of Epideictic Rhetoric." *College English* 58 (1996): 765–94. Print.

Short, Mick. *Exploring the Language of Poems, Plays and Prose*. London: Longman, 1996. Print.

Shoufani, Elias. "The Reaction in Israel to the Sadat Initiative." *Journal of Palestine Studies* 7.2 (1978): 3–25. Print

Shuqruf, 'Abd al-Mun'im M. *Al-Imām Muḥammad Māḍī Abū al-'Azā'im*. Cairo, Egypt: Dār al-Ṭibā'ah al-Ḥadīthah, 1972. Print.

Shriver, Donald W. "Where and When in Political Life Is Justice Served by Forgiveness?" *Burying the Past: Making Peace and Doing Justice after Civil Conflict*. Ed. Nigel Biggar. Washington, DC: Georgetown UP, 2001. 25–43. Print.

Simons, Herbert. *Persuasion: Understanding, Practice, and Analysis*. New York: McGraw-Hill, 1986. Print.

Simpson, Paul. *Language through Literature: An Introduction*. London: Routledge, 1997. Print.

Smeed, Judy L., et al. "Power Over, With and Through: Another Look at Micropolitics." *Leading and Managing* 15.1 (2009): 26–41. Print.

Smith, Daniel L. "The Rewards of Allah." *Journal of Peace Research* 26.4 (1989): 385–98. Print.

Stovel, Laura. "When the Enemy Comes Home: Restoring Justice after Mass Atrocity." Paper presented at the 6th International Conference on Restorative Justice, 2003. Vancouver. 17 November, 2006.

Stromberg, Ernest, ed. *American Indian Rhetorics of Survivance: Word Medicine, Word Magic*. Pittsburgh: University of Pittsburgh P, 2006. Print.

Tagliarina, Daniel. "Power, Privilege, and Rights: How the Powerful and Powerless Create a Vernacular of Rights." *APSA 2013 Annual Meeting Paper*. Social Science Research Network. 2013. http://ssrn.com/abstract=2301432.

Tannen, Deborah. *Talking Voices, Repetition, Dialogue and Imagery in Conversational Discourse*. 2nd ed. Cambridge: Cambridge UP, 2007. Print.

Taylor, Charles. "The Politics of Recognition." New Contexts of Canadian Criticism. Ed. Donna Ajay Heble, Palmateer Pennee, and J.R. Struthers. Ontario: Broadview P (1997). 25–73. Print.

Thompson, Geoff. *Introducing Functional Grammar*. New York: Arnold, 1996. Print.

Thye, Shane. "Power, Theories of." *Blackwell Encyclopedia of Sociology*. Ed. George Ritzer. Blackwell, 2007. Blackwell Reference Online. Web. 18 February 2013. http://www.blackwellreference.com.ezproxy.lib.utexas.edu/subscriber/tocnode.html?id=g9781405124331_chunk_g978140512433122_ss1–92.

Tiles, Mary. "Mastering Metaphors." *Linguistic Violence*. Spec. issue of *Peace Review*. 10.4 (1998): 517–22. Print.

Tucker, Robert. "Figure, Ground and Presence: A Phenomenology of Meaning in Rhetoric." *Quarterly Journal of Speech* 87.4 (2001): 396–414. Print.

Tull, Patricia K. "Rhetorical Criticism and Intertextuality." *To Each Its Own Meaning: An Introduction to Biblical Criticisms and Their Application*. Ed. S.L. McKenzie and S.R. Haynes. Louisville, KY: Westminster John Knox, 1999. 156–79. Print.

Tully, James. "Recognition and Dialogue: The Emergence of a New Field." *Critical Review of International Social and Political Philosophy* 7.3 (2004): 84–106. Print.

Türk, Volker, Selvi Supramaniam and Reuben Liew. "*Asylum and Islam*." *Refugee Survey Quarterly* 27.2 (2008). Print.

Turner, Victor W. "Betwixt and Between: Liminal Period in Rites de Passage." *Reader in Comparative Religion: an Anthropological Approach*. Ed. William Lessa Armand and Evon Zartman Vogt. 4th ed. New York: Harper & Row, 1979. 234–43. Print.

Tutu, Desmond. "Foreword by Chairperson." Truth and Reconciliation Commission Final Report, Volume 1, Chapter 1, Subsection 1, Paragraph 27. 1998. http://sabctrc.saha.org.za/reports/volume1/chapter1/subsection2.htm

Tutu, Desmond. *No Future without Forgiveness*. New York: Doubleday, 1999. Print.

Umbreit, Mark S. "Humanistic Mediation: A Transformative Journey of Peacemaking." *Conflict Resolution Quarterly* 14.3 (1997): 201–13. Print.

United Nations. "Chapter VI: Pacific Settlement of Disputes." *Charter of the United Nations*. Web. 4 Jan. 2009. https://www.un.org/en/documents/charter/chapter6.shtml.

United Nations. "Resolution 242: The Situation in the Middle East (22 Nov)." Security Council Resolutions-1967. Web. 10 Jan. 2008. http://unispal.un.org/unispal.nsf/0/7D35E1F729DF491C85256EE700686136.

United Nations. *The Universal Declaration of Human Rights*. 10 December 1948. 1 July 2010 http://www.un.org/en/documents/udhr/index.shtml.

United Nations. "Resolution 338 (1973) of 22 October 1973." Security Council Resolutions-1973. Web. 10 Jan.2008. http://unispal.un.org/unispal.nsf/0/7FB7C26FCBE80A31852560C50065F878.

Ury, William L., Jeanne M. Brett, and Stephen B. Goldberg. *Getting Disputes Resolved: Designing Systems to Cut the Costs of Conflict*. San Francisco: Jossey-Bass, 1988. Print.

Ushama, Thameem. "Is Islam a Religion of Moderation or Extremism? A Study of Key Islamic Teachings." *Asian Social Science* 10.8 (2014): 184–97. Print.

Vertovec, Steven "Conceiving and Researching Transnationalism." *Ethnic and Race Studies* 22.2 (1999): 447–62. Print.

Villa-Vicencio, Charles. "Now That the TRC Is Over: Looking Back, Reaching Forward." *Journal of Theology for Southern Africa* 18.1 (1999): 43–56. Print.

Villa-Vicencio, Charles. "Reconciliation." *Pieces of the Puzzle: Keywords on Reconciliation and Transitional Justice*. Ed. C. Villa-Vicencio, Erik Doxtader, and Richard Goldstone. Rondebosch, South Africa: Institute for Justice and Reconciliation, 2004. 6–8. Print.

Vitanza, Victor. "Historiographies of Rhetoric." *Encyclopedia of Rhetoric and Composition: Communication from Ancient to the Information Age*. Ed. Theresa Enos. New York: Garland, 1996. 324–25. Print

Vivian, Bradford. "Always a Third Party Who Says 'Me': Rhetoric and Alterity." *Philosophy and Rhetoric* 34.4 (2001): 343–54. Print.

Vivian, Bradford. *Public Forgetting: The Rhetoric and Politics of Beginning Again*. University Park: Penn State UP, 2010. Print.

Waldinger, Roger D., and David Fitzgerald. "Transnationalism in Question." *American Journal of Sociology* 109.5 (2004): 1177–95. Print.

Walker, Jeffery. "Aristotle's Lyric: Re-Imagining the Rhetoric of Epideictic Song." *College English* 51.1 (1989): 5–28. Print.

Wall, James A., and Ronda Roberts Callister. "Ho'oponopono: Some Lessons from Hawaiian Mediation." *Negotiation Journal* 11.1 (1995): 45–54. Print.

Walzer, Arthur, and David E. Beard. "Historiography and the Study of Rhetoric." *Sage Handbook of Rhetorical Studies*. Ed. Andrea Lunsford, Kirt Wilson, and Rosa Eberly. Thousand Oaks: Sage, 2009. 13–33. Print.

Wemmers, Jo-Anne. "Where Do They Belong? Giving Victims a Place in the Criminal Justice Process." *Criminal Law Forum*. 20.4 (2009): 395–416. Print.

Weyeneth, Robert R. "The Power of Apology and the Process of Historical Reconciliation." *Public Historian* 23.3 (2001): 9–38. Print.

Witty, Cathie J. "Disputing Issues in Shehaam: A Multireligious Village in Lebanon." *The Disputing Process-Law in Ten Societies*. Ed. L. Nader and H.F. Todd. New York: Columbia UP, 1978. 281–315. Print.

Worthington, Everett L. "Unforgiveness, Forgiveness, and Reconciliation and Their Implications for Societal Interventions." *Forgiveness and Reconciliation: Religion, Public Policy, and Conflict Transformation*. Ed. R.S. Helmick and R.L. Peterson. Philadelphia: Templeton Foundation P, 2001. 161–82. Print.

Xiaosui, Xiao. "From the Hierarchical *Ren* to Egalitarianism: A Case of Cross-Cultural Rhetorical Mediation." *Quarterly Journal of Speech* 82.1 (1996): 38–54. Print.

Yang, Xiaomei. "Categorical Imperatives, Moral Requirements, and Moral Motivation." *Metaphilosophy* 37.1 (2006): 112–29. Print.

Yildirim, Yetkin. "The Medina Charter: A Historical Case of Conflict Resolution." *Islam and Christian–Muslim Relations* 20.4 (2009): 439–50. Print.

Yildirim, Yetkin. "Peace and Conflict Resolution in the Medina Charter." *Peace Review: A Journal of Social Justice* 18.1 (2006): 109–17. Print.

Yusuf, Imtiyaz. "Dialogue between Islam and Buddhism through the Concepts Ummatan Wasaṭan (the Middle Nation) and Majjhima-Patipada (the Middle Way)." *Islamic Studies* 48.3 (2009): 367–94. Print.

Zahid, Mahmood. "Sadat and Camp David Reappraised." *Journal of Palestine Studies* 15.1 (1985): 62–87. Print.

Zarefsky, David. "Presidential Rhetoric and the Power of Definition." *Presidential Studies Quarterly* 34.3 (2004): 607–19. Print.

Zartman, I. William. *Negotiation and Conflict Management: Essays on Theory and Practice*. London: Routledge, 2008. Print.

Zehr, Howard. *The Little Book of Restorative Justice*. Intercourse, PA: Good Books, 2002. Print.

INDEX